The De Moneta of
Nicholas Oresme

and

English Mint Documents

Translated from the Latin with Introduction
and Notes by

Charles Johnson C.B.E. F.B.A.
sometime Scholar of Trinity College, Oxford

Thomas Nelson and Sons Ltd

London Edinburgh Paris Melbourne Toronto and New York

THOMAS NELSON AND SONS LTD
Parkside Works Edinburgh 9
36 Park Street London W1
312 Flinders Street Melbourne C1

302–304 Barclays Bank Building
Commissioner and Kruis Streets
Johannesburg

THOMAS NELSON AND SONS (CANADA) LTD
91–93 Wellington Street West   Toronto 1

THOMAS NELSON AND SONS
19 East 47th Street New York 17

SOCIÉTÉ FRANÇAISE D'EDITIONS NELSON
25 rue Henri Barbusse Paris V^e

———

First published 1956

CONTENTS

PREFACE

IT is a pleasure to acknowledge the substantial help which the translator has received in a task which, agreeable as it was, had difficulties for one who is neither an economist nor a numismatist. Professor R. A. B. Mynors has revised Wolowski's text of the *De Moneta* from a better selection of MSS, and has added a description of those which he has used. The two plates are due to the courtesy of Sir John Craig, to whom I am also indebted for leave to quote from his book on *The Mint*, and to the kindness of the Deputy-Master of the Royal Mint and of the Trustees of the British Museum. I must also thank those friends who have helped me by their knowledge of coins : Mr C. E. Blunt, Mr P. Grierson and Mr R. H. M. Dolley. I owe much to their aid, but they are not responsible for my blunders. The editors of the Medieval Series and the publishers have also done everything in their power to make my task easier.

CHARLES JOHNSON

INTRODUCTION

THE aim of this volume is to give an account of the theory and practice of coinage in the thirteenth and fourteenth centuries. For the theory, Nicholas Oresme's *De Moneta* presents the scholastic doctrine derived from Aristotle's *Politics*. For the practice, it seemed best to translate the treatise preserved in the *Red Book of the Exchequer*, and presumably written by William de Turnemire, Master of the Mint in 1279, with other documents from Hargrave MS 313 and from some of the registers of Bury St Edmund's Abbey, relating to the recoinages of 1247, 1279 and 1300, and to the gold coinage of Edward III.

I

NICHOLAS ORESME

Nicholas Oresme [1] is supposed to have been born about the year 1320 at the village of Allemagne near Caen, but the earliest certain fact about him is that he was a 'bursar' of the college of Navarre in the University of Paris from 1348 to 4 October 1356, when he was appointed Master. He is described as a Norman. He studied in Theology, but it is not known when he took his degree of Master in Theology. He remained Master of the college till 4 December 1361, when he was forced to resign. He became a canon of Rouen, 23 November 1362, and dean 18 March 1364. He preached a celebrated sermon before Pope Urban V on Christmas Eve 1363,

[1] For the details of Oresme's life I have followed the *Essai sur la Vie et les Ouvrages de Nicole Oresme* by François Meunier (Paris 1857), supplemented by the biographical and bibliographical sections of E. Borchert's 'Die Lehre von der Bewegung bei Nicolaus Oresme' in *Beiträge zur Gesch. der Philos. und Theol. des Mittelalters* xxi. 3 (1934), and by Émile Bridrey's *La Théorie de la Monnaie au xive Siècle* (Paris 1906).

denouncing the corruption of the world and the Church, and calling for repentance. Some time before 1370 he became one of the chaplains of Charles V (1364-80), since he undertook the translation of the *Ethics* (1370) and *Politics* and *Economics* of Aristotle at the king's request. The treatise on Money in its Latin and French forms is earlier than these translations, since it is mentioned in the preface to the *Politics*.[1] Oresme became bishop of Lisieux 16 November 1377 and was consecrated 28 January 1378. He died at Lisieux 11 July 1382.

Besides the works mentioned above, Oresme translated Aristotle's *De Caelo et Mundo*, and wrote several books directed against the claim of astrologers to predict the future as well as sermons and theological tracts. The translations were not from the Greek, but from the Latin versions of Grosseteste and William of Moerbeke. The treatise on money, though based on the *Politics*, was an economic tract provoked by the successive debasements of the coinage by Philip VI and John II and the consequent derangement of trade and social relations. It has been suggested that it brought its author to the notice of Charles V, who was then acting as regent during his father's captivity in England. But it is more likely that he was already employed in the king's service, as he is stated to have been engaged in raising a loan in Normandy in 1360, and there was a halt in the debasement of the coinage from 1360 to 1385.

In his treatise Oresme takes the Aristotelian view that a coin is a definite weight of precious metal, the quantity and fineness of which is guaranteed by the stamp of the authority issuing it. The currency does not belong to the issuing authority, but to the public which uses it for the purpose of exchange of goods. The prince has therefore no right to vary the standard

---

[1] M. Bridrey (op. cit. p. 47) argues that it was written before the end of 1355 because (1) the *Gabelle* was extended to the whole kingdom at the end of that year, and Oresme would not have dared to attack it as he does in Chapter X, and (2) Oresme's suggestion that trial-plates should be kept was accepted in an *Ordonnance* of 28 December in the same year.

or the weight or (if two metals are, as usually, employed) the bimetallic ratio ; though the last may be done if the relative value of the metals is materially altered by a new source of supply. And any necessary alteration must be by agreement of the whole community. Debasement is condoned as a temporary political expedient, but the true values must be re-established as soon as possible. It is remarkable that Oresme takes no account of credit, nor of bills of exchange, which were already extensively used by Italian bankers at the beginning of the fourteenth century. Paper money (which Goethe credits Mephistopheles with inventing) had not yet appeared to complicate the question. In an age in which inconvertible paper is the rule, there is something particularly apposite in Oresme's arguments ; and it is not surprising that a German translation by Dr Edgar Schorer (Jena 1937) lays some stress on this in an introduction.

It is curious that Oresme takes no account (pp. 13–14, 19–20) of what must have been a powerful motive for a gradual debasement of the coinage in the Middle Ages, the wear of the current coin. There was always a temptation to make the new coin approximate in value to the average worth of the coin in daily use. It was necessary either to call in all the old coin, and throw the loss upon the holders of it, or to see the new coin disappear into private hoards. And before the introduction of milled edges, the loss from wear was very heavy. The evidence of the mint officials estimated it at about 20 per cent in the early years of Richard II, when there had been no coinage of silver on a large scale for nearly thirty years, and there was a great lack of halfpence and farthings. Their estimate may have been too high, but the deterioration must have been considerable. To Oresme, to whom the maintenance of the standard was of supreme importance, there was little or no difference between such an adjustment of the new money and deliberate debasement ; but he makes no provision for the

gradual withdrawal of light money from circulation and its replacement by sound currency. A complete recoinage, the remedy which he proposes, throws the whole burden of the loss on the holders, at the moment, of the old money.

Oresme has been credited with the anticipation of ' Gresham's Law ' on the strength of a passage in the French translation describing the effect of debasement on the coinage. But this passage comes from an addition to Oresme's own version, and is not contained in the two earliest MSS (Paris, Bibl. Nat. MSS fr. 5913 and 23,926), as M. Bridrey has pointed out.[1] It has been suggested that longer versions were added by officials of the Flemish mint, who had observed the failure of Charles V's attempt to reform the French coinage, and had frequent opportunities to repeat the observation in the Low Countries.[2] One MS at all events (MS fr. 5913) is written by a Flemish copyist, and reads (f. 3) ' et maintenant est au present en ce pays de Flandres et les voisins '.

II

THE TEXT OF ORESME'S TREATISE

(Contributed by R. A. B. Mynors)

For the *De Moneta* we have no original manuscript ; only a number of copies, whose making is spread out over the hundred years that followed the author's death. Taken together these agree so closely that we are rarely left in any doubt what the author wrote ; and where their testimony differs, one or more of the earlier will always produce a reading by which the demands of sense and latinity are satisfied. As individuals they vary widely in external appearance and in

---

[1] op. cit. p. 65n
[2] H. Laurent. ' Le Problème des Traductions françaises du Traité des Monnaies d'Oresme dans les Pays-Bas bourguignons ' in *Revue d'Histoire Economique et Sociale* xxi. pp. 13–24 (Paris 1933)

quality, and give us some idea of the circulation of the work before it appeared in print.

Our three oldest are Parisian, two from the Abbey of St Victor and one from St Germain des Prés, and take us back to the theology schools of the University of Paris at the end of the fourteenth century :

PARIS, *Bibliothèque Nationale lat. 14,579* (formerly St Victor 111), ff. 336–43. Paper, with occasional leaves of parchment, 295 × 215 mm., 2 columns of about 50 lines, in a small current hand using pale ink, with rough red capitals. Bound in the old boards, re-covered. This stands at the end of a large collectaneous volume of moral and theological treatises, in different but contemporary hands, by Petrus de Alliaco, Henricus de Alemannia, Johannes Gerson, Nicolaus de Lyra and others, including Oresme himself.[1]

PARIS, *Bibl. Nat. lat. 14,580* (formerly St Victor 100), ff. 213–20. Paper and parchment, 305 × 210 mm., about 45 lines, no ornament, rebound. A volume in appearance and contents very much like the last, acquired for the library of St Victor's under their active prior, Jean Lamasse. It had belonged to a Paris theologian, Germanus de Rungiaco, from whose executors it was bought for 48 sols. ; and their signatures to a receipt for the price, dated 4 August 1417, are still to be seen on f. 222v.

PARIS, *Bibl. Nat. lat. 13,965* (formerly St Germain 1103). Parchment, 240 × 170 mm., 13 leaves, about 35 lines, in a good small hand dated A.D. 1397, with one illuminated initial. The other contents of the volume, which has been rebound, are in a hand of the same date : a widespread collection of literary commonplaces (beginning : ' Ordo iuris expostulat ut amicorum . . .') and a collection of French proverbs, with Latin analogues from the Bible and other sources.

These three volumes are characteristic university books : the first two on paper in the rapid, much-abbreviated current hand, with no ornament, that looks like the work of a scholar writing for his own use, or to earn his keep, rather than of a professional scribe ; the third on parchment, obviously written by a professional, and with professional ornament, but still in the close

---

[1] It is the MS taken as a base for the text of Oresme's *De Communicatione Ydiomatum* by E. Borchert in *Beiträge* xxxv. 4/5, 1940.

abbreviated script used for philosophical and theological texts. The best of them, probably the best of all our manuscripts, is 14,580 ; for 14,579 is full of small deviations from the standard text, peculiar to itself and having no claims to authenticity. 13,965 can be neglected ; for it is evidently a copy of the same parent manuscript as 14,580, and a much less faithful copy.[1]

Next, probably, both in value and date come :

PARIS, *Bibliothèque Ste Geneviève 343*, ff. 139v–   . Paper, 385 × 285 mm., 2 columns of 55–60 lines, well written at the end of the fourteenth or early in the fifteenth century, with red headings and red and blue capitals, medieval binding. The first page of the volume, which contains works of canon law and political philosophy, is ornamented with a miniature in quite good style. Owned previously by the Carmelite house at Dijon.

POITIERS, *Bibliothèque de la Ville 93 (243)*, ff. 50–70v. Paper, 215 × 150 mm., about 30 lines to the page, in a small fifteenth-century current hand, with red headings and red and blue capitals. Part of a rather miscellaneous volume, all of the same date, in its original white skin binding, complete with four ties and a book-marker. On the flyleaf is an inscription of ownership which might be legible, and ' Iste liber est episcopi Lingonensis ex dono subprioris beati Remigii Remensis sibi facto '. It belonged later to the Jesuit College at Poitiers.

The first of these, though written on paper, shows a high standard of finish, and may well have been ordered by some well-endowed canon lawyer ; the other belonged to a bishop of Langres, who has been identified as Gui Bernard (1453–81). They correspond closely in text, and there is at least one place where they are right and all our other copies wrong.

In our next group, we find at least one copy written for a wealthy layman :

---

[1] The two scribes found some difficulties in the text of their common exemplar. On p. 1, for *cessante scrupulo 14,580* has *et sante scrupulo ; 13,965*, rather than transcribe nonsense, leaves a gap. Twice, on pp. 5 and 17, they both for *a ueteribus* read *(h)abentibus* ; in the parent the words were so written that the *u* looked like a *b*, and the abbreviation-mark after the *t*, intended to signify *er*, could be taken to stand over the preceding *e*, where it could only signify *n*.

PARIS, *Bibl. Nat. lat. 8681* (formerly Fonds du Roi 5200). Parchment, 255 × 175 mm., 16 leaves, 34 long lines, in a good fifteenth-century 'lettre bâtarde', with space left for illuminated capitals, which have never been filled in. Old red velvet binding.

PARIS, *Bibl. Nat. lat. 8733A.* Parchment, 210 × 145 mm., 44 leaves (with blank quires before and after), 22 lines ruled in red, with red headings and illuminated capitals, paragraph-marks and space-fillers. Illuminated frontispiece showing moneyers at work striking coins (their elegant attire suggests that realism is not intended) ; in the border, the motto and badge (two bombards discharging their cannon-balls) of Louis de Bruges, Seigneur de la Gruthuyse, the great Flemish bibliophile who died in 1492, and the arms and porcupine badge of Louis XII of France. Modern binding, retaining the characteristic gauffered edges.[1]

PARIS, *Bibl. Nat. 18,205* (formerly Carmes de la Place Maubert 10), ff. 103–21. Paper, 210 × 150 mm., about 30 lines, in a fifteenth-century current hand, with simple capitals in red and blue. Original binding, rebacked. The other contents are theological treatises, mostly by or ascribed to Johannes Gerson. Owned previously by the Paris Carmelites.

It sometimes happens that the more expensive the appearance of a literary manuscript, the worse its text ; but this copy made for Louis de Bruges is very good, right two or three times where all the rest are wrong. I group 8681 with it, because though not particularly close in text, they are externally similar : parchment books, in 'lettre bâtarde', containing the *De Moneta* by itself, meant for the bibliophile rather than the scholar. As for 18,205, it groups itself with 8733A by an obvious textual relationship ; but it is a poor relation, and can be disregarded.

There is another fifteenth-century paper manuscript, of which at present I know nothing :

UTRECHT, *University Library 318* ; the *De Moneta* is ff. 114–28 of a volume of most miscellaneous contents.

---

[1] On Louis de Bruges, see L. Delisle, *Le Cabinet des MSS de la Bibl. Impériale* I (Paris 1868) 40–46. Two frontispieces with his device are reproduced by Philip Hofer in the *Harvard Library Bulletin* VII (1953), plates i and ii. Our MS has rather pretty subdued capitals in grey on a black ground diapered in gold ; once, on f. 20v, it suddenly lapses into an *M* in blue and red which would not have looked out of place a hundred years earlier.

And, to conclude this account of the manuscripts, here is one which looks forward into a different world :

BRUSSELS, *Bibliothèque Royale 9899* (being ff. 204–13 of a volume numbered 9896–9901). Paper, 290 × 200 mm., 45 lines, very neat hand with coloured penwork capitals, written in the last twenty years of the fifteenth century, and, as the context indicates, in Louvain. The other contents of this volume, which has been rebound, are primarily of humanistic interest, and some of them are *printed* : *Valerius Maximus* (no. 133 in Paul Thomas's catalogue of the classical MSS in Brussels) dated Louvain June 1483 ; *Isocrates ad Demonicum* in the version of Rodolphus Agricola and his *De Regno* in that of Leonardo Bruni, the latter dated Louvain 5 February 1499 ; Oresme, undated ; Bruni's *Isagogicum,* produced ' non fluviali calamo sed arte quadam caracterizandi modernissima ' by John of Paderborn at Louvain, 10 June 1475 (GKW 5616 ; Polain 4076) ; and a printed copy, without date or place, of Persius's Satires with the commentary of Bartholomeus Fontius. It was previously owned by the Jesuit College in Louvain.

As far as its text goes, this Brussels copy has nothing to offer us ; indeed, it has, I think, been corrected against the edition printed at Cologne in 1484. But could one ask for a more appropriate bridge between manuscript and printed text ?

The first of the printed editions appeared in 1484, as part of the *Opera Johannis Gerson* (Cologne, Johann Koelhoff 1483–4 ; Hain 7621), vol. IV ff. 268v–80. It was a good text, resembling that of Paris lat. 8681 and 8733*A* ; unfortunately it remained unknown to later editors, who depend entirely upon its inadequate successor. This appeared in Paris, without date, but about the year 1511, as a sixteen-page small-quarto pamphlet, put out by a printer in a small way, Thomas Kees. The source was a manuscript very close to Paris lat. 14,579, with all its peculiar readings, but it lacked, it seems, one pair of leaves, so that in Kees's edition there are two large gaps, to which no attention is drawn ; he omits (pp. 24–8) ' casibus prius dictis . . . in indebita mutacione monete ', and (pp. 35–8) ' sicut de re . . . uelle ergo amouere'. Rare as it is now (the copy

PLATE I

COINS, AND A TRIAL PLATE FOR 1279 COINAGE

1. Henry III long-cross penny 1247–8.   2. Henry III gold penny 1257.   3. Edward I halfpenny 1280.   4. Edward I penny 1279.   5. Edward I penny (Hull) 1300–2. 6. Edward I farthing (base) 1279.   7. Edward I groat 1280–5.   8. Edward III gold noble 1346–51.   9. Surviving portion of standard of 1279 (enlarged 5:4).   This has the imprint of the old coinage, but that of the new is unfortunately missing, presumably because the pieces for assay were taken from that part.

All coins are silver, actual size, and London Mint, except where otherwise stated.

By kindness of the Deputy Master of the Royal Mint and of the Trustees of the British Museum

in the Bibliothèque Nationale is believed to be unique), Kees's text with these two gaps is the sole source for all its successors down to 1864, when manuscript evidence was again brought into play. The first reprint was that of the *Sacra Bibliotheca Sanctorum Patrum* of M. De la Bigne, vol. IX (Paris 1589), col. 1291–1310. This was repeated five or six times in the course of the seventeenth century at Paris, Cologne and Lyons, and the Oresme text was reprinted separately from the Paris print of 1610 in 1622 at Helmstadt and at Luneburg in 1625. An independent reprint of Kees, with a good deal of editorial alteration, was published in 1605 by Gothard Voegelin at Leyden, as part of the *De Re Monetaria veterum Romanorum* of Marquard Freher ; and there are said to be other editions, by Jacobus Genathius at Basle in the early seventeenth century and by David Thomas de Hagelstein in *Acta publica monetaria I* (Augsburg 1642, second edition 1692), which I have not seen.

This all suggests that a lively interest was taken in these currency problems in the seventeenth century, but there was no recourse to fresh evidence for the text ; the two gaps in Kees's edition are still there, camouflaged now by a renumbering of the chapters made in 1589. The credit of putting an end to this state of affairs belongs to L. Wolowski, who in 1864 produced the complete text for the first time for three hundred and eighty years : *Traictie de la premiere Invention des Monnoies de Nicole Oresme, textes français et latin,* using three of the less good copies in the Bibliothèque Nationale, and quoting carefully the variants of the edition of 1605, because he did not realise that they were mere inventions of its editor. Wolowski's edition of the French and Latin texts was the basis of the exhaustive study of the treatise by Emile Bridrey, *La Théorie de la Monnaie au XIVe siècle, Nicole Oresme* (Paris 1906), which with its xxxix+741 pages (and no index) is the fullest discussion of the *De Moneta* that has yet been or is ever likely to be published.[1]

[1] It must be read with the comments of R. Landry in *Moyen Âge* XXII (2e série XIII), 1909, 145–78.

2

The text here printed is based on the following MSS : V = Paris lat. 14, 579 ; W = Paris lat. 14,580 ; G = Paris, Ste Geneviève 343 ; P = Paris lat. 8681 ; C = Paris lat. 8733A.

They rarely leave one in any doubt of the correct reading, and give clear indications of spelling, though not of punctuation, in which the scribes seem to have taken little interest. It is clear however that their common ancestor was not the author's auto- graph, but a copy of it, for all alike show the same displacement of eight words on p. 47 ; and this may mean that there are other errors in the text which cannot now be detected. The French version printed by Wolowski, though made from a Latin which in one or two places was already defective, is occasionally useful.

There has been one previous translation into English, by an unknown hand, of which a few specimens are printed by Bridrey. It survives, so far as is known, only in a fifteenth-century paper manuscript of the Customs of London, now MS O. III. 11 in the library of Trinity College, Cambridge. But this seems to be little more than a curiosity : it is so literal as sometimes to be unintelligible unless one has the Latin in front of one, and its author was clearly an indifferent Latinist. His original had the same dislocation in the text on p. 47 as all our Latin copies, and for our purposes his version is of no importance.

III

ENGLISH MINT DOCUMENTS

The other contents of this volume consist of the entries relating to the coinage to be found in three Exchequer MSS : the *Red Book*, which came to the Public Record Office as one

of the treasures of the Queen's Remembrancer of the Exchequer, Hargrave MS 313 and Cotton MS Cleopatra A. 16 in the British Museum, which contain much of the *Red Book* material, the former being demonstrably copied from it, and so closely akin to it in style that it has obviously been an Exchequer MS. Both the *Red Book* and the Hargrave MS are mainly of the thirteenth century, though the *Red Book* has some later additions. The account of the trial of the Pyx for the coinage of 1248 is only found in the Hargrave MS, though we should have expected to find it in the *Red Book*. We do not know whether this is the earliest instance of such a trial. The assay described in the *Dialogus de Scaccario* probably served the same purpose.

A further description of these manuscripts will be found in Dr Hubert Hall's edition of the *Red Book of the Exchequer* (London 1896) pp. i–cxlviii, and in *Dialogus de Scaccario* (Oxford 1902), pp. 3–5. Some additional passages have been taken from cartularies of the abbey of St Edmund's, Bury, in the British Museum (Harl. MS. 645 and Add. MS. 14,847). These were printed by Lord Francis Hervey in *The Pinchbeck Register* (London 1925) from another cartulary of the abbey in the Cambridge University Library (Ee.3.60).

To put these documents into their proper context it is necessary to give a sketch of the history of the English coinage from the Conquest to the fourteenth century. The system which William the Conqueror inherited from Edward the Confessor was to permit the coinage of pence, the only coin then current, in the boroughs of the several counties, by licensed moneyers, the number of whom varied with the importance of the borough. Moneyers were a privileged class. Some had official residences, and they had jurisdiction over their workmen, for whom they were responsible. The moneyers bought in silver or old coin at suitable rates and paid out the new coin. The king received no direct profit from the recoining, but he

was paid a fee by the moneyer on appointment and a similar
fee every time the type of coin was changed, and part of the
annual 'farm' of the borough was a payment for the privilege
of coining.[1] If the mint had been granted, or belonged by
prescription, to a bishop or abbot, these fees were payable to
him. The types of coin were periodically changed, and new
dies purchased from London, where they were engraved. The
monopoly of engraving was hereditary since 1107 in the family
of Otto the Goldsmith. The dies were in two parts : the
'pile' or lower die, which had a spike on the end to drive into
a wooden block, and the 'trussel' which was placed over the
blank as it rested on the pile and hammered down. The
trussel was held in place by a twisted withe. The pile was
engraved with the design for the obverse of the coin, showing
the king's image, and the trussel with the reverse bearing a
cross with the name of the moneyer and the place of issue. The
trussel wore out much more quickly than the pile, and was
beaten into a shape rather like a mushroom by the hammering.
The names on the reverse enabled the maker of light or impure
coins to be identified, and the punishment inflicted on the
moneyer might be mutilation. The makers of false coin were
therefore given to alter the legend of the trussels by substituting
meaningless groups of letters for their names and those of the
boroughs where they coined.[2] The dies were not engraved in
the ordinary sense of the word, but made up after a set model
by means of punches, straight or curved, impressing on the die
the components of the letters or design on the coin.[3] Sir John
Craig says that the patterns of these punches were changed ten
times between the Conquest and Edward I to bring in new
styles of epigraphy.[4] Thus it seems probable that the introduction of 'serifs', the short finishing strokes seen in type,

---

[1] Allen, *Catalogue of English Coins in British Museum*, lxxviii *seq.*
[2] Brooke, *Catalogue of English Coins : Norman Kings* i. cxlix *seq.*
[3] Brooke, op. cit. i. ccxxxv *seq.*   Allen, op. cit. xxxv *seq.*
[4] Craig, *The Mint*, p. 18

involving the making of an extra punch, marks the reform of the coinage by Henry I in 1108.[1]

There is no direct evidence of any control of the moneyers by the reeves of the boroughs to which they belonged, or by the exchequer, in the period immediately after the Conquest. But reforms of the coinage took place from time to time, and the chroniclers record the punishments then inflicted on makers of bad money. As soon as payments in kind from the tenants of crown manors began to be replaced by money payments, and the payments made by the sheriffs were assayed at the exchequer in the manner described in the *Dialogus de Scaccario*, it must have been obvious that light or debased coin was in circulation. Whether the change of the type of the coin, possibly every three years, was connected with a periodical test of the coinage cannot certainly be known. But in any case, the sheriff whose payments were much over sixpence in the pound short of their nominal value, and who was surcharged with the difference, was not likely to shield the moneyers responsible, especially if the bulk of the money paid in was in new coin.[2] Although the institution of the assay of the farms of counties is attributed to Roger of Salisbury, it is clear from Domesday Book that assaying was in use at the Conquest, and it is likely that an assay was taken before each change of coin-type, in order to determine the relative value of old and new coins.

The periodical change of type ceased with the first of the ' cross and crosslet ' or ' Tealby ' issues of Henry II in 1158. After that the king's bust on the obverse was always facing, and not to right or left in profile. The scarcity of earlier coins in the hoards containing coins of Henry II suggests that the recoinage was complete. The wear of the coins must have been heavy, and the lack of a milled edge together with irregularities resulting from careless striking exposed them to clipping. It is worth noting that the author of the *Dialogus* insists that the

[1] Brooke, op. cit., i. clv   [2] *Dialogus* (Med. Ser.), pp. 39, 43

samples for assay must be well mixed, so that they may ' answer to the weight '. He knew he must expect a considerable proportion of light coins. Henry I, hearing that good money was being refused because the coins were cracked, is said by William of Malmesbury to have ordered that all pence should be nicked before they were issued. And a number of types of Henry's coins, dated roughly between 1108 and 1125 or a little later have a cut made in them accordingly.

The recoinage of 1180, which also appears to have involved the recall of earlier issues, was marked by an important change in policy. The changing of money, which had previously been the lawful privilege of the moneyers, was now ' nationalised ', i.e. brought under the direct control of the Crown. Moneyers had already ceased to work in some of the boroughs, and they were now replaced by a company of foreign workmen under the control of Philip Aimer of Tours, who was brought over from Barfleur by Richard of Ilchester, Bishop of Winchester, one of the principal members of the Exchequer. Philip and his men were described as the king's *cambitores*, or changers, but it is clear from the accounts in the Pipe Rolls that they were occupied in making the new money, and that the recoinage was completed in 1182. They seem to have returned to the Continent after their work was done. The new or ' short-cross ' type remained without alteration even of the king's name *Henricus* until the recoinage of 1247. After 1182 the Pipe Rolls contain notes of amercements for the offence of ' exchanging contrary to the assize '. The persons guilty are sometimes described as moneyers, but the earliest was sheriff of Northamptonshire. It is not very easy to determine whether the offence consisted in unlicensed exchanging or in false coining, but some of the cases seem to indicate that money of the old coinage had been given out in exchange. The close association of exchanges with mints caused *Cambium* to be used indifferently for both.

The next general recoinage took place in 1205 under the control of Reginald of Cornhill as Warden of the Exchange of all England. All coins earlier than the 'short-cross' coins were recalled, as well as any of the latter which had lost more than an eighth of their weight. There is not much information in the Pipe Roll about the extent of this recoinage, as the provincial mints were let to farm. But the London mint received £1,257 0s 1d from the treasury to start the recoinage.[1]

From 1205 until the recoinage of 1247 the exchanges and mints were usually let to farm. Thus, during the minority of Henry III, William Marshal the younger was appointed Warden in 1218 with control of all the exchanges and mints at a farm of 500 marks, during the king's pleasure. The officials under him are described as keepers of the dies, assayers and moneyers. The London mint was then in the hands of two foreign merchants, William, son of Benedict, and Herbert Bonamy, who probably retained its actual management under Marshal's orders.[2] Though no general recoinage took place until 1247 there was no doubt a certain amount of exchange business and coining being done. So we find in 1223 that merchants at Ypres, Arras, St Omer's and Ghent were warned that the exchange of silver-plate and bullion was limited to the cities of London and Canterbury.[3] And in 1232 a safe-conduct was promised to all merchants bringing silver to the same cities, while proclamation was also made that any Jew or Christian dealing in silver or exchanging new for old money or vice versa, except in the king's exchanges, was liable to severe penalties.

William Hardel, who was Warden of the mints of London and Canterbury for the most of this period, was ordered, on 19 June 1233, to call together the moneyers, assayers, keepers of the dies and workers of the two mints, and to provide enough workers for the king's business,[4] and we find him constantly

---

[1] *Pipe Roll for 1205*, p. 12
[3] ibid. p. 366
[2] *Patent Rolls, 1216–25*, p. 138
[4] *Close Rolls, 1231–4*, p. 230

being called upon to find money for payments in cash, or for the purchase of silver, gold and other expensive materials for plate or vestments from time to time. In 1238 he was authorised to borrow money, if he had not enough new money at his command, for the expenses of an envoy to the Roman court.[1] In 1234 the moneyers of London and Canterbury were exempted from the tallage levied in that year, in accordance with their prescriptive rights.[2] On 28 August 1235 a commission was appointed ' to hear and determine trespasses and other things pertaining to the office of the king's mint of London ', and a like commission for Canterbury. The Warden of the Mint and the constables of the Tower and of Canterbury respectively were to be the commissioners.[3] The death of three moneyers between 1235 and 1237 enables us to see how their places were filled up. The die was taken into the king's hand and the post was sold or given to a new moneyer. A new die was then cut with the name of the moneyer on the trussel.[4] In 1241 certain goldsmiths of London were made to take an oath in the presence of the Treasurer and the Warden of the Mint that they would not themselves, nor by any agent Christian or Jew, exchange, buy or sell silver, whether plate, ore or clippings (*in pl*[*ata*] *vel mina vel retonduris*) or otherwise, contrary to the assize and constitution of the Mint (*Cambii*).[5] Another indication that the mint was not working at its full capacity, is an order to the Barons of the Exchequer, dated 3 May 1242, to enrol a grant to Nicholas of St Albans, melter of the mints of London and Canterbury, that the farm of £90 a year which he paid for his post should be reduced to compensate for loss of business through war. War with France was then impending.[6] A note

---

[1] *Close Rolls, 1237–42*, p. 101
[2] *Close Rolls, 1231–4*, p. 375. See also op. cit. *1242–7*, p. 364 for the liberty of freedom from arrest (in 1245).
[3] *Patent Rolls, 1232–47*, p. 127
[4] *Close Rolls, 1234–7*, pp. 144, 270, 421. The purchaser of one of the Canterbury dies paid 10 marks.   [5] *Close Rolls, 1237–42*, p. 322
[6] ibid. p. 421

in the *Red Book* (p. 50 below) gives an account of the sources from which silver for coining might be derived. In the form of plate it might come from the French or Spanish lands bordering on the Pyrenees, from Germany, the Low Countries or Italy. The coins mentioned imply trade with the Low Countries and, probably through them, with Germany and Italy. No mention is made of Scottish coins which were of the English standard and were usually current in England.[1]

In 1247, when a new coinage was needed, Reyner of Brussels was empowered (August 28) to recruit workmen from abroad for the mint.[2] The king had not, it seems, enough treasure in hand to finance this operation. So on 27 July he had agreed to borrow 10,000 marks (£6,666 13s 4d) from his brother Richard, Earl of Cornwall, to be repaid by instalments on the security of the profits of the exchange and mint. At the same time the Earl was given, for seven years (afterwards extended to twelve) from 6 November 1247, the right to coin, with a half-share of the profits, with a provision that the earl should, before any profits accrued, have back the same amount of money by tale as he had brought in to be recoined.[3] It is to this recoinage that the memorandum on the duties of the mint officials printed below (p. 51) refers. The officers named are the changer, the moneyers with their workmen, the assayer, the keeper of the dies and the usher. The old money was received by weight and a deduction of 16 dwt. was made, sixpence for seignorage and tenpence for the average lack of fineness in the old coin. The moneyers had also a prescriptive right to add 6 dwt. of copper to each pound for mintage, three for the wages of the workmen and three for the rent of the foundry and the pay of the workmen there and elsewhere, for the dies, coals and other expenses. As it appears from the

[1] *Close Rolls, 1253–4*, p. 2. They were prohibited on 8 July 1251. *Close Rolls, 1247–51*, p. 549
[2] *Patent Rolls, 1232–47*, p. 508   [3] op. cit. pp. 505, 511

account of the trial of the new and old money on 11 March 1248, that the old lost sixpence on assay, this statement is confirmed. If the moneyers refused to accept the estimate of the changer as to the fineness of uncoined silver purchased by him, the silver was to be refined by the changer at the expense of the king and the Earl of Cornwall, the cost (a halfpenny per pound) being paid from the profit of the dies. If the silver was better than had been estimated, the profit went to the king and the earl. The assayer had to see that the blanks were of due weight and fineness and also to assay the coins as they come from the dies. Twenty dwt. should not lose more, or less, than a half-pennyweight. The keepers of the dies were responsible for seeing that the striking was accurate and the coins of good weight and fineness. They received one shilling per hundred pounds from the moneyers.

The old coinage was clearly in a bad state, since on 26 November 1247 it was ordered that all sheriffs south of Trent, except those of Hereford, Salop and Stafford, should proclaim that no clipped money should be current, and that any such money found should be pierced.[1] The new coinage seems to have been limited at first to the mints of London and Canterbury.[1] The monks of Bury St Edmunds got an order for the delivery of their die on 6 December 1247. In February 1248 an inquiry was ordered into the best way for a general reform of the coinage and the mayor of London was ordered to assemble twelve prominent citizens and twelve goldsmiths to consult with the Council on the steps to be taken. The inquiry was held before the king and the Earl of Cornwall, the Treasurer, Edward of Westminster, 'fusour' (or melter) of the Exchequer, William Hardel, Warden of the mints of London and Canterbury, Ralph of Ely, a Baron of the Exchequer and others. On 11 March an assay was made of both the old and the new money, the old losing tenpence in the fire and the new

[1] *Close Rolls, 1247–51*, p. 12

only sixpence, and the rate of exchange was accordingly fixed at tenpence, with the option of having the old money refined before purchase by the mint. The old standard of eighteen pence in the pound alloy was maintained and Sir John Craig estimates that the fineness of the coin should have been (making allowance for the inaccuracy of the assaying) about ·935,[1] but that this is improbable. About ·925 (a little above the result of Sir William Roberts-Austen's assay of a ' cross and crosslet ' coin of Henry II) seems a likely estimate.[2] To check clipping, the cross on the reverse of the coin was made to extend to the margin, and to make the new coin more readily recognisable the number III was added to the king's name on the obverse. Two trial-plates were made, each weighing half a pound, to be kept in the Treasury, one of ' pure silver ' and the other of standard silver ; and similar plates weighing two ounces each for the mints of London, Canterbury, Bury St Edmunds, Norwich, Oxford, Northampton, Lincoln, Winchester, Gloucester, Exeter, York and Ilchester. The mayors, reeves or bailiffs of the towns, other than London and Canterbury, where money was to be coined were subsequently ordered to elect for each town four moneyers, as many keepers of the dies, two assayers and one clerk ; and the names of the persons elected are given. This must have been done towards the end of the month, since Peter de Gannoc, who appears in the list of officers at York, was sent by a writ of 31 March to act as deputy to William Hardel. He is listed as a clerk *ex parte regis*. Mandates were sent to Shrewsbury, Wallingford, Carlisle, Wilton, Hereford, Bristol and Newcastle, as well as to the towns already named, and they also received trial-plates. The Earl

---

[1] Craig, *The Mint*, p. 25

[2] The proportion of alloy in the reign of Edward I is stated to be 18½ dwt. of copper to the pound, giving a nominal fineness of about ·923 (see p. 68). Sir John Craig's figure seems to assume that the old standard was supposed to be approximately pure silver, which it certainly was not. See *Dialogus de Scaccario* (Oxford 1902), p. 31, n. 1.

of Cornwall had already, on 1 March, had letters patent
providing that he should be repaid all money sent by him
to be coined, together with half the profits on the coining,
and giving him power to distrain if the towns should default.[1]
On 28 April William Hardel, Warden of the London and
Canterbury mints, was appointed Warden of the Mint (*Cambium*)
throughout England.[2] It is probable that of the persons named
in these lists only the assayers were skilled in metallurgy. The
actual coining must have been done mainly by foreign workmen, since on 16 July 1248 Jordan of Brunswick was empowered
to engage at the king's expense ' ministers cunning in any kind
of minting and exchange of silver (*monetarie et cambii argenti*) '
to be paid at the usual rates in the mint, and to have safe
conduct while staying and returning to their homes.[3] The
' moneyers ', whose names would appear on the reverse of the
coins,[4] were local men of some consequence. William Prior,
for instance, one of the moneyers of Winchester, became mayor
in 1251.[5] Geoffrey of Stockwell was mayor of Oxford in 1238.
And it is clear from entries in the Patent Rolls that a moneyer's
place at Canterbury was an office of profit which could be used
as a pension for one of the king's clerks.[6] Other moneyers paid
£5 a year for their dies.[7] On 2 March 1248 the Treasurer and
Barons of the Exchequer were ordered to hold an inquiry into
unlawful exchanging and three days later the sheriff of York-
shire was ordered to make proclamation that all money of the
realm should pass current, unless it were clipped or counterfeit.
The same instructions were given to the sheriff of Lincoln and
the bailiffs of Stamford with regard to the Stamford fair. The
' short-cross ' coins had clearly not yet been called in. When
William Hardel had been replaced as Warden of the Mint by
the king's clerk, John Silvestre (18 January 1249),[8] it was found

---

[1] *Patent Rolls, 1247–58*, p. 10 [2] ibid. p. 12 [3] ibid. p. 21
[4] *Close Rolls, 1259–61*, p. 351 [5] *Patent Rolls, 1247–58*, p. 117
[6] ibid. p. 408 [7] ibid. p. 449 [8] ibid. p. 36

necessary to take steps against clippers and counterfeiters of the coin. Commissions were appointed (2 February 1251) to inquire :

Who changed new money for old without warrant and how much each changed and for how much ?
Who changed new money for plates and how much ?
Whether any goldsmith bought any silver except broken plate (*vasa fracta*) from any but a king's changer and how much and for what ?
How much silver the goldsmiths changed of broken metal (*fractivo*) in ingots (*virgis*) and plates ?
How much silver each goldsmith bought of the king's changers and for how much ?
Whether any one of the changers changed any money without the king's change and to his own use ?[1] [i.e. any officer of the mint exchanging or coining unofficially on his own account.]

The recoinage for England was presumably complete in 1251, since similar steps were taken in Ireland on 8 May in that year. There, however, there appears to have been strong opposition from the Irish.[2] The Irish mint was closed on 8 January 1254.[3] The bishop's mint at Durham, which had been closed during the recoinage, was reopened in 1253 and sanction was given for the cutting of the necessary dies.[4]

The most interesting episode in the history of the coinage of Henry III has left no record in the *Red Book*. It is the king's attempt to establish in England a gold coinage on the model of the florin in Florence, issued in 1252, twenty-four years after the unsuccessful *augustale* of Frederick II, the first European gold coin since the Carolingian empire. Gold coins were not unknown, though the Exchequer of Henry I usually accepted silver in discharge of debts in gold at a ratio of nine to one. In the thirteenth century a ratio of ten to one had become normal. In 1255 the ratio was a little less than ten to one.[5] The coins

[1] ibid. p. 115   [2] ibid. pp. 94, 114   [3] *Close Rolls, 1253–4*, p. 13
[4] *Close Rolls, 1251–3*, p. 370   [5] *Close Rolls, 1254–6*, p. 178

in circulation in England were mostly 'besants' from the imperial mint at Constantinople, or 'obols of musk' of half their value.[1] Henry III needed gold for payments to be made abroad and for plate, as well as for offerings at the shrines of saints, and employed Edward of Westminster, melter of the Exchequer, to purchase it for him. In 1252, however, he asked Edward to find him a skilled man whom he could appoint as 'King's Goldsmith' at a salary.[2] William of Gloucester was appointed to the post and had exemption from tallage as 'King's Goldsmith' within a fortnight.[3] It does not appear at what precise date it was determined to issue a gold coinage, but the council was considering financial reform in April 1257, when 20,000 marks (£13,333 6s 8d) were appropriated to clearing the debts of the Wardrobe and £1,000 to the costs of work on Westminster Abbey.[4] These appropriations were given priority to all other debts at the Exchequer. It is probable that the new coinage had been planned before this date, since the new money was proclaimed as current on 16 August 1257.[5] It seems probable that the king's goldsmith, William of Gloucester, was responsible for striking the coin, since he was ordered to make payments out of it to William de Valence and another on 30 August.[6] The style and execution of the coin are considered to be above the usual standard of the mint at this date.[7] Gloucester was a moneyer, having succeeded Nicholas of St Albans in the London mint in 1255.[8] He bought a die in the Canterbury mint on 1 October, and on the same day was appointed Warden of the Mint for all England.[9] The new coin

[1] Thus Solomon le Evesque, a Jew of London, had 85 marks, 40 dwt. of gold, most of which was in either of these forms, though 26 marks, 40 dwt. were in leaf. (*Close Rolls, 1250–9*, p. 459.) Mr P. Grierson has identified 'obols of musk' with the Almohade *dinars* or gold halfpence. (*E.H.R.* lxvi (1951), pp. 75 *seq.*)   [2] *Close Rolls, 1251–3*, p. 433
[3] *Patent Rolls, 1247–58*, p. 168 (26 December 1252)
[4] *Close Rolls, 1256–9*, p. 46   [5] ibid. p. 88
[6] *Patent Rolls, 1247–58*, p. 576   [7] Craig, *The Mint*, p. 36
[8] *Patent Rolls, 1247–58*, p. 409
[9] ibid. p. 580. *Close Rolls, 1256–9*, p. 97

was not successful as it was held to be over-valued at its legal rate of twenty pence for a coin weighing two pennies, and it was accordingly withdrawn. William ceased to be Warden of the Mint on 18 January 1262.[1]

Bartholomew de Castello, the last Warden of the Mint under Henry III, was ordered to prove and assay the king's money throughout the realm, with the object of checking clipping and the importation of counterfeit coin on 1 July 1270.[2] He remained warden until the recoinage by Edward I in 1279. It is to this recoinage that most of the remaining documents in the *Red Book* relate. The prohibition of usury by the statute of 1275, which deprived the Jews of their main source of income, though it enabled them to become merchants or artisans, failed in its object because it gave no security against violence or fraud. The result was an increase in clipping and an increasing prejudice against the Jews, which led up to their final expulsion.[3] They were not, of course, the only offenders, and the coinage was in a bad state. A general arrest of the Jews throughout England was made on 18 November 1278, and a large number of them were hanged. The recoinage began in the following year. The total amount of bullion purchased in the first six years of the king's reign was a little under 85,000 lb., considerably less than was bought in the first nine months of the recoinage. The warden was still Bartholomew de Castello, who died 29 November 1278. The office remained vacant till 28 April 1279, when the king appointed Gregory de Rokesle, a prominent merchant, and mayor of London, and Orlandino di Poggio, who probably represented the company of the Riccardi of Lucca, as joint wardens. They had already been ordered to prepare the mint for its work in February 1279.[4] Philip of the Change (*de Cambio*) had been appointed master

---

[1] *Patent Rolls, 1258–66*, p. 197   [2] *Patent Rolls, 1266–72*, p. 438
[3] C. Roth, *History of the Jews in England*, pp. 70 *seqq.*
[4] *Patent Rolls, 1272–81*, p. 301

moneyer of the mints of London and Canterbury before the death of the late warden. He was replaced soon after the new wardens came into office by one Master Albert. Before Michaelmas Albert gave place to three master moneyers, the chief of whom came from Asti, and his two assistants from Marseilles,[1] and one of the latter, William de Turnemire contracted for the whole recoinage on 8 December in the same year. The 'Form of the New Money' can thus be assigned to the autumn of 1279. The most noticeable reform was the coinage of halfpence and farthings, which had previously been obtained by cutting the penny into halves and quarters. The new round farthings were called 'Lundreis' (Londoners) since they were only to be coined at London. They contained a larger proportion of alloy than the pence to make them easier to handle; but four farthings were to contain as much silver as a penny. Another innovation was the coining of groats (or fourpenny pieces), corresponding with the *Gros Tournois* of the French coinage. Trial plates were to be provided for both pence and farthings. These were to be kept at the Exchequer, and duplicates of the pence standard were probably sent to the provincial mints; but the abbot of St Edmunds was not allowed one, though he seems to have had one in 1247. The Warden of the Mint was to see that the coins were of correct weight; 243 pence to the pound. Arrangements were made for assay at regular terms and for a box (the 'Pyx') to hold samples of each batch of coin. The prohibition of changing money except at the king's exchange was renewed and goldsmiths were forbidden to buy silver, except worn plate, otherwise than at the same exchanges. They were to work publicly in the main streets of the towns. The new Masters of the Mint were to be sworn in before Michaelmas.

The silver for the new coin came from several sources. There was the silver and clippings arising from the arrest of

[1] ibid. pp. 313, 305

PLATE II

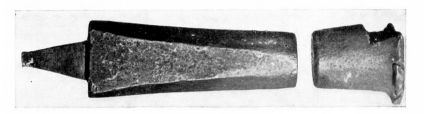

MEDIEVAL DIES (scale 1:2 approx.)
By courtesy of the Royal Mint

COINING IN PARIS *c.* 1500
(From a French print *c.* 1755)

the Jews and the value of the chattels of those who were con-
demned, the clipped coin brought in by merchants and others
and accepted by weight for recoinage, £2,000 borrowed from
Edmund, Earl of Cornwall in July 1279,[1] and silver purchased
abroad.[2] Orlandino's connection with the Riccardi must have
made it easier to purchase foreign silver, and Rokesle, who was
a goldsmith as well as a wool-merchant, would know of the
most likely English sources. The commissioners appointed on
5 January 1279 to punish clippers of coin were also bidden to
examine the various mints and to correct offences there, and the
preparations made in February were presumably the result of
their report.[3]

According to the new indenture with William de Turnemire,
mints were to work at London, Canterbury, Bristol and York.
The number of dies at London was not limited ; there were to be
eleven at Canterbury, including the Archbishop's three, and
twelve each at Bristol and York. The bishop of Durham had
his three dies sent him on 2 November 1279.[4] William was to
have deputy-masters at the three provincial mints, and was to
bear all charges, the king paying him 7d in the pound of new
money to cover all wages and expenses. The king was to find
the buildings needed and to pay the fees due to the FitzOtho
family for cutting the dies. He was also to lend William the
tools in use, to be replaced by William in as good condition as
when he received them. He was also to have any profit arising
from the saving of expense due to coining groats instead of
pence. On account of the extra alloy needed to make the
farthings large enough for use and of the extra labour in striking
them, it was estimated that the master would receive 10½d in
the pound for mintage. The king would have a shilling in
the pound for seignorage on all money coined. No mention is
made of halfpence, but the account for January to May 1280

---

[1] ibid. p. 321   [2] ibid. p. 322   [3] ibid. p. 338
[4] *Close Rolls, 1272–9*, p. 552

shows a mintage charge of 5½d in the pound for pence, 7d for halfpence and 10d for farthings.[1] Fazio Galgani mentioned in the indenture as the king's assayer, weigher and buyer of the mint, received his honourable discharge on 20 May 1281.[2] In 1280 new mints were opened at Lincoln, Newcastle and Chester. Peter Bertin de Turnemire, William's brother, appears as master-moneyer at York in August 1280, and it appears that both the York and Newcastle mints were furnished with new money for exchange from the Durham mint.[3] Surnak of Lucca is named as a master moneyer, possibly of one of the provincial mints in July 1281, and John Gyot, who may have succeeded Bonifazio Galgani, as assayer.[4]

The Treatise on the New Money, which is here attributed to William de Turnemire, was obviously written by a foreigner who was also Master of the Mint. This is clear from his allusion to the possibly conflicting interests of the Warden of the Mint, or the assayer who bought silver on his behalf, and the master. Moreover, the mintage rate of 5½d for pence and the allowance of three halfpence for the inferior fineness of the old money correspond with the figures in Turnemire's indenture. These two rates taken together add up to sevenpence, the rate which was paid to Turnemire before the memorandum of 10 February 1284, in which it was stated to have been reduced to 6½d. But this reduced rate is already shown in the account beginning 24 February 1281, so that the treatise may reasonably be assigned to the years 1279-81.

Another indication that this treatise was written by a foreigner will be found in his treatment of the proportion of alloy in the coin. He estimates the fineness of the silver for

---

[1] *Numismatic Chronicle, 4th Series XIII*, pp. 204 *seq.* As the total deduction was 19d on English silver and 17d on foreign, the seignorage must be over-estimated in the indenture. A change of mintage rates appears to have been made at Christmas 1280 (op. cit. p. 207), which is the date given by Sir John Craig (*The Mint*, p. 45) for the abandonment of the alloyed farthings.   [2] *Patent Rolls, 1272-81*, p. 448
[3] *Close Rolls, 1279-88*, pp. 32 *seq.*   [4] *Patent Rolls, 1272-81*, p. 448

the purposes of the assayer, not by the pound Tower of 5400 gr.
but by a pound of which the divisions correspond to those of
the pound Troy 5760 gr., giving a penny of 24 gr. instead of
22·5 gr. This has the convenience that the ratio of 1 gr. to half
an ounce is the same as that of a penny to the pound Tower,
and thus the number of grains lost on assay will correspond
with the number of pence in the pound to be reckoned as base
metal. These assay grains are described as ' light grains,' as
though the Tower and Troy pounds were of equal weight, but
that seems unlikely. It is more probable that the system of
division is borrowed from the pound which was more generally
used abroad by goldsmiths and apothecaries.

Sir John Craig credits Turnemire with improvements in
technique.[1] The dies, though making no attempt at a portrait,
are ' well modelled and graceful ', very different from the earlier
punched effigies, and the method of shearing and preparing
the blanks was altered. They had previously been cut from
ribbons of silver of the approximate thickness of the coin. The
silver was now made into rods whose cross-section was of about
the same area as the face of the coin, and the rods were cut into
slices a little heavier than a penny. These were ' held in
rouleaux by tongs and forged to roundness by beating in the
angles ', and then ' sized ' (i.e. trimmed and filed to the correct
weight). The workmen had 2½d per lb. for this task. The
blanks were checked for weight and fineness and returned to
the master, who handed them to the men who struck the coins.
Nothing of this is, however, described in the treatise. But it
seems clear that this was the traditional practice of the London
mint until machinery was introduced in 1663.[2] Sir John Craig
is satisfied that ' casting and cutting processes were certainly
revolutionised in 1279 ', though he mentions an MS in the Mint
Library which records a payment in 1299 (the next great

---

[1] Craig, *The Mint*, pp. 41 *seq.*   [2] ibid. p. 42, *n.* 1

recoinage) to ' another man called Guie for improvements of
coining methods '. It is tempting to identify this person with
the Guy de Turnemire (for that seems to be the name intended)
who was given £60 on 14 March 1300, for his work and advice
in connection with the new coinage.[1] He may have been a
son or nephew of William de Turnemire, who received letters
patent of honourable discharge on 28 January 1284.[2]

The treatise itself deals with the purchase of silver and the
kinds of silver likely to be offered for purchase, and proceeds
to the processes of alloying it to produce standard silver (with
an argument that the master should control the buying to
ensure that enough fine silver is bought to maintain the
standard), shearing and striking, and finally assaying, and the
Trial of the Pyx. A number of notes are appended which are
probably of later date. The last, at all events, which deals
with coinage of gold, must be assigned to c.1344.

Some of the Bury St Edmunds registers contain not only
a fuller account of the episode of the trial-plate, but also what
appears to be a revision of Turnemire's treatise made either
by the warden or by the changer, whose duty it was to purchase the silver for recoining. The order of the sections is
altered ; a great deal of technical matter relating to the rates
of purchase and the parallel between the grains in the half-
ounce assayed and the pence in the pound is omitted, as is the
complaint of the master about the possibility that he may be
defrauded if the warden does not buy enough good silver. On
the other hand more detail is given as to the supply and custody
of the dies and the testing of the coins for number to the pound
and weight of individual coins. And the purchase by the
changer is fully described and a set of specimen entries in the
Roll of Purchases is added. The date of the revision is not
certain. It must be after July 1290, when the deduction on

---

[1] *Close Rolls, 1297–1302*, p. 347   [2] *Patent Rolls, 1281–92*, p. 111

foreign silver was reduced from 16 dwt. to $11\frac{1}{2}$ dwt. It is also after the marriage of John de Botetourt to Maud, daughter of Thomas FitzOtho, of which the earliest mention is 27 June 1292.[1] As there is no mention of 'crockards and Pollards', it is probably earlier than the recoinage of 1300. It seems unnecessary to print it in full, but the additions to Turnemire's treatise have been translated and appended to the original work.[2]

Orlandino di Poggio ceased to be joint-warden on 15 July 1281, though he seems to have remained in England trading on behalf of the Riccardi till 1290, when he left for Italy and ceases to be mentioned on the Rolls.[3] It is probable that the Riccardi had no longer any financial interest in the mint. The form in which the account of it was presented at the Exchequer had been altered in the April before Orlandino's retirement. Henceforth Rokesle was sole warden. He remained so until his death in 1291.

The new coinage was not destined to last. Clipping began again even before the recoinage was finished. A case is recorded as early as 28 January 1280.[4] Gregory de Rokesle and Baroncino Gualtiere, a merchant of Lucca, were appointed commissioners on 1 March 1289, to enforce obedience to the proclamation against clipping.[5] Besides, the coins were too good. 'Sterlings' were not peculiar to England, and despite prohibitions against the importation of foreign coins, it seems clear that a penny (or rather a 'sterling') would pass current provided it appeared to be of fairly good weight, by whatever authority it was struck. A consequence of this was that, by Gresham's Law, the worse coins drove out the better, and England was flooded with 'sterlings' from the Low Countries

---

[1] *Close Rolls, 1288–96*, p. 235
[2] This version of the treatise was known to Stow, who quotes from it in his description of the Tower of London. [3] ibid. p. 367
[4] *Patent Rolls, 1272–81*, p. 412 [5] *Close Rolls, 1288–96*, p. 9

which received the nickname of ' crockards and pollards, eagles, lions, Brabantines'. Efforts were made to stop the importation of any foreign coin which resembled English, and on 14 October 1283 the use of bills of exchange was forbidden with the same object. The business of the mint had seriously declined as early as 1288, and in 1290 the deduction on foreign silver was reduced from 14½ dwt. to 11½ dwt. to encourage its being brought to the exchanges. It is probably a mere coincidence that this new provision took effect in the same month as the decree for the expulsion of the Jews. The most likely cause for the fall in the supply of foreign silver is the financial decline of the Riccardi, whose place was only gradually filled by merchants of Florence, Siena and Pistoja, of whom the most important were the Frescobaldi. In 1291 the use of imported counterfeit money was prohibited and any found was ordered to be pierced.[1] And when the king, needing money for the war with France in June 1294, sent commissioners to inspect money left on deposit in churches and monasteries, clipped and counterfeit money was probably sent to the mint.[2] It is, perhaps, significant that the account of the London mint for that year specifies £1,020 6s 8d (by weight) ' clipped money recoined without deduction '. The expedition to Flanders in 1297 probably brought a good deal of the coinage of the Low Countries into England, and it is clear from the Wardrobe Book of 1299–1300 that such coin was generally accepted as current until the ' Statute of Stepney ' (May 1299) which forbade the export of silver and the importation of foreign money.[3] A proclamation at Christmas 1299, ordained that these coins might pass at the value of a halfpenny until Easter, after which they were entirely demonetised.

---

[1] *Close Rolls, 1288–96*, p. 203
[2] Powicke, *The Thirteenth Century*, p. 670
[3] *Liber Quotidianus Contrarotulatoris Garderobae* . . . *A.D. MCCXCIX & MCCC* (London 1787), pp. 52 *seq.*

The first result of the Statute, which forbade the purchase of goods within the realm except by coin of the realm or hall-marked plate, was the sale of wool (for export) for crockards and pollards. A proclamation of 23 August 1299 made this a capital offence, but the death penalty was afterwards withdrawn.[1] The Frescobaldi had already received a pardon for the importation of such coin on 3 August.[2] When restrictions were relaxed and crockards were allowed to be accepted at half the nominal value, the Italian merchants bought them up and made a considerable profit. An examination of the cases recorded in the *Liber Quotidianus* in which parcels of crockards and pollards were taken to the mint and recoined shows an average value of about 72·5 per cent of the sums which they nominally represented.[3]

The order in council of 29 March 1300, which regulated the recoinage, contemplates an even bigger recoinage than that of 1280 ; thirty furnaces at London, eight at Canterbury, four at Hull, two at Newcastle, four at Bristol and two at Exeter, besides a separate establishment for Ireland of four furnaces at Dublin. This last, together with the mints at Hull, Newcastle and Exeter was leased to the Frescobaldi, who were to account for the issues to John de Sandale, Warden of the Mint, who in turn accounted to the king for them as well as for the mints of London, Canterbury and Bristol, and for the mint subsequently authorised at Chester. Sandale had power to oversee all the mints. A keeper of the dies was appointed at each mint who acted as controller on the king's behalf, and the changer of the London mint, Roger de Frowyk, appointed deputies for the mints of Canterbury and Bristol. At the others the exchange was in the hands of the Frescobaldi, who with the Bellardi of Lucca, seem to have been the main agents for the buying up

---

[1] *Patent Rolls, 1292–1301*, pp. 435, 473   [2] ibid. p. 430
[3] op. cit., pp. xxiii, 5, 57–60

of crockards and pollards. These were purchased as 'foreign silver' by the mint until 19 February 1300, from which date they paid the higher deduction as 'English silver'. The assayer of the London mint was to be allowed his travelling expenses when he visited provincial mints other than Canterbury. Extra clerks were to be employed during the period of extra pressure consequent on the demonetisation of the crockards and pollards.

A feature which all these recoinages have in common is the recruiting of foreign workmen from France, Italy or the Low Countries and their departure to their own homes when their job is completed. The men whom John de Sandale got together for the recoinage of 1300 [1] seem to have come from many different places and to have been sent in gangs to the various provincial mints and to Dublin. No doubt, like other medieval craftsmen such as masons, they were constantly on the move from place to place as the demand for their work shifted.[2] In the same way recoinages seem to have depended on the co-operation of the great Italian financial houses, the Riccardi, Frescobaldi, or the Bardi and Peruzzi, to whom the control of the mint was a speculation, comparable with the Constableship of Bordeaux, or the Irish Customs. Their international character would enable them to provide the necessary workman either from Italy or from their agencies in Bruges or Ghent or Cologne. Their importance in England suggests a parallel with the Welsers in Venezuela ; the Frescobaldi, at any rate, must have been almost as powerful until their expulsion in 1311.

The notes on the gold coinage which have been appended to Turnemire's treatise are probably of a date not long after the mint indenture of 27 January 1349, which is quoted in the first of them, although gold had been coined in London since 1344. They are concerned with the calculation of the

---

[1] *Close Rolls, 1297–1302*, p. 347   [2] Craig, *The Mint*, pp. 55 *seq.*

alloy in each coin, and consequently of the proportional allowance to be made in the assay for it and for the ' remedy ' within which a coin may pass if below or above standard fineness. The instructions given for making the assay describe fairly correctly the process of refining gold by cementation, as it may be found in a practical manual for chemical manu-facture (Gray's *Operative Chemist*) of 1828, and is stated to be then still in use at Venice, and probably at Constantinople and elsewhere in the East. The main differences are the addition of ' copperas heated to redness ' and the reduction of the time in the furnace from three days to eighteen to twenty-four hours. An addendum repeating the warning against depending on the touchstone, already given by Turne-mire in the case of silver, implies that there was no such systematic use of this method as was usual in the sixteenth century.[1]

[1] ibid. p. 70

LATIN TEXT
and
ENGLISH TRANSLATION

PART ONE

Tractatus de Origine, Natura
Jure, et Mutacionibus Monetarum

compositus per

Magistrum Nicolaum Oresme
Sacre Theologie Professorem

*

A Treatise on the Origin, Nature
Law and Alterations of Money

by

Master Nicholas Oresme
S.T.P.

[DE MONETA]

QUIBUSDAM uidetur quod aliquis rex aut princeps auctoritate propria possit de iure uel priuilegio libere mutare
monetas in suo regno currentes et de eis ad libitum
ordinare, ac super hoc capere lucrum seu emolumentum
quantumlibet ; aliis autem uidetur oppositum. Propter
quod intendo in presenti tractatu de hoc scribere, quid
secundum philosophiam Aristotilis principaliter michi
uidetur esse dicendum, incipiens ab origine monetarum ;
nichil temere asserendo, sed totum submitto correccioni
maiorum, qui forsan ex eis que dicturus sum poterunt
excitari ad determinandum ueritatem super isto, ita ut
omni cessante scrupulo omnes prudentes in unam possint
sentenciam pariter conuenire, et circa hoc inuenire quod
principibus et subiectis, ymo toti rei publice, proficiat
in futurum.[1]

[THE MINT]

SOME men hold that any king or prince may, of his own authority, by right or prerogative, freely alter the money current in his realm, regulate it as he will, and take whatever gain or profit may result : but other men are of the contrary opinion. I have therefore determined to write down in this treatise what seems to me from a philosophical and Aristotelian point of view, essentially proper to be said, beginning with the origin of money. I make no rash assertions, but submit everything to the judgment of my seniors. Perhaps my words will rouse them finally to settle the truth of this matter, so that the experts may all be of one mind, and come to a conclusion which shall be profitable both to princes and subjects, and indeed to the state as a whole.[1]

[1] See Appendix I

Incipiunt Capitula sequentis tractatus de origine et natura, iure et mutacionibus monetarum

2

CONTENTS

Expliciunt Capitula sequentis tractatus. Incipit Tractatus de origine et natura, iure et mutacionibus monetarum

[1] The translation into French adds to the table of contents :

Thus, then, from the preface and chapters above-mentioned, there appears a part, but not as yet the whole, of the scandals, damages and dis-

---

advantages which may arise, and are already beginning in the realm or country in which such abuses are allowed in the coinage, and in the noble metals of which it consists and ought to consist. And although I have no claim to interfere, being the meanest and most ignorant and unlearned of all men, I beg that this warning may be taken and understood to show my zeal and good will to the common wealth, and not be exposed to hasty abuse from its readers.

Capitulum I

Propter quid moneta sit inuenta

Quando diuidebat Altissimus gentes, quando separabat filios Adam, constituit terminos populorum.[1] Inde multiplicati sunt homines super terram, et possessiones prout expediebat diuise sunt. Ex hoc autem contigit, quod unus habuit de una re ultra suam necessitatem, alius uero de eadem habuit parum aut nichil, et de alia re econtrario fuit, sicut forsan pastor habundauit ouibus et pane indiguit, et agricola econuerso. Una eciam regio superhabundauit in uno, et defecit in alio. Ceperunt ergo homines mercari sine moneta, et dabat unus alteri ouem pro frumento, et alius de labore suo pro pane uel lana, et sic de aliis rebus. Quod adhuc longo postea tempore fuit in quibusdam ciuitatibus institutum, prout narrat Iustinus.[2] Sed cum in huiusmodi permutacione et transportacione rerum multe difficultates acciderent, subtiliati sunt homines usum inuenire monete, que esset instrumentum permutandi adinuicem naturales diuicias, quibus de per se subuenitur[a] humane necessitati. Nam ipse pecunie dicuntur artificiales diuicie ; contingit enim hiis habundantem mori fame, sicut exemplificat Aristotiles[3] de rege cupido, qui orauit ut quicquid ipse tangeret, aurum esset ; quod dii annuerunt, et sic fame periit, ut dicunt poete ; quoniam per pecuniam non immediate succurritur indigencie uite, sed est instrumentum artificialiter adinuentum pro naturalibus diuiciis leuius permutandis. Et absque alia probacione

---

[a] *After* subuenitur, V *adds* naturaliter
[1] Deut. xxxii. 8

Chapter I

Why Money was invented

' When the Most High divided to the nations their inheritance, when He separated the sons of Adam, He set the bounds of the people.' [1] Next, men were multiplied on the earth, and possessions were divided to the best advantage. The result of this was that one man had more than he needed of one commodity, while another had little or none of it, and of another commodity the converse was true : the shepherd had abundance of sheep and wanted bread, the farmer the contrary. One country abounded in one thing and lacked another. Men therefore began to trade by barter : one man gave another a sheep for some corn, another gave his labour for bread or wool, and so with other things. And this practice persisted in some states, as Justin [2] tells us, till long afterwards. But as this exchange and transport of commodities gave rise to many inconveniences, men were subtle enough to devise the use of money to be the instrument for exchanging the natural riches which of themselves minister to human need. For money is called ' artificial riches ' seeing that a man who abounds in it may die of hunger ; as appears from Aristotle's example of the greedy king,[3] who prayed that everything he touched should turn to gold, which the gods granted, and he perished of hunger, as the poets tell. For money does not directly relieve the necessities of life, but is an instrument artificially invented for the

---

[2] Perhaps a reference to the account of the Scythians in Justin II. 2. 3 ; cf. Aristotle Pol. I. ix. 6 (1257*a*24)   [3] Pol. I. ix. 11 (1257*b*16)

clare potest patere quod nummisma est ualde utile bone
communitati ciuili et rei publice usibus oportunum,
ymo necessarium, ut probat Aristotiles quinto Ethicorum,[1] quamquam de hoc dicat Ouidius : [2]

> Effodiuntur opes, irritamenta malorum,
> iamque nocens ferrum ferroque nocencius aurum
> prodierat, etc.

Hoc enim facit peruersa malorum cupiditas, non ipsa
pecunia, que est humano conuictui multum accomoda,
et cuius usus de per se bonus est. Inde ait Cassiodorus : [3]
' Pecunie ipse quamuis usu celeberrimo uiles esse uidean-
tur, animaduertendum est quanta tamen a ueteribus
racione collecte sunt, etc,' et in alio loco [4] dicit quod
constat monetarios in usum publicum specialiter esse
inuentos.

Capitulum II

De qua materia debet esse moneta

Et quoniam moneta est instrumentum permutandi
diuicias naturales, ut patet ex capitulo precedenti,
consequens fuit quod ad hoc tale instrumentum esset
aptum ; quod fit, si sit faciliter manibus attractabile
seu palpabile, leuiter portabile, et quod pro modica
ipsius porcione habeantur diuicie naturales in quantitate
maiori, cum aliis condicionibus que postea uidebuntur.
Oportuit ergo quod nummisma fieret de materia preciosa et rara, cuiusmodi est aurum. Sed talis materie
debet esse competens habundancia ; propter quod, ubi
aurum non sufficeret, moneta fit cum hoc de argento.

easier exchange of natural riches. And it is clear without further proof that coin is very useful to the civil community, and convenient, or rather necessary, to the business of the state, as Aristotle proves in the fifth book of the Ethics,[1] although Ovid [2] says :

> From earth we mine a source of future ill,
> First iron and then gold, more deadly still.

For that is caused by the perverse greed of wicked men, not by money itself, which is a convenience for human intercourse, and whose use is essentially good. Whence Cassiodorus says : ' However common money seems to us from our constant use of it, we should consider how good reason our forefathers had to amass it.' [3] And he says in another place that, ' It is certain that moneyers were established for the particular use of the public.' [4]

Chapter II

The Material of Money

Now, since money is an instrument for the exchange of natural riches, as appears from the preceding chapter, it follows that it must be a fit tool for the work. This implies that it must be easy to handle and to feel with the hands, light to carry and that a small portion of it should purchase a larger quantity of natural riches, with other conditions which will appear later. Coin must therefore be made of a precious and rare material, such as gold. But there must be enough of such material. Wherefore, if there is not enough gold, money is also

---

[1] Eth. V. v. 10–16 (1133a20) [2] Metamorphoses i. 140–2
[3] Variae I. 10. 5 [4] Variae V. 39. 8

Ubi autem ista duo metalla non sufficerent uel non
haberentur, debet fieri mixtio, aut simplex moneta de
alio puro metallo, sicut antiquitus fiebat ex ere, ut
narrat Ouidius in primo Fastorum,[1] dicens :

> Era dabant olim ; melius nunc omnis in auro est,
> uitaque concessit prisca moneta noue.

Similem eciam mutacionem promisit Dominus per
Ysaiam prophetam, dicens : *Pro ere afferam aurum, et pro
ferro afferam argentum.*[2]   Hec enim metalla sunt ad
monetam aptissima, et, ut Cassiodorus [3] inquit, ' primi
enim dicuntur aurum Eacus, argentum Indus rex
Sichie reperisse et humano usui summa laude tradidisse.'
Et ideo non debet permitti quod tantum ex eis in usus
alios applicetur, quod residuum non sufficiat pro
moneta.   Quod Theodoricus rex Ytalie recte aduertens,
aurum et argentum quod more gencium in sepulcris
mortuorum erat reconditum, iussit deponi, et usui
monete ad utilitatem publicam fecit afferri, dicens
' culpe genus esse inutiliter in abditis relinquere mortuorum, unde se uita potest sustentare uiuencium.' [4]
Rursum nec expedit policie quod talis materia sit nimis
habundans ; hac enim de causa moneta erea recessit
ab usu, ut ait Ouidius.   Forsan eciam quod ob hoc
humano generi prouisum est ut aurum et argentum,
que sunt ad hoc aptissima, non facile habeantur in copia,
neque possint per alkimiam leuiter fieri, sicut aliqui
temptant, quibus, ut ita dicam, iuste obuiat ipsa natura,
cuius opera frustra nituntur excedere.

---

[1] Fasti i. 221–2 ; the true text has *omen* for *omnis*, and *victaque*
[2] Isaiah lx. 17   [3] Variae IV. 34. 3
[4] Cassiodorus Variae IV. 34. 3

made of silver ; and where these two metals do not exist or are insufficient, they must be alloyed, or a simple money be made of another metal, without alloy, as was formerly the case with copper, as Ovid tells in the first book of the *Fasti*, saying :

> Men paid in copper once : they're now for gold,
> And the new money elbows out the old.[1]

A like change the Lord promised by the mouth of Isaiah [2] :

> For brass I will bring gold, and for iron I will bring silver.

For these metals are the fittest for coining. And, as Cassiodorus says [3] : ' Aeacus and Indus, king of Scythia, are said to have been the first to discover, one gold and the other silver, and to be praised for delivering them to man's use.' And therefore so much of them ought not to be allowed to be applied to other uses that there should not be enough left for money. It was this consideration that led Theodoric, king of Italy, to order the gold and silver deposited according to pagan custom in the tombs, to be removed and used for coining for the public profit, saying : ' It was a crime to leave hidden among the dead and useless, what would keep the living alive.' [4] On the other hand it is inexpedient that the material of money should be too plentiful ; for that, as Ovid says, was the reason for the disuse of copper. That may be the reason why Providence has ordained that man should not easily obtain gold and silver, the most suitable metals, in quantity, and that they cannot well be made by alchemy, as some try to do ; being, if I may say so, justly prevented by nature, whose works they vainly try to outdo.

Capitulum III

De diuersitate materie monetarum et mixtione

Moneta, ut dicit primum capitulum, est instrumentum mercature. Et quoniam communitati et cuilibet expedit mercaturam fieri aliquociens magnam seu grossam, quandoque uero minorem et plerumque de paruis uel paruam, inde est quod conueniens fuit habere monetam auream preciosam, que facilius portaretur et numeraretur, et que magis est habilis ad mercaturas maiores. Expediuit eciam habere argenteam, minus scilicet preciosam, que apta est ad recompensaciones et equiparancias faciendas, et pro empcione mercimoniorum minorum. Et quoniam aliquociens in una regione non satis est competenter de argento secundum proporcionem diuiciarum naturalium, ymo porciuncula argenti, que iuste dari deberet pro libra panis uel aliquo tali, esset minus bene palpabilis propter nimiam paruitatem, ideo facta fuit mixtio de minus bona materia cum argento, et inde habuit ortum nigra moneta, que est congrua pro minutis mercaturis. Et sic conuenientissime, ubi non habundat argentum, sunt tres materie monetarum : prima aurea, secunda argentea, et tercia nigra mixta. Sed animaduertendum est et notandum pro regula generali, quod nunquam debet mixtio fieri, nisi tantummodo in minus precioso metallo, de quo consueuit fieri parua *a* moneta, uerbi gracia, ubi habetur moneta ex auro et ex argento, mixtio nunquam facienda est in moneta aurea, si tamen aurum talis nature fuerit quod monetari possit inmixtum.[1] Et causa est, quoniam

---

[1] parua C, *and so the French version* (petite monnoie) ; minus preciosa V ; pura *the other MSS*

Chapter III

Of the Variety of Materials and of Alloy

Money, as was said in Chapter I, is the instrument of trade. And since both for communities or individuals, trade must sometimes be large, or in bulk, sometimes smaller, and more generally petty, or retail, it has been convenient to have precious money, made of gold, easy to carry and to count, and suitable for large transactions. It was also proper to have silver money, less precious, suitable for giving change and for adjustments of price, and for buying goods of lower value. And since a particular country is not always furnished with silver in proportion to its natural riches, besides which, the portion of silver which would be justly due for a pound of bread or the like, would be too small to hold in the hand, money came to be coined of a cheaper metal together with the silver, and that is the origin of our ' black ' money, which is suitable for petty dealings. And thus, where silver is not abundant, the best plan is to have three materials for money, gold, silver and the ' black ' alloy. But it should be observed and laid down as a general rule that no alloy should be permitted except in the least precious metal used for small change. For instance, where the money consists of gold and silver, the gold should never be alloyed if it can be coined pure.[1]

---

[1] The French translation adds : The gold which is unsuitable for coining florins because of its alloy can be made into rings or other jewellery. The same comment is found in one late MS of the Latin text. C *adds* aurum quidem non est aptum ad florenos si sit mixtum anuli fiant.

omnis talis mixtio de se suspecta est, nec facile possunt
auri substancia et eius quantitas in mixtione cognosci.
Propter quod nulla mixtio debet in monetis fieri, nisi
propter necessitatem iam tactam ; et tunc facienda est,
ubi suspicio est minor uel decepcionis minoris, et hoc
est in minus precioso metallo. Rursum nulla talis
mixtio facienda est, nisi dumtaxat pro utilitate communi,
racione cuius moneta inuenta est et ad quam naturaliter
ordinatur, ut patet ex prius dictis. Sed nunquam est
necessitas, nec apparet communis utilitas, faciendi
mixtionem in moneta aurea, ubi habetur argentea ;
nec uidetur posse bona intencione fieri, neque unquam
factum est in communitate prospere gubernata.

Capitulum IV

De forma uel figura monete

Cum primum cepissent homines mercari siue comparare diuicias mediante moneta, nundum erat in ea
aliqua impressio uel ymago, sed una porcio argenti uel
eris dabatur pro potu uel cibo, que quidem porcio
mensurabatur ad pondus. Et quoniam tediosum erat
ita crebro ad trutinam recurrere, nec bene poterat
pecunia mercaturis equiparari per pondus, cum hoc
eciam ut in pluribus uenditor non poterat cognoscere
metalli substanciam siue modum mixtionis, ideo per
sapientes illius temporis prudenter prouisum est, quod
porciones monete fierent de certa materia et determinati
ponderis, quodque in eis imprimeretur figura que

The reason is that all such mixture is naturally suspect because the proportion of pure gold in it cannot readily be determined. Consequently coins should not be alloyed except for the necessity above-mentioned. And this should only be done where the suspicion is least, or the fraud is of least importance, that is in the less precious metal. Again, no such mixture should be made except for the common good, on account of which money was invented and by which it is regulated as is shown above. But there is no necessity nor common advantage in alloying gold money where silver is also in use ; nor can it honestly be done, nor has it been done in any well governed community.

Chapter IV

Of the Form or Shape of Money

When men first began to trade, or to purchase goods with money, the money had no stamp or image, but a quantity of silver or bronze was exchanged for meat and drink and was measured by weight. And since it was tiresome constantly to resort to the scales and difficult to determine the exact equivalent by weighing, and since the seller could not be certain of the metal offered or of its degree of purity, it was wisely ordained by the sages of that time that pieces of money should be made of a given metal and of definite weight and that they should be stamped with a design, known to everybody,

cunctis notoria significaret qualitatem materie nummismatis et ponderis ueritatem, ut amota suspicione
posset ualor monete sine labore cognosci. Quod autem
impressio talis instituta sit nummis in signum ueritatis
materie et ponderis, manifeste nobis ostendunt antiqua
nomina monetarum cognoscibilium ex impressionibus
et figuris, cuiusmodi sunt libra, solidus, denarius, obolus,
as, sextula et similia, que sunt nomina ponderum
appropriata monetis, ut ait Cassiodorus.[1] Similiter
ciclus [a] est nomen monete, ut patet in Genesi,[2] et est
nomen ponderis, ut patet ibidem. Alia uero nomina
monete sunt impropria, accidentalia seu denominatiua
a loco, a figura, ab actore,[3] uel aliquo tali modo. Porciones autem monete, que dicuntur nummisma, debent
esse figure et quantitatis habilis ad contractandum et
ad numerandum, et de materia monetabili [b] ac eciam
ductibili atque receptibili impressionis, necnon et eius
impressionis retentiua siue tenaci. Et inde est quod
non omnis res preciosa apta est ut fiat nummisma ;
gemme enim, lazuleus, piper et talia non sunt ad hoc
apta nata, sed precipue aurum et argentum, sicut fuit
supra tactum.

CAPITULUM V

Cui incumbit facere nummisma

Adhuc autem fuit antiquitus racionabiliter ordinatum et propter decepcionem cauendam, quod non
cuilibet licet facere monetam, aut huiusmodi figuram
uel ymaginem imprimere in suo proprio argento uel

[a] *MSS have* actus, accus *or* acus
[b] *So* G *and the French version* (monnoyable) ; C *has* monetali, *the other MSS*
numerabili

to indicate the quality and true weight of the coin, so that suspicion should be averted and the value readily recognised. And that the stamp on coins was instituted as a guarantee of fineness and weight, is clearly proved by the ancient names of coins distinguishable by their stamp or design, such as pound, shilling, penny, half-penny, *as*, *sextula*, and the like, which are names of weights applied to coins, as Cassiodorus [1] says. Shekel, likewise, is the name of a coin, as appears in Genesis, [2] and also of a weight as appears in the same book. The other names of coins are not ' proper ' (i.e. derived from the essence), but accidental, or denominative from a place, a design or an authority, [3] or in some other way. But the pieces of money which are called coin (*nummisma*) should be of a shape and quantity suitable for handling and counting, and of a material capable of being coined, malleable and fit to receive and retain an impression. Hence not all precious substances are fit for coins : gems, lapis lazuli, pepper and the like are not naturally fit, but gold and silver eminently are so, as we said before.

Chapter V

Who has the Duty of Coining ?

Furthermore, it was ordained of old, with good reason, and to prevent fraud, that nobody may coin money or impress an image or design on his own gold and silver, but that the money, or rather the impression

---

[1] Variae VII. 32   [2] Genesis xxiii. 15
[3] e.g. ' Carolus,' ' Louis ' etc.

auro, sed quod moneta et caracteris impressio fieret per unam personam publicam, seu per plures a communitate quoad hoc deputatas ; quia, sicut premissum est, moneta de natura sua instituta est et inuenta pro bono communitatis. Et quoniam princeps est persona magis publica et maioris auctoritatis, conueniens est quod ipse pro communitate faciat fabricare monetam et eam congrua impressione signare. Hec autem impressio debet esse subtilis, et ad effigiendum seu contrafaciendum difficilis. Debet eciam prohiberi sub pena, ne aliquis aut extraneus princeps uel alter fabricaret monetam similem in figura et minoris ualoris, ita quod uulgus nesciret distinguere inter istam et illam. Hoc esset malefactum, nec aliquis potest de hoc habere priuilegium, quia falsitas est ; et est causa iuste bellandi contra talem extraneum.

Capitulum VI

Cuius sit ipsa moneta

Quamuis pro utilitate communi princeps habeat signare nummisma, non tamen ipse est dominus seu proprietarius monete currentis in suo principatu. Moneta siquidem est instrumentum equiualens permutandi diuicias naturales, ut patet ex primo capitulo. Ipsa igitur est eorum possessio, quorum sunt huiusmodi diuicie. Nam si quis dat panem suum uel laborem proprii corporis pro pecunia, cum ipse eam recepit, ipsa est sua, sicut erat panis uel labor corporis, qui erat in eius potestate libera, supposito quod non sit seruus. Deus enim a principio non dedit solis principibus libertatem et dominium rerum, sed primis parentibus et toti posteritati,

of its characteristic design, should be made by one or more public persons deputed by the community to that duty, since, as we have said, money is essentially established and devised for the good of the community. And since the prince is the most public person and of the highest authority, it follows that he should make the money for the community and stamp it with a suitable design. This stamp should be finely wrought and difficult to engrave or counterfeit. It should also be penal for a foreign prince or any other to coin money of like design but of lower weight, so that common people could not distinguish one from the other. This should be a crime ; nor can anyone have such a privilege, for it is forgery ; and it is a just cause for war.

Chapter VI

Who owns the Money ?

Although it is the duty of the prince to put his stamp on the money for the common good, he is not the lord or owner of the money current in his principality. For money is a balancing instrument for the exchange of natural wealth, as appears in Chapter I. It is therefore the property of those who possess such wealth. For if a man gives bread or bodily labour in exchange for money, the money he receives is as much his as the bread or bodily labour of which he (unless he were a slave) was free to dispose. For it was not to princes alone that God gave freedom to possess property, but to our first parents

ut habetur in Genesi.[1] Moneta igitur non est solius principis. Si quis autem uellet opponere per hoc, quod Saluator noster, ostenso sibi quodam denario, interrogauit dicens *Cuius est ymago et superscripcio hec*?[2], et cum responsum esset *Cesaris*, ipse sentenciauit et dixit : *Reddite ergo que sunt Cesaris Cesari, et que sunt Dei Deo*, ac si diceret : Cesaris est nummisma, ex quo ymago Cesaris in eo est impressa ; sed inspicienti seriem ewangelii patet facile, quod non ideo dicitur Cesari deberi denarius, quia erat Cesaris ymagine superscriptus, sed quoniam erat tributum. Nam, ut ait Apostolus, *Cui tributum tributum, cui uectigal, uectigal*.[3] Christus itaque per hoc signauit posse cognosci cui debeatur tributum, quia illi debebatur qui pro re publica militabat, et qui racione imperii poterat fabricare monetam. Est igitur pecunia communitatis et singularium personarum ; et ita dicit Aristotiles septimo Politice,[4] et Tullius circa finem ueteris Rethorice.[5]

Capitulum VII

Ad cuius expensas fabricanda sit moneta

Sicut ipsa moneta est communitatis, ita facienda est ad expensas communitatis. Hoc autem fit conuenientissime, si huiusmodi expense accipiantur super ipsam monetam, per hunc modum quod materia monetabilis, sicut aurum, quando traditur ad monetandum uel

---

[1] Genesis i. 28   [2] Matthew xxii. 20
[3] Romans xiii. 7. The French version translates *vectigal* as *betaille* (possibly by confusion with *taille*, a tax).
[4] Pol. vii. 8. ?   [5] Inv. ii. 56

and all their offspring, as it is in Genesis.[1]   Money,
therefore, does not belong to the prince alone.   But if
anyone object that our Saviour, when a penny was
shown Him, asked : ' Whose is this image and superscription ? ' [2] and when it was answered ' Caesar's,' gave
judgment : ' Render therefore unto Caesar the things
which are Caesar's, and unto God the things that are
God's ' (as though He meant ' The coin is Caesar's
because Caesar's image is stamped upon it '), it is clear
to anyone who reads the context that He does not say
that the money was due to Caesar because it bore
Caesar's image, but because it was ' tribute.'   For, as
the apostle says : ' Tribute to whom tribute is due ;
custom to whom custom.' [3]   Christ therefore showed
that the stamp was the means of knowing to whom the
tribute was due, namely the person who fought the
battles of the state, and by reason of his dominion had
the right to coin money.   Thus, money belongs to the
community and to individuals.   And so say Aristotle in
the seventh book of the Politics [4] and Cicero about the
end of the old Rhetoric.[5]

CHAPTER VII

Who bears the Expense of Coining ?

As money belongs to the community, it should be
coined at the expense of the community.   The most
appropriate way of doing this is to distribute the expense
over the whole coinage by causing the material, such as
gold, when it is brought to be coined or sold for coined
money, to be bought for less money than it could be

uenditur pro moneta, detur pro minori pecunia quam
possit fieri ex ea sub certo precio taxato : [1] uerbi gracia,
si ex marcha argenti possint fieri lxii solidi, et pro labore
et necessariis ad monetandum eam requirantur duo solidi,
tunc marcha argenti non monetata ualebit lx solidos,
et alii duo solidi [a] erunt pro monetacione. Hec autem
porcio taxata debet esse tanta quod sufficeret habundanter omni tempore pro fabricacione monete. Et si
moneta possit fieri pro minori precio, satis congruum
est quod residuum sit distributori uel ordinatori, scilicet
principi uel magistro monetarum, et sit quasi quedam
pensio. Sed tamen huiusmodi porcio debet esse moderata, et sufficeret satis parua, si monete sufficerent debito
modo, ut dicetur postea. Et si talis pensio uel porcio
esset excessiua, hoc foret in dampnum et preiudicium
tocius communitatis, sicut potest unicuique faciliter
apparere.

Capitulum VIII

De mutacionibus monetarum in generali

Ante omnia sciendum est, quod nunquam sine
euidenti necessitate immutande sunt priores leges,
statuta, consuetudines seu ordinaciones quecumque
tangentes communitatem. Ymo, secundum Aristotilem
in secundo Politice,[2] lex antiqua positiua non est abro-
ganda pro meliori noua, nisi sit multum notabilis
differencia in bonitate earum, quoniam mutaciones
huiusmodi diminuunt ipsarum legum auctoritatem et
reuerenciam, et multo magis si frequenter fiant. Ex hoc

---

[a] V *omits* tunc . . . alii duo solidi, *a slip which Kees's editor tries to mend by
inserting* lxiiii *after* monetacione.

coined into and at a certain fixed rate [1] : e.g. if a mark
of silver can be coined into sixty-two shillings, and two
shillings are needed for labour and other necessaries in
minting, the mark of silver will be worth sixty shillings
and the other two will be paid for the minting. But
the rate should be fixed high enough to cover the cost
of coining at all times. And if the money can be made
at a lower price, it is reasonable that the balance should
go to the distributor or ordainer, to wit, the prince or
the master of the mint, as a sort of pension. But this
rate should be a moderate one, and need only be quite
small if money is adequately plentiful, as shall be said
later. And if such a rate or pension were excessive it
would be to the damage and prejudice of the whole
community, as any man may easily see.

Chapter VIII

On Alterations in Coinage in general

First of all we must know that the existing laws,
statutes, customs or ordinances affecting the community,
of whatever kind, must never be altered without evident
necessity. Indeed, as Aristotle says in the second book
of the Politics,[2] an ancient positive law is not to be
abrogated in favour of a better new law, unless there is
a notable difference in their excellence, because changes
of this kind lessen the authority of the laws and the
respect paid them, and all the more if they are frequent.

---

[1] The French version says ' fixed by the Lords and officers versed in the
matter '.   [2] Pol. II. viii. 23 (1263a18)

enim oritur scandalum et murmur in populo, et periculum inobediencie ; maxime autem, si tales mutaciones
essent in peius, nam tunc forent intollerabiles et iniuste.
Nunc autem ita est, quod cursus et precium monetarum
in regno debet esse quasi quedam lex et quedam ordi-
nacio firma. Cuius signum est, quod pensiones et
quidam redditus annuales taxati sunt ad precium pecunie,
scilicet ad certum numerum librarum uel solidorum. Ex
quo patet, quod nunquam debet fieri mutacio monetarum, nisi forsan emineret necessitas, aut euidens
utilitas pro tota communitate. Unde Aristotiles quinto
Ethicorum de nummismate loquens, ' Uerumptamen,
inquit, uult manere magis.' [1] Mutacio uero monete,
prout possum in generali perpendere, potest ymaginari
fieri multipliciter : uno modo in forma seu in figura
precise, alio modo in proporcione, alio modo in precio
uel appellacione, alio modo in quantitate uel pondere,
et alio modo in substancia materie. Quolibet enim
istorum quinque modorum sigillatim aut pluribus simul
potest mutari moneta. Bonum est ergo istos modos
discurrendo declarare et per racionem inquirere, si
aliquo eorum potest iuste mutari moneta, et quando, et
per quem, et qualiter, et propter quid.

Capitulum IX

De mutacione monete in figura

Figura impressa seu caracter monete potest dupliciter
innouari. Uno modo, non prohibendo cursum monete
prioris, ut si princeps in moneta que fit suo tempore

---

[1] Eth. V. v. 14 (1133*b*14)

For hence arise scandal and murmuring among the
people and the risk of disobedience. Especially if such
changes should be for the worse, for then they would be
intolerable and unjust. Now it is the case, that the
course and value of money in the realm should be, as it
were, a law and a fixed ordinance. This is indicated by
the fact that pensions and yearly rents are reckoned
according to the value of money, i.e. in a certain number
of pounds or shillings. From which it is clear that a
change in money should never be made, unless perhaps
under eminent necessity or for the obvious advantage of
the whole community. Wherefore Aristotle, in the fifth
book of the Ethics [1] speaking of coin, says : ' It aims at
remaining of the same value.'

But alteration in money (considering the matter
generally) may be regarded as being made in various
ways : first, to put it shortly, in form or shape ; then,
in bimetallic ratio ; in value and denomination ; again,
in quantity or weight, and lastly in material substance.
For money may be altered in any one or more of these
five ways. We had better then, discuss these ways, and
reasonably inquire whether money can justly be altered
in any of them, and, if so, when, by whom, how and for
what reason.

CHAPTER IX

Change of Form

The impressed form or stamp of the money can be
altered in two ways. One is, without demonetising the
old money ; as, if a prince should inscribe his own
name on the money issued during his reign, allowing

inscriberet nomen suum, permittendo semper cursum
precedentis ; et hoc non est proprie mutacio, nec est
magna uis si hoc fiat, dum tamen non implicetur cum
hoc alia mutacio. Alio modo potest innouari figura,
faciendo nouam monetam cum prohibicione cursus
antique ; et est proprie mutacio, et potest fieri iuste
propter alteram duarum causarum. Una est si aliquis
princeps extraneus, uel aliqui falsarii, maliciose effigiaue-
rint uel contrafecerint modulos seu cuneos monetarum,
et inueniatur in regno moneta sophistica, falsa et similis
bone in colore et figura ; tunc, qui non posset aliter
remedium apponere, expediret mutare modulos et figuram impressionis monete. Alia causa posset esse, si
forsan antiqua moneta esset uetustate nimia impeiorata
uel in pondere diminuta ; tunc cursus eius deberet
prohiberi, et in noua meliore esset facienda impressio
differens, ut uulgus sciret per hoc distinguere inter
istam et illam. Sed non uidetur michi quod princeps
posset inhibere cursum prioris monete sine altera istarum
causarum ; alias enim talis mutacio esset preternecces-
saria, scandalosa et communitati dampnosa. Nec
apparet quod princeps ad talem mutacionem faciendam
posset aliunde moueri, nisi propter alterum duorum :
aut uidelicet quia uult ut in quolibet nummismate
inscribatur nomen suum et nullum aliud, et hoc esset
facere irreuerenciam predecessoribus suis et ambicio
uana, aut quia uult plus fabricare de moneta, ut ex hoc
habeat plus de lucro, iuxta illud quod tactum est
supra in capitulo septimo, et hoc est praua cupiditas, in
preiudicium et dampnum tocius communitatis.

the old money to pass current. This is not strictly an alteration, nor is it a great matter if it is done, unless another alteration is involved.

The form may be changed in another way, by making new money and demonetising the old. That is definitely an alteration and can justly be made for one of two reasons. One is, if a foreign prince or false coiners maliciously copy or counterfeit the moulds or dies of the money and there is found in the realm a forged, false money, like the good in colour and form. Then, if no other remedy could be applied, it would be well to change the moulds and the form of the stamp. Another reason might be if perchance the old money was too much injured by age or reduced in weight. Its currency should then be forbidden and the new and better money should be given a different stamp, so that the common people should be able to know one from the other.

But I do not think that the prince should be able to demonetise the old money except for one of these reasons, for such a change would otherwise be unnecessary, scandalous and to the damage of the community. Nor does it appear that the prince could be induced to make such a change but for one of two reasons : either because he wishes to have no other name than his own inscribed on the coins, which is a slight to his pre-decessors, and empty ambition ; or because he wants to get a larger profit by coining more money, as was mentioned in Chapter VII, and that is covetousness and to the prejudice and loss of the whole community.

Capitulum X

De mutacione proporcionis monetarum

Proporcio est rei ad rem comparacio uel habitudo, sicut in proporcione[a] monete auree ad monetam argenteam debet esse certa habitudo in ualore et precio. Nam secundum hoc quod aurum est de natura sua preciosius et rarius argento, et ad inueniendum uel habendum difficilius, ipsum aurum equalis ponderis debet preualere in certa proporcione : sicut forsan esset proporcio xx ad unum, et sic una libra auri ualeret xx libras argenti et una marcha xx marchas et una uncia xx uncias, et sic semper conformiter. Et possibile est quod sit una alia proporcio, sicut forte xxv ad tria, uel queuis alia. Verumptamen ista proporcio debet sequi naturalem habitudinem auri ad argentum in preciositate, et secundum hoc instituenda est huiusmodi proporcio, quam non licet uoluntarie transmutare, nec potest iuste uariari, nisi propter causam realem et uariacionem ex parte ipsius materie, que tamen raro contingit ; ut si forsan notabiliter minus inueniretur de auro quam ante, tunc oporteret quod esset carius in comparacione ad argentum, et quod mutaretur in precio et ualore. Si parum aut nichil mutatum sit in re, hoc eciam nullo modo potest licere principi. Nam si huiusmodi proporcionem ad libitum immutaret, ipse per hoc posset attrahere sibi indebite pecunias subditorum, ut si taxaret aurum ad paruum precium, et illud emeret pro argento, deinde augmentato precio

---

[a] *So* C ; VWG *have* in proposito, P imposicio

Chapter X

Change of Ratio

Ratio is the comparison or habitual relation of one thing to another, just as in the proportion of gold money to silver money there ought to be a definite relation in value and price. For as gold is naturally more precious and scarcer than silver, and more difficult to find and to get, gold of the same weight ought to excel silver in value by a definite proportion. The ratio, for instance, might be twenty to one, and thus one pound of gold would be worth twenty pounds of silver, one mark twenty marks, one ounce twenty ounces, and so forth. And another proportion is possible, such as twenty-five to three, or any other. But this proportion ought to follow the natural relation in value of gold to silver, and a ratio should be fixed, not to be arbitrarily changed, nor justly varied except for a reasonable cause and an alteration arising from the material, a thing which rarely happens. Thus, if it were notorious that less gold was being found than before, it would have to be dearer as compared with silver, and would change in price and value. But if there were little or no material change, the prince would not be free to make such a change in price. For if he were to alter the ratio arbitrarily, he might unfairly draw to himself his subjects' money, for instance, by fixing a low price for gold and buying it for silver, and then raising the price when he sold his gold or gold money ; or by doing the same with silver.

rursum uenderet aurum suum uel monetam auream, uel
conformiter de argento ; illud esset simile, sicut si
poneret precium in toto frumento sui regni, et emeret,
et postea uenderet pro maiori precio. Quisque certe
potest clare uidere quod ista esset iniusta exaccio et
uere tyrannis ; ymo uideretur uiolencior et peior quam
illa fuerit, quam fecit Pharao in Egypto, de qua Cassiodorus [1] inquit : ' Ioseph legimus contra famem funestam
emendi quidem tritici dedisse licenciam, sed tale posuisse
precium ut sue subuencionis [a] auidus populus se uenderet, pocius alimoniam mercaturus. Quale fuit, rogo,
tunc miseris [b] uiuere, quibus acerba subuencio libertatem suam uidebatur adimere, ubi non minus ingemuit
liberatus quam potuit flere captiuus ? Credo uirum
sanctum hac necessitate constrictum, ut et auaro principi
satisfaceret et periclitanti populo subueniret.' Hec
ille. Istud autem monopolium monetarum adhuc esset
uerius tyrannicum, eo quod foret magis inuoluntarium
et communitati non necessarium, sed precise dampno-
sum. Si quis autem dicit quod non est simile de frumento, quia aliqua spectant specialiter ad principem,
in quibus potest statuere precium prout placet, sicut
dicunt aliqui de sale, et forciori racione de moneta ;
istud autem monopolium seu gabella salis, aut cuiuscumque rei necessarie communitati, iniusta est, et si qui
principes statuerint leges hoc eis concedentes, ipsi sunt
de quibus Dominus per Ysaiam prophetam dicit *Ve
qui condunt leges iniquas et scribentes iniusticias scripserunt*,
etc.[2] Rursum ex primo et sexto capitulis satis patet,
quod pecunia est ipsius communitatis ; ideoque, et ne
princeps possit maliciose fingere causam mutacionis

---

[a] VC *have* subieccionis, *and so apparently the French version* (affin que le
glout peuple vensist a sa subjection)
[b] *So* PC *and the 1484 edition ; all other MSS* miserum

It would be like fixing a price for all the corn in his kingdom, buying it and selling again at a higher price. Everyone can clearly see that this would be an unjust exaction and actually tyranny : indeed, it would appear outrageous and worse than that which Pharaoh did in Egypt, of which Cassiodorus says [1] :

'We read that Joseph gave leave to buy corn, to meet the deadly famine, but set such a price that the people, hungry for relief, sold themselves into slavery to him to buy themselves food. What a miserable life it must have been for those to whom the bitter bread of relief seemed to take away their freedom, where the freed man groaned no less than the captive wept. I believe the holy man to have been compelled by the necessity both of satisfying a greedy prince and of helping a perishing people.'

So Cassiodorus.

But the monopoly of coinage of which we spoke would be even more tyrannous, being more involuntary and not for the need of the community, but literally to its harm. But if anyone should say that corn is not a fair parallel, because certain commodities are the private property of the prince for which he may set his own prices, as some say is the case with salt and *a fortiori* with money, we answer that a monopoly or *gabelle* of salt, or any public necessity, is unjust. And that princes who have made laws to give themselves this privilege are the men of whom the Lord says, in the words of the prophet Isaiah [2] : 'Woe unto them that decree un-righteous decrees, and write grievousness which they have prescribed.' Again, it is clear from our first and sixth chapters, that money is the property of the common-wealth. Therefore, and lest the prince should unfairly

---

[1] Variae XII. 28, 7   [2] Isaiah x. 1

proporcionis monetarum in presenti capitulo assignatam,
ipsi soli communitati spectat decernere, si et quando,
qualiter et usquequo immutanda est huiusmodi proporcio, nec princeps hec sibi debet quomodolibet
usurpare.

Capitulum XI

De mutacione appellacionis monete

Sicut fuit dictum capitulo quarto, quedam sunt appel-
laciones seu nomina accidentalia monetarum, denominatiua ab actore uel loco, et ista quasi nichil aut modicum
faciunt ad propositum. Sed alia sunt magis essencialia
et appropriata nummismati, sicut denarius, solidus,
libra et similia, que denotant precium siue pondus, et
que fuerunt alta consideracione et magno misterio ab
antiquis imposita. Unde Cassiodorus [1] ' Animaduertendum est ' inquit ' quanta racione ipse pecunie a
ueteribus collecte sunt. Sex milia denariorum solidum
esse uolebant,[2] scilicet ut radiantis metalli formata
rotunditas etatem mundi, quasi sol aureus, conuenienter
includeret. Senarium uero, quem non immerito per-
fectum antiquitas docta diffinit,[3] uncie, que mensure
primus gradus est, appellacione signauit, quam duo-
decies similitudine mensium computatam in libre pleni-
tudinem ab anni curriculo collegerunt. O inuenta
prudencium ! O prouisa maiorum ! Exquisita res
est, que et usui humano necessaria distingueret, et
tot archana nature figuraliter contineret. Merito ergo
dicitur libra, que tanta rerum est consideracione truti-
nata.' Hec ille. Si autem alio modo utamur pro

[1] Variae I. x. 5

put forward the reason given in this chapter for altering
the ratio, the community alone has the right to decide
if, when, how, and to what extent this ratio is to be
altered, and the prince may not in any way usurp it.

Chapter XI

Change of Name

As was said in Chapter IV, there are certain names
or non-essential denominations of money which indicate
the author or the place of coinage, and these have little
or nothing to do with our subject.   But others are
essential or proper to coin, e.g. penny, shilling, pound
and the like, which denote the value or weight and
were given by our forefathers after deep thought and
with great mystery.   Of which Cassiodorus [1] says :

It is remarkable on how rational a plan money was
brought together by the ancients.   They would have six
thousand pence to be a shilling (*solidus*),[2] in order that
the round shape of radiant metal, like a golden sun,
might correspond numerically with the age of the world.
But the number six (*senarius*) (which learned antiquity
defined not undeservedly as perfect [3]) it signified by the
name of ounce (*uncia*), the first degree of measurement,
and multiplying it by twelve to match the months,
brought it up to a pound to correspond with the year.
What a wise invention !   How far-seeing were our
elders !   It was most ingenious to devise measures for
human use and at the same time symbolise so many of
the secrets of nature.   That, therefore, is deservedly
called a pound which has been so weightily considered.

So far Cassiodorus.

---

[2] i.e. the Roman *solidus*, worth 25 *denarii*   [3] As being 1 + 2 + 3

nunc istis nominibus et nummis, nunquam tamen immutanda sunt frustra. Sint ergo, gratia exempli, tres modi nummismatis : primum ualeat unum denarium, secundum unum solidum, et tercium unam libram. Si ergo appellacio unius immutetur et non alterius, iam uariabitur proporcio. Sicut qui uocaret uel faceret ualere primum nummisma duos denarios, aliis non mutatis, proporcio esset uariata ; quod non licet fieri, ut patet ex capitulo precedenti, nisi forsan rarissime, et de hoc ad presens non curo. Oportet igitur, si proporcio remaneat immutata, et unum nummisma mutet appellacionem, quod aliud eciam proporcionaliter immutetur ; ut si primum uocetur duo denarii, secundum uocetur duo solidi, et tercium due libre. Si autem non fieret alia mutacio, oporteret mercimonia ad maius precium proporcionaliter comparare seu appellare. Sed talis mutacio nominum fieret frustra, et non facienda est, quia scandalum esset et appellacio falsa. Illud enim uocaretur libra, quod in ueritate non esset libra ; quod est inconueniens, ut nunc dictum est. Verumptamen nullum aliud inconueniens sequeretur, ubi non essent pensiones uel aliqui redditus ad pecunie numerum assignati ; ubi uero essent, statim patet quod cum inconuenientibus predictis huiusmodi redditus ex tali mutacione proporcionaliter minuerentur aut crescerent, irracionabiliter et iniuste, ac eciam in preiudicium multorum. Nam ubi pensiones uel redditus aliquorum essent nimis parui, deberent per alium modum specialem augeri, et non isto modo preiudiciabili et dampnoso. Hec ergo appellacionis mutacio precisa nunquam est facienda, et maxime princeps in nullo casu debet hoc attemptare.

But although we now apply these names differently to our coins, they must not be changed to no purpose. Suppose, for example, that there are three kinds of coins, the first worth a penny, the second a shilling and the third a pound. Then if the description of one is altered but not that of any other, that will change their proportionate value. So, if anyone were to call or fix the value of the first kind at two pence without altering the others to match, the proportionate value would be changed, a thing which is not lawful (as appears in the preceding chapter), except in very rare cases with which I am not concerned at present. It is necessary, then, that if the proportion is to remain unchanged, and one coin changes its denomination, the others should be changed in proportion, so that if the first coin is called two pence, the second shall be two shillings and the third two pounds. And if no other change were made, it would be necessary for goods to be bought or priced at proportionately higher rates. But such a change would be to no purpose, and must not be made, because it would be scandalous and a false denomination. For that would be called a pound which really was not a pound, which is, as we have said, improper. But no other impropriety would ensue, except where pensions or rents were appointed in terms of money. For in that case it is immediately apparent that besides the impropriety which we have named, such rents by this change would either be reduced or would increase unreasonably and unjustly and to the damage of many people. For where some people's pensions or rents were inadequate, they should be augmented by another special measure, and not this prejudicial and hurtful one. Therefore this change of denomination should never be made ; least of all should the prince attempt to make it.

Capitulum XII

De mutacione ponderis monetarum

Si pondus nummismatis mutaretur, et cum hoc uariaretur proporcionaliter precium, et appellacio cum figura, hoc esset facere aliud genus monete, sicut qui faceret de uno denario duos obolos uel aliquid tale, sine perdicione uel lucro. Et istud posset aliquociens licite fieri propter aliquam transmutacionem realem in materia monetabili, que non potest nisi rarissime contingere, sicut de quadam alia mutacione dictum est in capitulo decimo. Nunc autem uolo dicere de precisa mutacione ponderis seu quantitatis monete, que fieret appellacione et precio non mutatis. Et uidetur michi quod talis mutacio est simpliciter illicita, potissime principi, qui nullo modo potest hoc facere, nisi turpiter et iniuste. Primo namque, quoniam ymago siue superscripcio in nummismate per principem ponitur ad designandum certitudinem ponderis et materie qualitatem, sicut fuit ostensum capitulo quarto, ergo, si non corresponderet ueritas in pondere, patet statim quod esset falsitas uilissima et decepcio fraudulenta. Sepe enim mensure bladi et uini et alie signate sunt publico signo regis, et si quis in istis fraudem committat, reputatur falsarius. Omnino autem consimiliter superscripcio nummismatis significat mensuram ponderis et materie ueritatem. Quam ergo sit iniquum,[1] quam detestabile, precipue in principe, sub eodem signo pondus minuere, quis sufficeret explicare? De hoc enim ad istud propositum Cassiodorus v° [a] Variarum [2] sic inquit : 'Quid enim tam nepharium, quam pre-

---

[a] *So* WP ; uero C, libro VG

Chapter XII

Change of Weight

If the weight of a coin be changed and its value proportionately altered and also its denomination and its form, a new variety of money is created, as if a penny were made into two halfpence, involving neither loss nor gain. This may lawfully sometimes be done by reason of a real change in the value of the material, a thing which very rarely happens, as was said in Chapter X, speaking of another kind of change. But I am now speaking of a definite alteration of the weight or quantity of money without any change of name or value. And it seems to me that such a change is plainly unlawful, especially in a prince, who cannot do it without disgraceful injustice. Because, in the first place, the prince's image or superscription is placed by him on the coin to guarantee the weight and standard of the material, as was proved above in Chapter IV. Consequently, if the weight is not true, this is at once seen to be a foul lie and a fraudulent cheat. For measures of corn and wine and other measures are frequently stamped with the king's public mark, and any man tampering with these is held to be a forger. In exactly the same way, the inscription on a coin indicates its weight and the purity of its material. Can any words be too strong [1] to express how unjust, how detestable it is, especially in a prince, to reduce the weight without altering the mark ? Cassiodorus says on this point, in the fifth book of his *Variae* [2] :

---

[1] The French version had ' who can trust a prince who reduces etc. ? '
[2] Variae V. 39. 5

sumptoribus liceat eciam in *a* ipsa trutine qualitate pec-
care, ut quod est iusticie proprium datum, hoc per fraudes
noscatur esse corruptum ? ' *b* Adhuc autem princeps
per hunc modum sibi posset acquirere pecuniam alienam,
nec aliunde potest moueri ad mutacionem huiusmodi
faciendam. Reciperet enim nummismata boni ponderis,
et ex eis fabricaret et traderet nummismata tempore *c*
mutilato pondere. Et hoc non est aliud, quod in multis
locis sacre Scripture prohibetur a Deo. Inde ait Sapiens :
Pondus et pondus, mensura et mensura, utrumque abhominabile
apud Deum [1] et in Deuteronomio dicitur, quod Dominus
abhominabitur eum qui facit hec. [2] Et ideo diuicie taliter
congregate in malum domini sui consumuntur in breui,
quia, sicut ait Tullius, ' male parta male dilabuntur.' [3]

Capitulum XIII

De mutacione materie monetarum

Aut materia nummismatis est simplex aut mixta,
ut patuit ex capitulo tercio. Si simplex, ipsa potest
propter defectum dimitti, ut, si nichil aut modicum auri
posset inueniri, oporteret ipsum desinere monetari, et
si de nouo reperiretur sufficiens habundancia eius,
incipiendum esset facere monetam ex ipso, sicut aliquociens fuit factum. Rursum aliqua materia deberet
dimitti monetari propter habundanciam excessiuam.
Propter hoc enim erea moneta olim recessit ab usu, ut
dictum fuit in eodem capitulo tercio. Sed huiusmodi

---

a MSS except C omit in
b The 1605 edition here inserts, without reason given, an excerpt from Cassiodorus,
Variae I. 10
c So the MSS ; the 1484 edition omits the word, and two late copies have ipse
and ipso

' For what is so criminal as to permit oppressors to sin against the very nature of the balance, so that the very symbol of justice is notoriously destroyed by fraud ? '

Secondly, the prince can in this way get possession of other people's money, nor can there be any other reason why he should make such a change. For he would receive money of good weight, recoin it and pay out coins of short weight. And this is the very thing which God forbids in sundry places of Holy Scripture. Of this Solomon says : ' Divers weights and divers measures, both of them are alike abomination to the Lord.' [1] And in Deuteronomy it is said that : ' All that do such things . . . are an abomination unto the Lord.' [2] Therefore riches thus gathered to their lord's hurt are soon consumed, because, as Cicero says [3] : ' Ill-gotten goods never prosper.'

Chapter XIII

Change of Material

The material of money is either simple or mixed, as appeared in Chapter III. If simple, it may be abandoned as insufficient ; for instance if little or no gold could be found, it must needs cease to be coined : and if it again were found in sufficient plenty, money would again begin to be coined of it, as has sometimes happened. Again, a particular material might have to cease to be coined because it was too abundant. It was for that reason that copper money formerly went out of use, as was said in Chapter III. But such causes occur

---

[1] Proverbs xx. 10   [2] Deut. xxv. 16
[3] Philippics II. 65 (quoting Naevius)

cause eueniunt rarissime, et in nullo alio relinquenda
est uel assumenda nouiter pura siue simplex materia
monetarum. Si autem in tali materia sit mixtio, ipsa
debet fieri solum in minus precioso metallo per se
monetabili, ut probatum fuit in eodem capitulo tercio,
et in nigra moneta, ut cognoscatur purum a mixto.
Hec eciam mixtio debet esse secundum certam proporcionem, sicut decem de argento contra unum, uel
contra tria de alio metallo, uel alio modo, sicut expedit,[1]
secundum prius dicta in capitulo tercio. Et ista proporcio potest mutari propter aliquam proporcionem seu
uariacionem realem in natura materie uel equiualentem,[a]
et dupliciter ; aut propter defectum materie, sicut qui
non haberet argentum nisi multum notabiliter minus
quam ante, tunc posset diminui proporcio argenti ad
reliquum metallum in nigra moneta ; aut si haberetur
de argento habundanter plus quam ante, tunc plus de
eo deberet poni in illa mixtione. Sed, sicut predictum
est, iste cause ualde raro contingunt ; et si forsan
talis casus aliquociens eueniret, adhuc huiusmodi proporcionis siue mixtionis mutacio facienda est per
communitatem ad maiorem securitatem habendam et
decepcionis maliciam euitandam, sicut de mutacione
proporcionis monetarum dictum est in capitulo decimo.
In nullo uero alio casu debet mutari mixtio talis siue
proporcio mixtionis ; potissime nunquam potest hoc
licere principi, propter raciones factas in capitulo
precedenti, que de directo faciunt ad istud propositum,
quoniam impressio monete est signum ueritatis materie
et huiusmodi mixtionis ; hanc igitur mutare esset monetam falsificare. Preterea in quibusdam nummis inscri-
bitur nomen Dei[b] uel alicuius sancti, et signum crucis ;

---

[a] equiualentis V, equiualenciam G
[b] *The 1605 edition adds the words* uel B. Virginis

rarely, and in no other way is a material for money, pure or mixed, to be abandoned or newly adopted. But if the material be mixed, it should be so only in the less precious of the metals which are coined pure (as was proved in Chapter III), and in black money, that the pure may be distinguished from the mixed. And the mixture (or alloy) must be made in a fixed proportion, such as ten parts of silver to one, or to three, of some other metal, as is convenient,[1] as we said in Chapter III. And this proportion may be altered on account of a real or corresponding proportion or variation in the nature of the material, and in two ways. Either owing to the lack of material, like having no silver, or conspicuously less than before, in which case the proportion of silver to the other metal in the black money may be diminished ; or, if silver were much more abundant than before, the quantity of silver in the mixture should be raised. But, as has been said, such causes are very rare and, if the case occurs, such a change in proportion should be made by the community, for greater safety and to prevent fraud, as was said in Chapter X of the change in the (bimetallic) ratio. But in no other case should the mixture, or its proportion, be changed, least of all by the prince, for the reasons given in the last chapter, which are directly applicable to the present question since the stamp on the coin denotes the genuineness of the material and its proportions, and so to change these is to falsify the coinage. Besides, some coins are inscribed with the name of God or of some saint and with the sign of the cross, which was devised and

---

[1] The French version adds, ' and ordained by the wise lords expert in the matter '.

quod fuit inuentum et antiquitus institutum in testimonium ueritatis monete in materia et pondere. Si ergo princeps sub ista inscriptione immutet materiam siue pondus, ipse uidetur tacite mendacium et periurium committere, et falsum testimonium perhibere, ac eciam preuaricator fieri illius legalis precepti quo dicitur : *Non assumes nomen Domini Dei tui in uanum.*[1] Ipse eciam abutitur hoc uocabulo *moneta* ; [a] nam secundum Hugucionem [2] moneta dicitur a *moneo*, quia monet ne fraus in metallo uel pondere sit. Rursum princeps per hunc modum potest ad se trahere populi substanciam indebite, sicut fuit dictum de mutacione ponderis in priori capitulo, et multa alia inconueniencia sequerentur. Ymo pro certo ista falsitas esset peior quam in mutacione ponderis, quia magis est sophistica et minus perceptibilis, et potest magis nocere et plus ledere communitatem. Et propter hoc, ubi fit talis mixtio uel nigra moneta, communitas debet custodire penes se, in loco uel locis publicis, exemplar istius proporcionis et qualitatis mixtionis, pro uitandis periculis, ne uidelicet princeps (quod absit) aut monetarii mixtionem huiusmodi occulte falsificarent, sicut eciam apud communitatem seruantur quandoque aliarum exemplaria mensurarum.

Capitulum XIV

De mutacione composita monetarum

Mutacio monete composita est, quando plures mutaciones simplices implicantur in unam, sicut qui mutaret simul proporcionem monete uel mixtionem materie, uel

---

[a] *So* W ; *the other MSS* hoc uocando monetam

appointed of old as a witness of the genuineness of the
money in material and weight.   If the prince, then,
despite this inscription, should change the material or
the weight, he would seem to be silently lying and
forswearing himself and bearing false witness, and also
transgressing that commandment which says : ' Thou
shalt not take the name of the Lord thy God in vain.' [1]
Also he misuses the word ' money ', for Uguccio [2] says :
' *Moneta* is so called from *moneo* (to warn) ' because it
warns us against fraud in metal or weight.   Again, a
prince by this means could wrongfully draw to himself
the wealth of his people, as was said in the last chapter
on change of weight, and many other anomalies would
result.   This fraud indeed would surely be worse than
that of change of weight, because it is more cunning
and less apparent and does more harm and injury to
the community.   And for this reason, where such alloy
or black money exists, the community ought to keep in
some public place or places a sample of this proportion
or quality of alloy, to prevent the prince (which God
forbid) or the moneyers secretly committing this fraud
in the alloy, just as examples of other measures are
frequently kept in charge of the community.

Chapter XIV

Compound Change of Money

There is a compound change of money when more
simple changes than one are combined, as by changing
at the same time the (bimetallic) ratio or the mixture

---

[1] Exodus xx. 7
[2] Uguccione of Pisa, Bishop of Ferrara, in his *Derivationes magnae*

cum hoc eciam pondus, et sic multiplicantur *ᵃ* combina-
ciones possibiles quinque mutacionum simplicium superius positarum. Et quoniam nulla mutacio simplex
debet fieri, nisi propter reales et naturales causas iam
dictas, que rarissime accidunt, sciendum quod adhuc
rarius, ymo forte nunquam, contingit uera occasio
faciendi mutacionem monete compositam. Et si forsan
contingeret, adhuc forciori racione quam de simplici
talis mutacio composita nunquam debet per principem
fieri, propter pericula et inconueniencia prius tacta, sed
per ipsam communitatem. Nam si ex mutacionibus
simplicibus indebite factis tot abusiones sequuntur,
sicut predictum est ante, multo maiores et peiores
sequerentur ex mutacione composita. Moneta namque
debet esse uera et iusta in substancia et pondere, quod
nobis signatum est in sacra Scriptura, ubi de Abraham
dicitur, quod ipse emit agrum, pro quo dedit *cccc ciclos
argenti probate monete publice.*[1] Si ipsa ergo foret bona, et
non mutaretur indebite, cum ipsa sit longo tempore
durabilis, non oporteret multum de ea fabricare, nec
plures monetarios ad expensas communitatis habere ;
et in hoc esset utilitas communis, sicut tactum fuit
capitulo septimo. Uniuersaliter ergo ex premissis concludendum est, quod nulla monete mutacio, siue simplex
siue composita, est sola principis auctoritate facienda, et
maxime ubi hoc uellet facere propter emolumentum uel
lucrum ex tali mutacione sumendum.

ᵃ multipliciter WP, multipliciter ferent C

of materials and possibly the weight as well. There
would thus be a number of possible combinations of the
five simple changes already described. And since no
simple change ought to be made except for the real and
natural causes mentioned which very rarely occur, it is
obvious that the occasion for a compound change will
even more rarely, or perhaps never, happen. And if it
should, *a fortiori* such a compound change must never
be made by the prince, because of the dangers and
disadvantages already named, but only by the community. For if so many abuses result from simple
changes wrongly made, as we have said, much greater
and worse would follow from a compound change. For
money ought to be true and just in substance and in
weight, as is shown us in the Holy Scriptures, where it
is said of Abraham that he bought a field for which he
gave 400 shekels of silver of approved public money.[1]
If then the money were good and were not unnecessarily
altered, since it would last a long time, there would not
be any need to make a great deal of it nor to have many
moneyers at the public expense. And this would be to
the public advantage, as was suggested in Chapter VII.
On the whole then, we must conclude from the premises
that no change of the money, simple or compound, is to
be made on the sole authority of the prince, especially
where he wishes to do it for the sake of the profit and
gain to be got from the change.

---

[1] Genesis xxiii. 16

Capitulum XV

Quod lucrum quod prouenit principi ex mutacione monete est iniustum

Videtur michi quod principalis et finalis causa propter quam princeps sibi uult assumere potestatem mutandi monetas, est emolumentum uel lucrum quod inde potest habere ; aliter enim frustra faceret tot mutaciones et tantas. Volo ergo adhuc plenius ostendere, quod talis acquisicio est iniusta. Omnis enim mutacio monete, preterquam in rarissimis casibus prius dictis, falsitatem et decepcionem includit, et non potest principi pertinere, sicut probatum est ante. Ex quo ergo princeps hanc rem de se iniustam usurpat iniuste, impossibile est quod ibi capiat emolumentum iuste. Preterea, quantum ibi princeps capit de lucro, tantum necesse est ipsam communitatem habere de dampno. Quidquid autem princeps facit in dampnum communitatis, iniusticia est et factum tyrannicum, non regale, ut ait Aristotiles.[1] Et si ipse diceret, sicut solent mentiri tyranni, quod ipse tale lucrum conuertit in publicam utilitatem, non est credendum sibi, quia pari racione posset michi tunicam amouere et dicere quod ipse indiget ea pro communi commodo. Eciam secundum Apostolum non sunt facienda *mala ut eueniant bona.*[2] Nichil ergo debet turpiter extorqueri, ut postea in pios usus fingatur expendi. Rursum, si princeps potest de iure facere unam simplicem mutacionem monete et ibi capere aliquod lucrum, pari racione potest facere maiorem mutacionem et capere maius lucrum, et mutare pluries et adhuc plus habere de lucro, et facere mutacionem uel mutaciones com-

Chapter XV

That the Profit accruing to the Prince from Alteration of the Coinage is unjust

I am of opinion that the main and final cause why the prince pretends to the power of altering the coinage is the profit or gain which he can get from it ; it would otherwise be vain to make so many and so great changes. I propose therefore to give fuller proof that such gain is unjust. For every change of money, except in the very rare cases which I have mentioned, involves forgery and deceit, and cannot be the right of the prince, as has previously been shown. Therefore, from the moment when the prince unjustly usurps this essentially unjust privilege, it is impossible that he can justly take profit from it. Besides, the amount of the prince's profit is necessarily that of the community's loss. But whatever loss the prince inflicts on the community is injustice and the act of a tyrant and not of a king, as Aristotle [1] says. And if he should tell the tyrant's usual lie, that he applies that profit to the public advantage, he must not be believed, because he might as well take my coat and say he needed it for the public service. And Saint Paul says that we are not to do evil that good may come.[2] Nothing therefore should be extorted on the pretence that it will be used for good purposes afterwards. Again, if the prince has the right to make a simple alteration in the coinage and draw some profit from it, he must also have the right to make a greater alteration and draw more profit, and to do this more than once and

---

[1] Pol. V. x. 10 (1310*b*40) ; cf. Eth. ix (1160*b*2)   [2] Romans iii. 8

positas, et semper augere lucrum secundum modos prius
tactos ; et uerisimile est quod ita procederet ipse uel
successores sui, aut proprio motu aut per consiliarios,
ex quo istud liceret, quia natura humana inclinatur et
prona est ad augendum sibi diuicias, quando hoc potest
leuiter facere, et sic tandem princeps posset sibi attrahere
quasi totam pecuniam siue diuicias subditorum et eos
in seruitutem redigere, quod esset directe tyrannizare,
ymo uera et perfecta tyrannis, sicut patet per philosophos
et per historias antiquorum.

Capitulum XVI

Quod lucrari in mutacione monete est innaturale

Quamuis omnis iniusticia sit quodammmodo contra
naturam, uerumptamen accipere lucrum ex mutacione
monete est quodam speciali modo iniustum *a* innaturale.
Naturale enim est quibusdam naturalibus diuiciis se
multiplicare, sicut cerealia grana

> que sata cum multo fenore reddit ager,

ut ait Ouidius ; [1] sed monstruosum est et contra naturam
quod res infecunda pariat, quod res sterilis a tota specie
fructificet uel multiplicetur ex se, cuiusmodi est pecunia.
Cum igitur ipsa pecunia affert lucrum, non exponendo
eam in mercacione naturalium diuiciarum et in usum
proprium ac sibi naturalem, sed eam transmutando in
semetipsam, sicut mutando unam in aliam uel tradendo
unam pro alia, tale lucrum uile est et preter naturam.

a V *has* iniustum et
[1] Epp. ex Ponto I. v. 26

make still more, and also to make one or more compound alterations, constantly making more profit in the ways already described. And it is probable that he or his successors would go on doing this either of their own motion or by the advice of their council as soon as this was permitted, because human nature is inclined and prone to heap up riches when it can do so with ease. And so the prince would be at length able to draw to himself almost all the money or riches of his subjects and reduce them to slavery. And this would be tyrannical, indeed true and absolute tyranny, as it is represented by philosophers and in ancient history.

CHAPTER XVI

That such Profit is unnatural

Although all injustice is in a way contrary to nature, yet to make a profit from altering the coinage is specifically an unnatural act of injustice. For it is natural for certain natural riches to multiply, like grains of corn, ' which,' as Ovid says, ' when sown, the field with ample interest repays.' [1] But it is monstrous and unnatural that an unfruitful thing should bear, that a thing specifically sterile, such as money, should bear fruit and multiply of itself. Therefore when profit is made from money, not by laying it out in the purchase of natural wealth, its proper and natural use, but by changing it into itself, as changing one form of it for another, or giving one form for another, such profit is vile and unnatural. It is by this reasoning that Aristotle

Per hanc enim racionem probat Aristotiles primo Politice [1] quod usura est preter naturam, quoniam naturalis
usus monete est, quod ipsa sit instrumentum permutandi
diuicias naturales, ut sepe dictum est. Qui ergo utitur
ea alio modo, ipse abutitur contra institutionem naturalem monete ; facit enim, ut ait Aristotiles, quod denarius
pariat denarium, quod est contra naturam. Adhuc
autem, in istis mutacionibus ubi capitur lucrum, oportet
uocare denarium illud quod in ueritate non est denarius
et libram illud quod non est libra, et ita de aliis sicut
dictum fuit ante. Constat autem quod hoc non est aliud
nisi nature et racionis ordinem perturbare, unde Cassiodorus ait : [2] ' Da certe solidum, et aufer inde si preuales ;
trade libram, et aliquid si potes minue ; cuncta ista
nominibus ipsis constat esse prouisum ; aut integra
tribuis, aut non ipsa que dicuntur exsoluis. Non
potestis omnino nomina integritatum dare et scelestas
imminuciones efficere. Talia ergo nature secreta uiolare,
sic certissima uelle confundere, nonne [a] ueritatis ipsius
uidetur crudelis ac feda laceracio ? Constet prius pondus
ac mensura probabilis, quia cuncta turbantur, si inte-
gritas cum fraudibus misceatur.' Rursum in libro
Sapiencie dicitur quod *omnia* Deus disposuit *mensura,*
pondere et numero,[3] sed in mutacione monete lucrum non
capitur, nisi fraus in istis rebus certissimis committatur,
sicut prius declaraui. Ergo Deo et nature derogat, qui
sibi ex huiusmodi mutacionibus lucrum captat.

---

[a] *All MSS have an abbreviation here which looks like* numine *or* minime,
rather than nonne ; *possibly for* numne ?

[1] Pol. I. x. 5 (1258*b*7)   [2] Variae I. 10. 7 and 6
[3] Wisdom xi. 21

proves, in the first book of the Politics,[1] that usury is against nature, because the natural use of money is as an instrument for the exchange of natural wealth, as has frequently been said. Anyone therefore who uses it otherwise, misuses it against the natural institution of money, for he causes money to beget money, which, as Aristotle says, is against nature. And, besides, in these changes by which profit accrues it is necessary to call something which in truth is not a penny, a penny, and which is not a pound, a pound, as has already been said in another connexion. But it is clear that this is no less than to disturb the order of nature and of reason, of which Cassiodorus says [2] :

' Pay your shilling, and keep something back if you are strong enough ; deliver a pound, and make it less if you can. In all such cases, as the names themselves show, you pay in full, or you are not giving what you say you give. You cannot by any means use the names of whole units and yet make fraudulent deductions. Is not such a violation of nature's secrets, such an attempt to obscure the greatest certainties, plainly a cruel and disgraceful wound to truth itself ? Weight and measure are the first things to prove, for all is chaos where there is deceit in the unit of measurement.'

Again, it is said in the book of Wisdom [3] that God ordered all things by measure, weight and number ; but in changing of money there is no profit unless fraud is committed in these most certain things, as I have declared before. Therefore he who seeks to profit from such changes of money sins against God and against nature.

Capitulum XVII

Quod lucrari in mutacione monete peius est quam usura

Tres sunt modi, prout michi uidetur, quibus aliquis potest in moneta lucrari, absque hoc quod exponat eam in usu suo naturali : unus per artem campsoriam, custodiam uel mercanciam monetarum, alius est usura, tercius monete mutacio. Primus modus uilis est, secundus malus, et tercius peior. De primis duobus fecit Aristotiles mencionem,[1] et non de tercio, quia tempore suo talis malicia nundum fuerat adinuenta. Quod autem primus sit uilis et uituperabilis, hoc probat Aristotiles per racionem iam tactam in precedenti capitulo ; hoc enim est quodammodo facere pecuniam parere. Artem eciam campsoriam uocat *obolostaticam,*[a] quod uulgariter solet dici ' pictauinagium ', propter quod sanctus Matheus apostolus, qui fuerat campsor, non est reuersus ad priorem operam post resurreccionem Dominicam, sicut fecit sanctus Petrus qui fuerat piscator ; et in assignando causam huiusmodi, dicit beatus Gregorius [2] quod ' aliud est uictum per piscacionem querere, aliud thelonei lucris pecunias augere. Sunt enim, inquit, pleraque negocia que sine peccatis aut uix aut nullatenus exerceri possunt,' etc. Nam sunt quedam artes banause, que maculant corpus, sicut est cloacaria,[3] et alie que maculant animam, sicut est ista. De usura uero certum est quod mala est, detestabilis et iniqua, et ista habetur ex sacra Scriptura. Sed nunc

---

[a] abolostaticam, *all MSS*

Chapter XVII

That Profit from the Change of Money is worse than Usury

It seems to me that there are three ways in which profit may be made from money, without laying it out for its natural purpose ; one is the art of the money-changer, banking or exchange, another is usury, a third alteration of the coinage. The first way is contemptible, the second bad and the third worse. Aristotle mentioned the first two,[1] but not the third, because in his times such wickedness had not yet been invented. That the first is contemptible and disreputable, Aristotle proves by the reasons given in the last chapter, for this is as it were to make money beget money. He also calls exchange ' obolostatic ', what we commonly call *Poitevinage*. It was for that reason that Saint Matthew, the apostle who had been a moneychanger, did not return to his former calling after our Lord's resurrection, as Saint Peter, who had been a fisherman, did. And in giving this reason, the Blessed Gregory says [2] : ' It is one thing to earn a living by fishing, and another to amass money from the profits of receipt of custom. For there are many trades which can scarcely if ever be practised without sin, etc.' For there are certain vulgar crafts which defile the body, such as cleaning the sewers,[3] and others which, like this, defile the soul. As to usury, it is certainly bad, detestable and unjust, and Holy

---

[1] Pol. I. x. 4–5 (1258*b*1–8)
[2] Homiliae in Evangelia xxiv (col. 1184*c*)
[3] The French adds ' chimneys '.

restat ostendere quod lucrum sumere in mutacione
monete adhuc peius est quam usura. Usurarius uero
tradidit pecuniam suam ei qui recipit eam uoluntarie,
et qui postea potest ex ea se iuuare ac inde sue necessitati
succurrere, et illud quod dat alteri ultra sortem est ex
contractu uoluntario inter partes. Sed princeps in
indebita mutacione monete accipit simpliciter inuolun-
tarie pecuniam subditorum, quia prohibet cursum
prioris monete melioris, et quam quilibet plus uellet
habere quam malam.[a] Deinde preter necessitatem
absque utilitate, que ex hoc posset prouenire subditis,
ipse reddit eis pecuniam minus bonam. Et si faciat
meliorem quam ante, hoc tamen est ut deterioretur in
posterum, et tribuet eis minus equiualenter de bona quam
receperat de alia, et qualitercumque sit, ipse retinet [b]
partem pro se. In hoc ergo quia ipse supra pecuniam
recipit incrementum, contra et preter naturalem ipsius
usum, ista acquisicio par est ipsi usure, sed peior quam
usura, eo quod est minus uoluntaria uel magis contra
uoluntatem subditorum, et absque hoc quod possit eis
proficere, et preter necessitatem penitus ; et quoniam
lucrum feneratoris non tantum excedit, nec est ita preiudiciabile generaliter multis, sicut istud quod contra et
supra totam communitatem impositum non minus
tyrannice quam dolose, ita ut sit michi dubium an
pocius debeat dici uiolenta predacio uel exaccio fraudulenta.

a V *has* aliam, W malam uel aliam
b *After* retinet, V *inserts* perfecte, *which the 1605 edition emends to* profecto

Scripture says so. But it remains to show that gaining money by altering the coinage is even worse than usury. The usurer has lent his money to one who takes it of his own free will, and can then enjoy the use of it and relieve his own necessity with it, and what he repays in excess of the principal is determined by free contract between the parties. But a prince, by unnecessary change in the coinage, plainly takes the money of his subjects against their will, because he forbids the older money to pass current, though it is better, and anyone would prefer it to the bad ; and then unnecessarily and without any possible advantage to his subjects, he will give them back worse money. And even if he makes better money than before, it is only with a view to a future debasement, and that he may give them (meanwhile) less of the good money than the corresponding value of the old. In either case he keeps back part for himself. In so far then as he receives more money than he gives, against and beyond the natural use of money, such gain is equivalent to usury ; but is worse than usury because it is less voluntary and more against the will of his subjects, incapable of profiting them, and utterly unnecessary. And since the usurer's interest is not so excessive, or so generally injurious to the many, as this impost, levied tyrannically and fraudulently, against the interest and against the will of the whole community, I doubt whether it should not rather be termed robbery with violence or fraudulent extortion.

Capitulum XVIII

Quod tales mutaciones monetarum, quantum est ex se, non sunt permittende

Aliquociens, ne peius eueniat, et pro scandalo euitando, permittuntur in communitate aliqua inhonesta et mala, sicut lupanaria publica. Aliquando eciam pro aliqua necessitate uel oportunitate permittitur aliqua negociacio uilis, sicut est ars campsoria, uel eciam praua, sicut est usura. Sed de tali mutacione monete pro lucro accipiendo, non apparet aliqua causa mundi, quare tantum lucrum malum debeat aut possit admitti, quoniam per istud non euitatur scandalum sed pocius generatur, ut patet satis ex octauo capitulo, et multa inconueniencia inde sequuntur, quorum aliqua iam tacta sunt et adhuc alia postea uidebuntur, nec est aliqua necessitas neque oportunitas hoc faciendi, neque potest rei publice expedire. Cuius rei manifestum signum est, quod mutaciones huiusmodi sunt nouiter adinuente, sicut iam tactum est in capitulo precedenti. Nunquam enim sic factum est in ciuitatibus aut regnis olim uel modo prospere gubernatis, nec unquam reperi historiam que de hoc faceret mencionem, hoc excepto quod in quadam epistola Cassiodori scripta nomine Theodorici regis Ytalie, una parua mutacio monete in pondere facta durissime reprehenditur, et multum efficaciter reprobatur, quam quidam arcarius[a] fecerat pro quibusdam stipendiariis persoluendis. Unde predictus rex Boecio de hoc scribens inter cetera dixit[1] : ' Quapropter prudencia uestra leccionibus erudita dogmaticis scelestam falsitatem a consorcio ueritatis eiciat, ne cui sit

---

[a] *So the 1605 edition* ; quidam efficarius WP, quidem efficacius VGC

Chapter XVIII

That such Alterations of Money are essentially not permissible

Sometimes, lest worse befall and to avoid scandal, dishonourable and bad things such as public brothels are allowed in a community. Sometimes also, from necessity or for convenience, some contemptible business like money-changing is permitted, or some evil one, like usury. But there seems to be no earthly cause why so much gain should be allowed from alteration of the coinage for profit. It does not avoid scandal, but begets it, as appears in Chapter VIII, and it has many awkward consequences, some of which have already been mentioned, while others will appear later, nor is there any necessity or convenience in doing it, nor can it advantage the commonwealth. A clear sign of this is that such alterations are a modern invention, as was mentioned in the last chapter. For such a thing was never done in cities or kingdoms formerly or now well governed. Nor have I found any mention of it in history except that in a letter of Cassiodorus written in the name of Theodoric, king of Italy, a slight change of weight, which a certain treasurer had made in paying some soldiers, is severely blamed and thoroughly censured. Writing of this to Boetius, the king says [1] : ' Wherefore let your prudence, learned in philosophic doctrines, expel wicked lying from the company of truth, lest anyone should be tempted to diminish its integrity.' And, a little later, he

---

[1] Cassiodorus Variae I. x.2

appetibile aliquid de illa integritate subducere.' Et
quibusdam interpositis rursum inquit : ' Mutilari certe
non debet, quod laborantibus datur, sed a quo actus
fidelis exigitur, compensacio imminuta *a* prestetur, etc.'
Si uero Ytalici seu Romani tales mutaciones finaliter
fecerunt, sicut uidetur ex quadam praua moneta ueteri
que quandoque reperitur in campis, hec forte fuit una
de causis, quare eorum nobile dominium deuenit ad
nichilum. Sic igitur patet quod iste mutaciones tam
male sunt, quod de natura sua non sunt aliquatenus
permittende.

Capitulum XIX

*De quibusdam inconuenientibus tangentibus principem, que
sequuntur ex mutacionibus monetarum*

Multa et magna inconueniencia oriuntur ex taliter
mutando monetas, quorum aliqua principalius respiciunt principem, alia totam communitatem, et alia magis
partes ipsius. Unde breui tempore nuper transacto
quamplurima talia in regno Francie uisa sunt euenire,
aliqua eciam iam tacta sunt ante, que tamen expedit
recitare. Primo namque nimis detestabile et nimis
turpe est principi fraudem committere, monetam falsificare, aurum uocare quod non est aurum et libram
quod non est libra, et sic de talibus prius positis duode-
cimo et terciodecimo capitulis. Preterea sibi incumbit
falsos monetarios condempnare. Quomodo ergo satis
potest erubescere, si reperiatur in eo, quod in alio
deberet turpissima morte punire? *b* Rursum magnum
scandalum est, sicut dicebatur octauo capitulo, et uile
principi, quod moneta regni sui nunquam in eodem

a So P ; munita W, minuta VC, minuta non G   *b* puniri GPC

continues : ' The wages of labourers must not be docked,
but payment must be made in full to him of whom
faithful service is required.' If the Italians or Romans
did in the end make such alterations, as appears from
ancient bad money sometimes to be found in the
country, this was probably the reason why their noble
empire came to nothing. It appears therefore that these
changes are so bad that they are essentially impermissible.

Chapter XIX

Of certain Disadvantages to the Prince resulting from Alterations of the Coinage

Many great disadvantages arise from such alterations
in the coinage, some of which specially affect the prince,
others the whole community, and others particular parts
of the community. Many of these have lately been seen
to occur in the realm of France, and some have already
been named, which must nevertheless be recapitulated.
First, it is exceedingly detestable and disgraceful in a
prince to commit fraud, to debase his money, to call
what is not gold, gold, and what is not a pound, a
pound, and so forth as in Chapters XII and XIII.
Besides, it is his duty to condemn false coiners. How can
he blush deep enough, if that be found in him which
in another he ought to punish by a disgraceful death ?
Again, it is a great scandal, as was said in Chapter VIII,
and contemptible in a prince, that the money of his
kingdom never remains the same, but changes from day
to day, and is sometimes worth on the same day more
in one place than in another. Also, as time goes on and
changes proceed, it often happens that nobody knows

statu permanet, sed de die in diem uariatur, et quandoque
in uno loco ualet plus quam in alio pro eodem tempore.
Item sepissime ignoratur durantibus hiis temporibus uel
mutacionibus, quantum ualeat hoc nummisma uel
illud, et oportet mercari seu emere uel uendere monetam,
seu alterari *a* de precio, contra eius naturam ; et sic rei
que debet esse certissima nulla est certitudo, sed pocius
incerta et inordinata confusio in uituperium principantis.
Item absurdum est et penitus alienum a regia nobilitate,
prohibere cursum uere et bone monete regni et ex
cupiditate precipere, ymo cogere subditos ad utendum
minus bona moneta, quasi uelit dicere quod bona est
[et] mala et econuerso ; cum tamen talibus dictum sit
a Domino per prophetam, *Ve qui dicitis bonum malum et
malum bonum.*[1] Et iterum, dedecus est principi irreuereri
predecessores suos ; nam quilibet tenetur ex Dominico
precepto honorare parentes. Ipse autem progenitorum
detrahere uidetur honori, quando bonam monetam
eorum abrogat, et facit eam cum eorum ymagine
scindere, et loco monete auree, quam ipsi fabricauerant,
facit monetam eream in parte. Quod uidetur fuisse
figuratum in tercio Regum, ubi legitur quod rex Roboam
abstulit *scuta aurea, que fecerat* pater eius *Salomon, pro
quibus fecit scuta erea.*[2] Idem quoque Roboam perdidit
quinque partes populi sui, pro eo quod ipse uoluit in
principio nimis grauare subiectos. Adhuc autem rex
nimis debet abhorrere tyrannica facta, cuiusmodi est
mutacio talis, ut predictum est sepe ; que eciam est
preiudiciabilis et periculosa pro tota posteritate regali,
sicut in sequentibus diffusius ostendetur.

a The 1605 edition prints altercari, *an attractive suggestion, but not supported
by the French version*

[1] Isaiah v. 20

what a particular coin is worth, and money has to be
dealt in, bought and sold, or changed from its value, a
thing which is against its nature. And so there is no
certainty in a thing in which certainty is of the highest
importance, but rather uncertain and disordered confusion, to the prince's reproach. Also it is absurd and
repugnant to the royal dignity to prohibit the currency
of the true and good money of the realm, and from
motives of greed to command, or rather compel, subjects
to use less good money ; which amounts to saying that
good is evil and vice versa, whereas it was said to such
from the Lord, by his prophet [1] :

> Woe unto them that call evil good and good evil.

And again, it is a disgrace to a prince to dishonour his
predecessors, for we are all bound by the Lord's commandment to honour our parents. But he seems to
detract from the honour of his ancestors when he cries
down their good money, and has it, and with it their
image, cut up and in place of the gold money which
they coined makes money which is partly brass. This
seems to be foreshadowed in the first book of Kings [2]
where we read that King Rehoboam took away the
golden shields which his father Solomon had made, in
exchange for which he made brazen shields. That
same Rehoboam lost five-sixths of his people because he
tried at the beginning of his reign to overtax his subjects.
Furthermore, the king ought exceedingly to abhor
tyrannical acts, of which as we have said before alteration of the coinage is one. And that is prejudicial and
dangerous to all the king's posterity, as shall be shown
more at length later.

---

[2] 1 Kings xiv. 27 (D. V. 3 Kings). It was Shishak, in fact, who took
away the golden shields.

CAPITULUM XX

De aliis inconuenientibus totam communitatem tangentibus

Inter multa inconueniencia ex mutacione monete
ueniencia, que totam communitatem respiciunt, unum
est quod prius tangebatur capitulo quintodecimo principaliter, quia uidelicet princeps per hoc posset ad se
trahere quasi totam pecuniam communitatis et nimis
depauperare subiectos. Et quemadmodum quedam
egritudines cronice sunt aliis periculosiores, eo quod
sunt minus sensibiles,[1] ita talis exaccio, quanto minus
percipitur, tanto periculosius exercetur ; non enim ita
cito grauamen ipsius sentitur a populo, sicut per unam
aliam collectam. Et tamen nulla fere talia *a* potest esse
grauior, nulla generalior, nulla maior. Rursum aurum
et argentum propter tales mutaciones et impeioraciones
minorantur in regno, quia non obstante custodia deferun-
tur ad extra, ubi carius allocantur. Homines enim
libencius conantur suam monetam portare ad loca, ubi
eam credunt magis ualere. Ex hoc igitur sequitur
diminucio materie monetarum in regno.[2] Item illi de
extra regnum aliquociens contrafaciunt et afferunt
similem monetam in regno, et sic attrahunt sibi lucrum,
quod rex ille credit habere. Adhuc eciam forsitan ipsa
monete materia in parte consumitur, fundendo eam et
refundendo tociens quociens solet fieri, ubi mutaciones
huiusmodi exercentur. Sic ergo materia monetabilis
tripliciter minuitur occasione mutacionum predictarum.

---

a talis V, *and so the French version* (telle ou semblable)

[1] The French has ' because some sicknesses are so contagious and more
dangerous than others because they are more perceptible and affect the
nobler members '.

Chapter XX

Of other Disadvantages to the Community as a whole

Among the many disadvantages arising from alteration of the coinage which affect the whole community,
is one which was the main subject of Chapter XV,
namely that the prince could thus draw to himself almost
all the money of the community and unduly impoverish
his subjects. And as some chronic sicknesses are more
dangerous than others because they are less perceptible,[1]
so such an exaction is the more dangerous the less
obvious it is, because its oppression is less quickly felt by
the people than it would be in any other form of
contribution. And yet no tallage can be heavier, more
general or more severe.

Again, such alterations and debasements diminish
the amount of gold and silver in the realm, since these
metals, despite any embargo, are carried abroad, where
they command a higher value. For men try to take
their money to the places where they believe it to be
worth most. And this reduces the material for money
in the realm.[2]

Again, foreigners frequently coin similar counterfeit
money and bring it to the country where the debased
coin is current and thus rob the king of the profit which
he thinks he is making. It may be, too, that some of
the material is consumed in the constant melting and
re-melting which goes on where such alterations are
made. There are thus three ways in which the material

---

[2] The French adds ' and the coining of money in the land where the
debasement occurs '.

Ergo non possunt, ut uidetur, longo tempore permanere, ubi non exuberaret materia monetabilis in mineris uel aliunde, et sic tandem princeps non haberet, unde facere posset sufficienter de bona moneta. Item propter istas mutaciones bona mercimonia seu diuicie naturales de extraneis regnis cessant ad illud afferri, in quo moneta sic mutatur, quoniam mercatores ceteris paribus prediligunt ad ea loca transire, in quibus reperiunt monetam certam et bonam. Adhuc autem intrinsecus in tali regno negociacio mercatorum per tales mutaciones perturbatur et multipliciter impeditur ; preterea hiis mutacionibus durantibus, redditus pecunie, pensiones annuales, locagia, censure et similia non possunt bene et iuste taxari seu appreciari, ut notum est. Item nec pecunia potest secure mutuo dari uel credi, et sic de talibus ; ymo multi nolunt ista caritatiua subsidia facere propter tales mutaciones. Et tamen sufficiencia materie monetabilis, mercatores et omnia predicta sunt aut necessaria aut ualde utilia nature humane, et opposita sunt preiudiciabilia et nociua toti communitati ciuili.

Capitulum XXI

De aliis inconuenientibus, que tangunt partes communitatum

Quedam partes communitatis occupate sunt in negociis honorabilibus aut utilibus toti rei publice, ut in diuiciis naturalibus [a] ad crescendum uel tractandum pro necessitate communitatis,[1] cuiusmodi sunt uiri ecclesiastici, iudices, milites, agricole, mercatores, artifices et similes. Sed alia pars auget diuicias proprias uili questu,

---

[a] *After* naturalibus, C *adds* ad orandum et sustinendum

of money is lessened by these alterations. They cannot therefore last long unless the material is abundant in mines or otherwise, and so the prince would at last be unable to coin enough good money. Again, because of these alterations, good merchandise or natural riches cease to be brought into a kingdom in which money is so changed, since merchants, other things being equal, prefer to pass over to those places in which they receive sound and good money. Furthermore, in such a kingdom internal trade is disturbed and hindered in many ways by such changes, and while they last, money rents, yearly pensions, rates of hire, cesses and the like, cannot be well and justly taxed or valued, as is well known. Neither can money safely be lent or credit given. Indeed many refuse to give that charitable help on account of such alterations. And yet a sufficiency of metal for coin, merchants and all these other things mentioned are either necessary or highly useful to humanity, and their opposites are prejudicial and hurtful to the whole civil community.

Chapter XXI

Of Disadvantages to part of the Community

Some sections of the community are occupied in affairs honourable or profitable to the whole state, as in the growing of natural wealth or negotiating on behalf of the community.[1] Such are churchmen, judges, soldiers, husbandmen, merchants, craftsmen and the

---

[1] '. . . as by acquiring natural wealth, by prayers and supplications for divine help, by maintaining justice and by dealing with certain matters for common need or profit '. Fr. Vers., and there are traces of this wording in one late MS of the Latin.

sicut sunt campsores, mercatores monete siue uillona-
tores ; que quidem negociacio turpis est, prout dicebatur
capitulo octauodecimo. Isti ergo, qui sunt quasi
preternecessarii rei publice, et quidam alii, sicut recep-
tores et tractatores pecunie et tales, capiunt magnam
partem emolumenti siue lucri prouenientis ex mutacionibus monetarum, et maliciose aut fortuite ditantur
inde contra Deum et iusticiam, quoniam ipsi sunt tot
diuiciis immeriti [1] et tantis bonis indigni. Alii uero
depauperantur ex hoc, qui sunt optime partes illius
communitatis, ita quod princeps plures et meliores
subditos suos per istud dampnificat et nimium grauat,
et tamen non totum lucrum peruenit ad ipsum, sed
magnam partem habent isti predicti, quorum negociacio
uilis est et admixta cum fraude. Rursum, quando
princeps non facit prescire populo tempus et modum
future mutacionis monete quam intendit facere, aliqui
per cautelas aut per amicos hoc secrete preuident, et
tunc emunt mercimonia pro moneta debili, et postea
uendunt pro forti, et subito fiunt diuites et nimium
lucrantur indebite contra naturalis mercacionis legitimum
cursum.[2] Et uidetur esse quoddam genus monopolii, in
dampnum et preiudicium totius communitatis residue.
Adhuc autem per tales mutaciones necesse est redditus
taxatos ad numerum pecunie aut iniuste minui aut
iniuste saltim augeri, sicut tactum fuit ante in capitulo
de mutacione appellacionis monete. Item princeps
per tales diuersificaciones et sophisticaciones monetarum
dat malis occasionem faciendi falsam monetam, aut
quia minus est contra conscienciam eorum ipsam
falsificare, ex quo apparet eis quod ita facit princeps, aut
quia eorum falsitas non ita cito deprehenditur, et

---

[1] Fr. Vers. ' en moult grande richesse emiclopes ' (*enveloppes* ?). Could
the Latin have been *immersi* ?

like. But another section augments its own wealth by unworthy business, as do money-changers, bankers or dealers in bullion : a disgraceful trade as was said in Chapter XVIII. These men, then, who are as it were unwanted by the state, and some others such as receivers and financial agents, etc., take a great part of the profit or gain arising from changes in coinage and by guile or by good luck, draw wealth from them, against God and Justice, since they are undeserving [1] of such riches and unworthy of such wealth. But others, who are the best sections of the community, are impoverished by it ; so that the prince in this way damages and overburdens the larger and better part of his subjects and yet does not receive the whole of the profit ; but the persons above-mentioned, whose business is contemptible and largely fraudulent, get a large part of it. Again, when the prince does not announce beforehand the date and the scheme of the alteration which he means to make, some persons, by their own cunning or through their friends, secretly foreknow it, and buy up merchandise with the weak money to sell again for the sound, get rich quickly, and make an excessive and undue profit against the lawful course of normal trade.[2] And this seems to be a kind of monopoly to the prejudice and damage of all the rest of the community. Furthermore, by such changes rents assessed in terms of money are necessarily unjustly lessened or unjustly raised, as was said before in Chapter XI on change of name. The prince, also, by such variations and sophistications of coin gives scoundrels an opportunity to coin false money, either because they consider that the prince has already done so and it is thus less against their conscience, or because the

---

[2] Fr. Vers. adds ' at which St Augustine is amazed and much marvels '.

possunt facilius et plura mala hiis stantibus perpetrare,
quam si semper curreret bona moneta. Preterea, istis
durantibus, quasi innumerabiles perplexitates, obscuri-
tates, errores et inextricabiles difficultates accidunt in
compotis, de mis[i]is et receptis. Oriuntur eciam inde
materie litigiorum et uarie questiones : male persolu-
ciones debitorum, fraudes, inordinaciones, abusiones
quamplurime et inconueniencia multa, que nescirem
explicare, forsan quibusdam enumeratis prius maiora
et deteriora *a* ; neque mirum, quia, sicut ait Aristotiles,[1]
uno inconuenienti dato multa sequuntur, et hoc non
est difficile uidere.

Capitulum XXII

Si communitas potest facere tales mutaciones monete

Cum moneta sit communitatis, ut ostensum est
capitulo sexto, uidetur quod communitas ipsa possit
de ea ad libitum ordinare. Ergo eam potest quomodolibet uariare, et super hoc capere quantum placeat, et
de ea facere sicut de re sua, maxime autem si pro
guerra uel pro redempcione sui principis de captiuitate
uel aliquo tali casu fortuito ipsa communitas indigeret
una magna pecunie summa. Ipsa enim tunc posset eam
leuare per mutacionem monete, nec esset contra naturam
aut sicut usura, ex quo hoc non faceret princeps, sed
ipsa communitas cuius est ipsa moneta. Per hoc enim
cessarent *b* nec haberent hic locum multe raciones prius

a V *has* deteriora, et hoc est difficile uidere, *omitting the rest*
b *For* cessarent, V *has* ipsa cessarent multa inconueniencia adducta,
which makes good sense, but needs support from other MSS or the French version

forgery is less quickly found out and they can more
easily commit more crimes in these conditions than if
good money were constantly current. Besides, in these
circumstances, what innumerable perplexities, obscuri-
ties, errors and insuperable difficulties occur in accounts
of expenditure and receipts ! Hence also arise matters
for lawsuits and various issues, insufficient payments of
debts, frauds, disorders, manifold abuses and sundry
disadvantages more than I can describe and possibly
worse and greater than some that have been mentioned.
And no wonder, for as Aristotle says [1] : ' One error has
many consequences ' as may easily be seen.

Chapter XXII

Whether the Community can make such Alterations

Since the coinage is the property of the community
as was shown in Chapter VI, it appears that the community can dispose of it as it pleases. It can therefore
alter it after any fashion, make what gain it will from it
and treat it as its own, especially if it needs a large sum
of money for war or for the ransom of its prince from
captivity or some accident of the kind. For in that case
it might raise the sum by an alteration of the coinage
nor would this be unnatural or like usury, because it
would not be done by the prince but by the community
to which the money belonged. For in this way many of
the objections to the alteration of the coinage already
made would drop and have no place. And it appears

---

[1] Top. ii. 5. ?

facte contra mutaciones monete. Nec solum uidetur
quod communitas hoc facere potest, sed eciam quod
hoc deberet, ex quo necessaria est collecta, quoniam in
tali mutacione aggregari uidentur quasi omnes bone
condiciones requisite in aliqua talia seu collecta ; nam
in breui tempore multum lucrum affert, facillima est
ad colligendum et distribuendum seu assignandum, sine
occupacione multorum et sine fraude colligencium et
cum paruis expensis. Nulla eciam potest ymaginari
magis equalis seu proporcionalis, quia fere qui plus
potest, plus soluit, et est secundum sui quantitatem
minus perceptibilis seu sensibilis, et ideo magis porta-
bilis sine periculo rebellionis et absque murmure populi.
Est eciam generalissima, quia neque clericus neque nobi-
lis ab ea se potest per priuilegium uel alias eximere, sicut
multi uolunt de aliis collectis, unde oriuntur inuidie,
dissenciones, lites, scandala et multa alia inconueniencia
que non ueniunt ex tali mutacione monete. Ergo in
casu predicto ipsa potest et debet fieri per ipsam communitatem. De isto autem, saluo meliori iudicio, michi
uidetur ad presens sic posse dici, quod uidelicet aut
illa summa pecunie, qua communitas indiget, trans-
ferenda est uel exponenda in remotis partibus et inter
gentes cum quibus non habetur communicacio, et
eciam tanta est quod materia monetabilis ex hoc diu
erit notabiliter minor in ista communitate ; et in isto
casu potest fieri collecta per mutacionem monete in
materia uel in mixtione, quia si fieret aliter, talis mutacio
esset postea facienda propter causam assignatam et
secundum modum positum capitulo terciodecimo. Si
uero summa predicta non sit ita magna, uel si taliter
exponatur, quomodocumque sit, quod de materia
monetabili non sit diu notabiliter minus in communitate
propter istud, dico quod preter inconueniencia incepta

not only that the community might do this, but also that it ought, assuming that the contribution is necessary, for such an alteration seems to unite almost all the good conditions required by any tallage or contribution. For it brings in much profit in little time, is very easy to collect and assess or share without employing a large staff or risking fraud in collection, and is cheap to collect. Nothing, either, can be devised more fair or proportional, since he who can afford most pays most. And it is, for its amount, less seen or felt and more endurable without danger of rebellion or popular discontent. For it is universal : neither clerk nor noble can escape it by privilege or otherwise, as many try to escape other contributions, causing envyings, dissensions, litigation, scandals and many other evils which do not arise from such an alteration of the coinage. Therefore, in the case presupposed, it can and should be done by the community.

But in this matter it seems to me now, with all respect for wiser heads, that it may be laid down that the money needed by the community should be exported to, or spent in distant lands and among people with whom there is no intercourse, and also be so much as to cause a notorious lack of the materials for money in the community for a long time. And if so, the sum may be raised by lightening or alloying the coin, because if this were not done, the alteration would have to be made later for the reason and in the way given in Chapter XIII. But if the sum be not so great or be otherwise expended, or in any other way be such as not to cause a notable and long lack of material for money in the community, I maintain that besides the disadvantages hinted at in the present chapter, such an alteration of the coinage would involve more, and worse things than those above

in presenti capitulo, adhuc sequerentur plura et peiora
quam superius explicata de tali mutacione monete
quam de una alia collecta ; et potissime sequeretur
periculum, ne tandem princeps uellet hoc sibi attribuere,
et tunc reuerterentur omnia inconueniencia prius dicta.
Nec obstat racio prima in qua dicebatur quod pecunia
est communitatis, quia nec communitas nec aliquis
iuste potest abuti re sua seu illicite uti ea, sicut faceret
communitas si taliter mutaret monetas. Et si forsan
communitas ipsa qualitercumque faceret talem mutacionem, tunc moneta cicius quam potest reducenda est ad
statum debitum et permanentem, et cessare debet capcio
lucri super ipsam monetam.

CAPITULUM XXIII

In quo arguitur quod princeps possit mutare monetas

Solet dici quod in casu necessitatis omnia sunt
principis. Ipse ergo de monetis regni sui potest quantum
et qualiter sibi uidetur expediens accipere pro imminenti
uel instanti necessitate seu pro defensione rei publice
aut principatus sui regni. Modus uero colligendi
pecuniam per mutacionem monete est ualde conueniens
et ydoneus, ut probaretur per ea que dicta sunt capitulo
precedenti. Adhuc autem, supposito quod princeps non
posset taliter mutare monetas et tantum emolumentum
super hoc sumere de iure ordinario uel communi, tamen
diceretur quod hoc ipse potest alio priuato iure, ut puta
priuilegio speciali a papa uel ecclesia uel imperatore
Romano uel eciam a communitate olim sibi hereditarie
concesso propter bona merita sua. Item moneta est

explained, than would any other contribution. And
the worst danger would be lest the prince should at last
assume the right to do this and then all the before-
mentioned evils would come back again. Nor does it
matter that, as we began by saying, the money belongs
to the community, because neither the community nor
anyone else has the right to misuse or unlawfully use his
own property, as the community would be doing if it
made such an alteration in the coinage. And if the
community, rightly or wrongly, should make such a
change, the money must with all speed be brought back
to its due and permanent state, and all taking of profit
from it must cease.

Chapter XXIII

An Argument that the Prince may alter the Coinage

It is usually said that in an emergency all things
belong to the prince. Therefore in an imminent or
instant emergency, he may take as much of the money
of his realm as he chooses, in any way he likes, for the
defence of the commonwealth or of his own position as
prince. And alteration of the coinage is an appropriate
and fitting way of doing this, as may be proved from
what is said in the previous chapter. Again, supposing
that the prince has no right at the common or ordinary
law so to alter the coinage and take such a profit from
it, it might be said that he can do so in virtue of a prerogative, for instance a special privilege from the Pope,
or the Church, or the Roman Emperor, or even from the
community, granted to him of old as a heritage for his
services.

ipsius communitatis, ut patet ex capitulo sexto, et ipsa
potest eam sic mutare ut dictum est capitulo precedenti ;
ergo ipsa communitas potest aut potuit auctoritatem
taliter mutandi monetas principi concedere et se ipsam
spoliare iure ordinacionis et mutacionis monete, et
partem monete principi dare ab eo capiendam, quomodo
uellet. Item si de iure communi spectat ad communitatem ordinare de monetis, ut dictum est sepe, et ipsa
propter discordiam multitudinis non potuit conuenire
in unum modum, nonne ipsa potuit in hoc condescendere
quod totalis disposicio monete ex tunc et de cetero staret
in principis uoluntate ? Certe sic, et quod racione huius
ipse caperet emolumentum in mutacione siue ordinacione monete. Item in septimo capitulo dicebatur,
quod certa pensio debet esse taxata pro faccione monete,
et quod de et super illa pensione princeps potest aut
debet aliquid habere. Ergo pari racione potest habere
uel accipere super hoc plus et plus, et per consequens
tantum sicut per mutacionem monete. Ergo eodem
modo per tales mutaciones potest illud emolumentum
leuare. Item oportet principem habere redditus certos
et magnos super communitatem, unde ipse possit tenere
statum nobilem et honestum, prout decet magnificenciam
principalem siue regiam maiestatem. Oportet eciam
quod isti redditus sint de dominio principis seu de iure
proprio corone regalis. Possibile est ergo, quod una et
magna pars istorum reddituum olim fuerit assignata
super factum monetarum taliter quod liceret principi
lucrum recipere mutando monetas. Possibile est eciam
quod isto dempto residui redditus nunquam sufficerent
pro statu principi pertinenti. Velle ergo amouere sibi
potestatem mutandi monetas est contra honorem regni
attemptare principem exhereditare, ymo ipsum depauperare et a statu debite magnificencie destituere, non tam

The money, also, is the property of the community, as appears from Chapter VI, and the community can change it as was said in the last chapter ; therefore it can, or could, grant the authority to make such a change to the prince, renounce the right to ordain or change the coinage, and give part of the money to the prince to take in any way he pleased. Again, if by the common law it rests with the community, as has been said, to regulate the coinage, and it, owing to popular discord, has failed to agree on a plan, may it not compromise by leaving the regulation of the coinage henceforward and for ever to the will of the prince ? It may surely do so, and allow him on this account to take a profit from the change or regulation of the coinage. It was said, too, in Chapter VII that a certain ' pension ' ought to be fixed to cover the expense of coining and that the prince may have something out of or in excess of that ' pension ' for himself. Therefore, by parity of reasoning, he may have or take more and more from this and consequently as much as he would get from an alteration in the coinage. He may, therefore, in the same way, raise that profit by such alterations. Besides, the prince ought to have a large settled revenue from the community with which to maintain a noble and honourable estate as becomes princely magnificence or royal majesty. These revenues, then, must be attached to the princely dominion or the prerogative of the royal crown. It is therefore possible that a considerable part of these revenues was formerly charged on the coinage, so that it would be lawful for the prince to make a profit by altering the coin. It is also possible that if this right were taken away the rest of the revenue would not be enough for a princely state. Consequently to propose to take from him the power of altering the coinage, is an attack on

iniuste quam eciam uituperabiliter pro tota communitate, quam non decet habere principem, nisi excellenti
statu pollentem.

Capitulum XXIV

Responsio ad predicta et conclusio principalis

Quamuis in solucione primi argumenti forsan multe
difficultates possent occurrere, uerumptamen breuiter
transeundo pro nunc occurrit michi quod, ne princeps
fingeret talem necessitatem esse quando non est, sicut
fingunt tyranni, ut dicit Aristotiles,[1] determinandum
est per communitatem aut per ualenciorem eius partem,
expresse uel tacite, quando qualis et quanta necessitas
eminet. Expresse dico, quia ad hoc debet congregari
communitas, si adsit facultas ; tacite uero, si fuerit
tam festina necessitas quod populus uocari non possit,
et tam euidens quod postea appareat notorie. Tunc
enim licet principi aliqua recipere de facultatibus
subditorum non per mutacionem monete sed per modum
mutui, de quo postea facienda est restitucio plenaria.
Ad aliud, cum dicitur quod princeps potest habere
priuilegium mutandi monetas, primo non intromitto
me de potencia pape, sed puto quod nunquam hoc
concesserit nec concederet, quoniam sic ipse daret
licenciam malefaciendi, quam nullus bene operando
meretur accipere. De imperatore autem Romano dico,
quod ipse nulli principi potuit unquam priuilegium dare
faciendi illud quod sibimet non liceret, sicut est talis

---

[1] Perhaps referring to the demand for a body-guard. Polit. iii. 10. 10
(1286*b*.39–40)

the honour of the king, a disherison of the prince, it is
indeed impoverishing him and robbing him of his magnificence, not only unjustly, but disgracefully to the
whole community which cannot with decency have a
prince unless he maintains his dignity.

Chapter XXIV

Reply to the previous Chapter and main Conclusion

Although there might possibly be many difficulties
in meeting the first argument, I will pass over them
briefly, as it occurs to me now that, lest the prince
should pretend such an emergency when there is none,
as Aristotle says tyrants do,[1] it should be determined by
the community or the better part of it, expressly or tacitly,
when, what and how great an emergency threatens.
I mean by ' expressly ', that the community should be
assembled, if there is the opportunity ; ' tacitly ', if the
emergency is so imminent that the people cannot be
called together and so plain that it is subsequently
notorious. For in such a case the prince may take some
part of the property of his subjects, not by changing the
coinage, but by way of a loan to be repaid in full later.
On the second point, that the prince may have a privilege to change the money, first, I will not discuss the
Pope's powers, but I think he never has made or would
make such a grant since he would be giving a licence
to do evil, which no possible good deeds could qualify a
man to receive. As for the Roman Emperor, I say that
he never had power to give any prince the privilege to
do what he could not lawfully do himself, e.g. such a

monete mutacio, ut patet ex prius dictis. De communitate eciam dictum est capitulo uicesimo secundo,
quod ipsa non potest mutare monetas, nisi in certo
casu ; et tunc si ipsa committeret hoc principi cum
limitacione racionabili, que potest ex eodem capitulo
et aliis apparere, iam hoc non faceret princeps tanquam
principalis auctor, sed sicut ordinacionis publice executor.
Ad aliud autem, cum arguitur quod communitas, cuius
est moneta, potest se spoliare suo iure et illud totum
principi tradere, et sic totum ius monete deuolueretur
ad principem : primo uidetur michi quod hoc nunquam
faceret communitas bene consulta, nec eciam sibi
liceret quomodolibet mutare monetas aut male uti re
sua, ut dictum est capitulo uicesimo secundo. Item
communitas ciuium, que naturaliter est libera, nunquam
scienter se redigeret in seruitutem aut se subiceret iugo
tyrannice potestatis. Si igitur ipsa, decepta aut minis
territa uel coacta, concedat principi tales mutaciones,
non aduertens inconueniencia que sequuntur, et ex hoc
seruiliter se fore *a* subiectam, ipsa potest hoc statim
aut quomodolibet reuocare. Item res que spectat
alicui quasi de iure naturali quandoque non potest ad
alterum iuste transferri ; sic autem pertinet moneta
ipsi libere communitati, ut satis patet ex capitulis primo
et sexto. Sicut ergo communitas non potest concedere
principi quod ipse habeat auctoritatem abutendi uxori-
bus ciuium quibuscumque uoluerit, ita non potest ei
dare tale priuilegium monetarum, quo ipse non posset
nisi male uti, exigendo tale lucrum super mutacione
earum, ut satis patet ex multis precedentibus capitulis.
Per hoc eciam patet ad illud, quod addebatur ulterius
de communitate non concordi in ordinacione monete,
que potest condescendere, quantum ad hoc, in principis

a For se fore, W *has* nouerit se esse

change in the money, as appears from what has been said. As to the community, it has been said in Chapter XXII that it cannot change the money except in a particular case, and then, if it should entrust the task to the prince, within reasonable limits which are apparent from that chapter and from others, the prince would still not be doing it of his own authority but as the executor of a public ordinance. In answer to another argument, that the community which owns the money may divest itself of its right and transfer it to the prince, it seems, in the first place, that no well advised community would do such a thing ; and secondly that it is unlawful even for itself to alter the coinage or to misuse its own property in any way, as was said in Chapter XXII. Again, a community of citizens which is naturally free would never knowingly reduce itself to slavery or submit itself to the yoke of a tyranny. If, therefore, it were cheated or terrified and coerced into granting the prince such alterations without foreseeing the resulting evils, and that this would amount to slavery, it can immediately or otherwise revoke the grant. Again, anything belonging to anyone as of natural right cannot justly be transferred to another ; but that is how money belongs to the free community, as is clear enough from Chapters I and VI. So, just as the community cannot grant to the prince authority to misuse the wives of any of its citizens he will, it cannot give him such a privilege over the coinage as he can only misuse, by exacting a profit from changing it, as appears from several earlier chapters. The same argument applies to what was added about a disagreement in the community in the regulation of the coinage and its compromising in so far on the prince's decision. I admit it can do so for some purposes and on some occasions ; but not by giving him the power to

arbitrio. Dico quod sic potest quantum ad aliqua et ad
tempus, sed non sibi concedendo potestatem tanti lucri
sumendi super indebitis mutacionibus supradictis. Ad
aliud argumentum, sumptum ex capitulo septimo, de
hoc quod princeps potest aliquod emolumentum habere
super monetam, respondetur faciliter, quod hoc est
quasi quedam pensio parua et limitata, que non potest
quantumlibet augeri per mutaciones predictas, sed stat
sine mutacione quacumque. Ad aliud conceditur, quod
princeps potest habere redditus, et debet habere magni-
ficum et honestissimum statum ; sed isti redditus
possunt et debent alibi assignari et aliter sumi quam
per tales mutaciones indebitas, ex quibus tanta mala et
tot inconueniencia oriuntur, sicut ostensum est ante.
Posito eciam, quod aliqua porcio istorum reddituum
esset super monetam, ipsa tamen debet esse certe et
determinate quantitatis, sicut supra quamlibet mar-
cham que monetaretur duo solidi uel sic ;[1] et tunc
istud esset absque quacumque mutacione siue lucri
augmento irracionabili et enormi, quod potest prouenire
ex detestabilibus mutacionibus sepe dictis. De quibus
uniuersaliter concludendum est, quod princeps non
potest eas facere aut taliter lucrum accipere, nec de iure
communi seu ordinario nec de priuilegio siue dono,
concessione, pacto seu quauis alia auctoritate uel alio
quocumque modo, nec potest esse de suo dominio,
aut sibi quomodolibet pertinere ; ideoque[a] istud sibi
denegare non est ipsum exhereditare aut maiestati regie
contraire, sicut menciuntur falsiloqui adulatores, sophis-
tici, et rei publice proditores. Rursum, cum princeps
teneatur hoc non facere, ipse non meretur habere
aliquam pensionem seu donum pro abstinendo a tali
abusiua exaccione ; hoc enim non uidetur aliud esse

[a] ideoque W, ideo V, item quia GC, item quod P

take such undue profit from the said unnecessary alterations. To another argument, borrowed from Chapter VII, that the prince may have some profit from the coinage, the answer is easy, namely that this is a small and limited pension, which is not to be at all augmented by alteration of the coinage, but is independent of any change. In reply to another argument, that the prince may have revenues and ought to have a magnificent and honourable estate, such revenues can and should be appropriated and drawn from other sources than such undue alterations from which, as has previously been shown, such great evils and disadvantages arise. And supposing that some part of such revenue is charged on the coinage, it must be fixed and limited in amount, say two shillings or so on every mark coined [1] and so forth, which would not involve any alteration or unreasonable and enormous increase in profit arising from the detestable changes of which we have spoken.

The general conclusion from all this is that the prince cannot make these changes or receive profit in this way either by the regular common law or by privilege, gift, grant, bargain or any other authority or means whatever, nor can it be his right in virtue of his lordship or otherwise. Also that the denial of such a right is no disherison or infringement of his majesty as is falsely alleged by flatterers, intriguers and traitors to the commonwealth. Again, since the prince is bound not to do this, he deserves no pension or gift for refraining from such an improper exaction, for this seems nothing less than a

---

[1] Fr. Vers. ' as of every mark of gold, six shillings and of every mark of silver, one shilling, or other liberal rate '

nisi precium redempcionis a seruitute, quod nullus rex aut bonus princeps debet a subditis exigere. Item, supposito et non concesso quod ipse haberet priuilegium capiendi aliquid supra monetam pro faciendo eam bonam et pro tenendo eam in eodem statu, adhuc ipse deberet priuilegium tale perdere in casu in quo tantum abuteretur, quod ipse mutaret et falsificaret monetam pro suo lucro non minus cupide quam turpiter adaugendo.

CAPITULUM XXV

Quod tyrannus non potest diu durare

In istis duobus capitulis intendo probare, quod exigere pecuniam per tales mutaciones monete, est contra honorem regni et in preiudicium tocius regalis posteritatis. Sciendum est ergo quod inter principatum regium et tyrannicum hoc interest, quod tyrannus prediligit et plus querit proprium commodum quam commune conferens subditorum, et ad hoc nititur ut teneat populum sibi seruiliter subiugatum ; rex autem econtrario utilitati priuate publicam prefert, et super omnia post Deum et animam suam diligit bonum et libertatem publicam subditorum. Et hec est uera utilitas atque nobilitas principantis, cuius dominium tanto est nobilius, tanto melius, quanto est magis liberorum siue meliorum, ut ait Aristotiles,[1] et eo diuturnius, quo in tali proposito intencio regis perseuerat, dicente Cassiodoro : [2] ' Disciplina imperandi est amare quod multis expedit.' Quociens enim regnum in tyrannidem uertitur, non longo post tempore custo-

ransom from slavery, which no king or good prince ought to exact from his subjects. Also, supposing, but not admitting, that he may have the privilege of drawing a profit from the coinage as a return for coining good money and maintaining its standard, even so he must forfeit the privilege if he so abuses it as to change and debase the money for the greedy and disgraceful enhancement of his own profit.

Chapter XXV

That a Tyrant cannot be lasting

In this and the following chapter I propose to prove that raising money by such alterations of the coinage is dishonourable to the kingdom and to the damage of all the king's posterity. You must know, therefore, that the difference between kingdom and tyranny is that a tyrant loves and pursues his own good more than the common advantage of his subjects, and aims at keeping his people in slavery ; a king, on the contrary, prefers the public good to his own and loves above all things, after God and his own soul, the good and public freedom of his subjects. And this is the true usefulness and nobility of the princely power, whose lordship is the nobler and the better, as Aristotle says,[1] the more it is over freer and better men, and endures the longer for the king's steadfastness in following that principle. As Cassiodorus says [2] : ' The art of governing is to love the interests of the many.' For whenever kingship approaches tyranny it is near its end, for by this it becomes ripe for division,

---

[1] Pol. III. iv. 14 ?   [2] Variae ix. 9. 5

ditur, quia per hoc ad diuisionem,[a] translacionem aut
perdicionem omnimodam preparatur, maxime in regione temperata et remota a seruili barbaria, ubi sunt
homines conuersacione, moribus et natura liberi, non
serui nec sub tyrannide per consuetudinem indurati,
quibus seruitus foret inexpediens, inuoluntaria, et oppres-
sio tyrannica simpliciter uiolenta, ergo non diu per-
mansura, quia, sicut ait Aristotiles,[1] 'uiolenta citissime
corrumpuntur.' Ideo dicit Tullius [2] quod ' nulla uis imperii tanta est, que premente metu possit esse diuturna,'
et Seneca in tragediis inquit : [3]

> Violenta nemo imperia continuit diu ;
> moderata durant.

Unde principibus destitutis improperabat Dominus per
prophetam, dicens quod *imperabant* subditis *cum austeri-
tate et potencia.*[4] Adhuc autem propositum aliter declara-
tur ; ait enim Plutarchus ad Traianum imperatorem,[5]
quod ' res publica est corpus quoddam, quod diuini
numinis instar beneficio animatur et summe equitatis
agitur nutu, et regitur quodam moderamine racionis.'
Est ergo res publica siue regnum sicut quoddam corpus
humanum, et ita uult Aristotiles quinto Politice.[6] Sicut
ergo corpus male disponitur, quando humores excessiue
fluunt ad unum eius membrum, ita quod illud membrum
sepe ex hoc inflammatur [b] et nimium ingrossatur, reli-
quis exsiccatis et nimis attenuatis, tolliturque debita
proporcio, neque tale corpus potest diu uiuere ; ita
conformiter est de communitate uel regno, quando
diuicie ab una ipsius parte attrahuntur ultra modum.
Communitas namque uel regnum, cuius principantes in
comparacione ad subditos, quantum ad diuicias poten-

[a] diminucionem VC
[b] *So VC and the French version* (enflammé) ; inflatur *the other MSS*

change of dynasty or total destruction, especially in a
temperate climate, far from a slavish barbarism, where
men are habitually, morally and naturally free, not
slaves, nor habituated to tyranny ; to whom slavery
would be unprofitable and unacceptable, and tyranny
nothing less than unnatural and therefore short-lived,
since as Aristotle says [1] : ' Things contrary to nature
most quickly decay.' So, too, Cicero says [2] : ' That no
empire is strong enough to last if it is full of fear.'
And Seneca in his tragedies says [3] :

> No-one can prolong
> Enforced empires : moderate empires last.

Wherefore the Lord by his prophet [4] reproached the
deposed princes, saying : ' With force and with cruelty
have ye ruled them.' And the same thing is said elsewhere, for Plutarch says to the emperor Trajan that
' the state is a body, living as it were by a gift of the
gods, actuated by the decision of the highest justice, and
governed by the restraint of reason.' [5] The state or
kingdom, then, is like a human body and so Aristotle
will have it in Book V of the Politics.[6] As, therefore,
the body is disordered when the humours flow too
freely into one member of it, so that that member is
often thus inflamed and overgrown while the others are
withered and shrunken and the body's due proportions
are destroyed and its life shortened ; so also is a commonwealth or a kingdom when riches are unduly attracted
by one part of it. For a commonwealth or kingdom

---

[1] Metaph. iv. 5. ?   [2] De officiis ii. 25
[3] Troades 258-9. The same quotations occur together in the last
paragraph of Oresme's *Contra Astrologos*.   [4] Ezek. xxxiv. 4
[5] Inst. Trajani ii. Oresme is probably quoting from the *Policraticus* of
John of Salisbury, by whom this work is thought to have been invented ;
see *Journal of the Warburg and Courtauld Institutes*, vi. (1943) 33-9 and xii.
(1949) 189-90.   [6] Pol. V, iii. 66 (1302*b*35)

tiam et statum, enormiter crescunt, est sicut unum
monstrum, sicut unus homo cuius caput est tam magnum,
tam grossum, quod non potest a reliquo debili corpore
sustentari. Quemadmodum ergo talis homo non potest
se iuuare nec sic diu uiuere, ita neque regnum permanere
poterit, cuius princeps trahit ad se diuicias in excessu,
sicut fit per mutaciones monete, ut patuit capitulo
uicesimo. Rursum, sicuti in mixtione uocum non
placet nec delectat equalitas, et inequalitas*a* nimia uel
indebita totam consonanciam destruit et deturpat ;
ymo requiritur proporcionata inequalitas et commen-
surata, qua perseuerante emiscent leti blanda modula-
mina chori : sic eciam uniuersaliter, quoad omnes partes
communitatis, equalitas possessionum uel potencie non
conuenit nec consonat, sed et nimia disparitas armoniam
rei publice dissipat et corrumpit, ut patet per Aristotilem
quinto Politice.[1] Potissime uero ipse princeps, qui est
in regno ueluti tenor et uox principalis in cantu, si
magnitudine excedat et a reliqua communitate dis-
cordat,*b* regalis policie dulce melos tunc erit turbatum.
Propter quod secundum Aristotilem adhuc est alia
differencia inter regem et tyrannum, quia tyrannus uult
esse potencior tota communitate, cui presidet uiolente ;
regis uero temperancia est tali moderamine comparata,*c*
quod ipse est maior atque potencior quam aliquis eius
subditus, est tamen tota ipsa communitate inferior
uiribus et opibus,*d* et sic in medio constitutus. Sed
quoniam potestas regia communiter et leuiter tendit in
maius, ideo maxima cautela adhibenda est et peruigil
custodia, ymo altissima et principalis prudencia requiri-

---

a equalitas et *is omitted by* C *and the French version,* et inequalitas *by* VW
b discordet *the 1484 edition, perhaps rightly*
c *So* W ; moderata V, temperata GPC
d opibus GP, operibus *the other MSS and the French version* (œuvres et
forces)

whose princes, as compared with their subjects, increase
beyond measure in wealth, power and position, is as it
were a monster, like a man whose head is so large and
heavy that the rest of his body is too weak to support it.
And just as such a man has no pleasure in life and cannot
live long ; neither can a kingdom survive whose prince
draws to himself riches in excess as is done by altering
the coinage, as appeared in Chapter XX. Again, as in
a chorus unison has no power to please and excessive
or improper dissonance destroys and spoils the whole
harmony, but a proportional and measured difference of
tone is needed to produce the sweet melody of a joyous
choir : so also, generally, equality of possessions or
power in all sections of the community is inconvenient
and inconsistent, but too great a disparity destroys and
spoils the harmony of the state, as appears from Aristotle in Politics, Book V.[1] But especially if the prince,
who is, as it were, the tenor and leading voice in singing,
is too great and is out of tune with the rest of the commonwealth, the sweet melody of the kingdom's constitution
will be disturbed. And this, as Aristotle says, is another
difference between a king and a tyrant. For a tyrant
wishes to be more powerful than the whole community
over whom he rules by force : but a king's moderation
is restrained by the fact that he is greater and more
powerful than any of his subjects, but of less power or
wealth than the whole community, and so stands in the
middle. But because the king's power commonly and
easily tends to increase, the greatest care and constant
watchfulness must be used, indeed extreme and supreme
prudence is needed, to keep it from degenerating into

---

[1] Pol. V. i. (1304a26)

tur ad eam preseruandam, ne labatur ad tyrannidem,
precipue propter adulatorum fallacias, qui semper
principes ad tyranniam impulerunt, ut ait Aristotiles.[1]
Ipsi enim, sicut in libro Hester legitur, *aures principum
simplices et ex sua natura alios estimantes, callida fraude
decipiunt*, et eorum *suggestionibus regum studia deprauantur*.[2]
Sed quoniam eos euitare aut extirpare difficile est, ipse
Aristotiles [3] dat aliam regulam, per quam regnum potest
longo tempore conseruari ; et est, quod princeps non
multum amplificet dominium supra subditos, exacciones
capciones non faciat, libertates eis dimittat aut concedat,
nec eos impediat, neque utatur plenitudine potestatis
sed potencia legibus et consuetudinibus limitata uel
regulata. Pauca enim, ut ait Aristotiles,[4] sunt iudicis
uel principis arbitrio relinquenda. Aristotiles eciam
adducit exemplum de Theopompo Lacedemoniorum
rege,[5] qui, cum multas potestates atque tributa populo
remisisset ab antecessoribus imposita, ipse quidem
uxori ploranti atque improperanti, turpe esse regnum
minoris emolumenti filiis traditurum quam suscepisset
a patre, respondit dicens : ' Trado diuturnius.' O
diuinum oraculum ! O quanti ponderis uerbum, et in
palaciis regiis literis aureis depingendum ! Trado,
inquit, diuturnius, ac si diceret : Plus auxi regnum
duracione temporis quam sit diminutum moderacione
potestatis. *Ecce plus quam Salomon hic.*[6] Nam si Roboam,
de quo supra memini, a patre suo Salomone regnum
sic compositum recepisset et tenuisset, nunquam decem
de duodecim tribubus Israel perdidisset, nec sibi impro-
peratum fuisset Ecclesiastici xlvii : *Prophanasti semen tuum
inducere iracundiam ad liberos tuos, et ceteris stulticiam tuam,*

---

[1] Pol. V. xi. 3 (1314*a*2)   [2] Esther xvi. 6–7 (in the Vulgate)
[3] Pol. V. xi. 2 (1313*a*18)   [4] Pol. III, xvi. 11

tyranny, especially because of deceitful flatterers who
have always, as Aristotle says, urged princes to be
tyrants.[1] For they cunningly deceive the simple ears of
princes (as we read in the book of Esther), who judge
other men's characters by their own, and by their
suggestions kings' minds are turned to evil.[2] But since
it is hard to avoid them or to root them out, Aristotle
gives another rule by which a kingdom may long
survive.[3] That is that the prince should not enlarge his
dominion over his subjects, should not overtax them or
seize their goods, should allow or grant them liberties
and should not interfere with them or use his plenary
powers but only a power regulated and limited by law
and custom. For few things, as Aristotle says,[4] should be
left to the decision of a judge or a prince. For he adduces
the example of Theopompus, king of the Lacedae-
monians,[5] who, after having given back to the people
many powers and imposts, when his wife wept and
reproached him, saying, 'He should be ashamed to
hand on to his sons a less profitable kingdom than he
had received from his father,' replied, 'I leave them a
more permanent one.' Surely an oracle of God ! How
weighty a saying, fit to be written in golden letters in
kings' palaces ! ' I leave them a more permanent one ' :
as he might have put it, 'I have made the kingdom
greater in duration than I have made it less by limiting
its power.' A greater man than Solomon is here.[6] For
if Rehoboam, whom I mentioned above, had received
from his father Solomon a kingdom so limited, he would
never have lost ten of the twelve tribes of Israel, nor
would he have been reproached thus in Ecclesiasticus :
' Thou didst profane thy seed, to bring wrath upon thy

---

[5] Pol. V. xi. 3 (1313*a*26–33)   [6] Luke xi. 31

ut faceres imperium bipertitum.[1]   Sic ergo ostensum est, quod dominium quod ex regno in tyrannidem uertitur, oportet ut celeriter finiatur.

Capitulum XXVI

Quod capere lucrum ex mutacione monetarum preiudicat toti regali posteritati

Declarare propono quod mutaciones predicte sunt contra honorem regis et generi regio preiudicant. Pro quo tria premitto. Primum est, quod illud est in rege uituperabile et successoribus eius preiudiciabile, per quod regnum perdicioni disponitur, aut ut ad alienigenas transferatur ; nec rex posset satis dolere uel flere, qui esset ita infelix, ita miserabilis, quod per negligenciam suam aut per malum regimen eius aliquid fieret, unde ipse uel heredes sui perderent regnum tot uirtutibus auctum, tanto tempore gloriose seruatum.   Necnon in periculo anime sue gloriose foret, si ex defectu sui populus pateretur tot pestilencias, tot calamitates et tantas, quot et quante solent accidere in dissipacione siue in translacione regnorum.   Secundo suppono quod per tyrannizacionem regum *a* regnum perdicioni exponitur,*b* sicut declaratum est in capitulo precedenti, et quoniam, sicut in Ecclesiastico scribitur, *Regnum a gente in gentem transfertur propter iniusticias et iniurias et contumelias et diuersos dolos,*[2] tyrannis autem iniuriosa est et iniusta. Cum hoc eciam, ut ad specialia descendam, absit quod in tantum degenerauerint Francigenarum libera corda,

---

a regum *is omitted by* VWC   *b* disponitur W, *perhaps rightly*

children ; and I was grieved for thy folly ; so that the
sovereignty was divided.' [1]

It has thus been proved that a dominion which is
turned from a kingdom to a tyranny is bound to have a
speedy end.

Chapter XXVI

*That the taking of Profit from Alteration of the Coinage
injures the whole Royal Succession*

I propound the thesis that the alterations before-
mentioned are dishonourable to the king and prejudicial
to the royal house. To prove this I lay down three
premisses :

First that that is a reproach to a king and to the
prejudice of his successors by which a kingdom is exposed
to destruction or to being given over to strangers. Nor
could a king grieve or weep enough who should be so
unhappy, so wretched as by his carelessness or mis-
government to do anything that brought him or his heirs
to lose a kingdom ennobled by so many great deeds and
so long gloriously maintained. Nor would it be without
danger to his glorious soul, if by his fault his people should
suffer so many plagues, so many great misfortunes as
usually accompany the fall or the conquest of kingdoms.

Secondly, I submit that tyranny exposes a kingdom
to ruin, as was set forth in the last chapter and since, as
it is written in Ecclesiasticus,[2] ' Sovereignty is transferred
from nation to nation, because of iniquities and deeds
of violence and greed of money,' while tyranny is
iniquitous and violent. Furthermore, to come to par-

---

[1] Ecclus. xlvii. 20-21   [2] Ecclus. x. 8

quod uoluntarie serui fiant. Ideoque seruitus eis imposita durare non potest, quoniam, etsi magna sit tyrannorum potencia, est tamen liberis subditorum cordibus uiolenta et aduersus alienos inualida. Quicumque ergo dominos Francie ad huiusmodi regimen tyrannicum quoquo modo traherent, ipsi regnum magno discrimini exponerent, et ad terminum prepararent. Neque enim regum Francie generosa propago tyrannizare didicit, nec seruiliter subici populus Gallicus consueuit. Ideo, si regia proles a pristina uirtute degeneret, proculdubio regnum perdet. Tercio suppono, tanquam iam probatum et sepius repetitum, quod capere uel augere lucrum super mutacione monete est factum dolosum, tyrannicum et iniustum, cum hoc eciam, non posse continuari in regno, quod quidem regnum iam non sit, quoad alia multa, in tyrannidem uersum. Unde non solum inconueniencia sequuntur ex isto, sed oportet quedam alia mala esse preuia, alia concomitancia ; quia hoc non potest a uiris consuli qui non sint in intencione corrupti atque ad omnem fraudem et nequiciam tyrannicam consulendam parati, ubi uiderent principem ad hoc inclinari uel posse flecti. Dico itaque recolligendo, quod res per quam regnum perdicioni disponitur, turpis est et preiudiciabilis regi et heredibus suis, et hoc fuit primum suppositum ; *a* sed hoc est protrahi et conuerti in tyrannidem, et hoc fuit secundum ; et ad hoc uertitur per mutaciones monete, ut dicit tercium. Igitur exaccio que fit per tales mutaciones est contra honorem regis, et preiudiciabilis toti posteritati regali ; quod erat probandum.

Hec igitur, ut premisi, sine assercione dicta sint et cum correccione prudentium, nam, secundum Aristotilem,[1]

---

a The eight words et heredibus... suppositum *stand in all MSS and editions after* conuerti

ticulars, God forbid that the free hearts of Frenchmen should have so degenerated that they should willingly become slaves ; and therefore a slavery thrust upon them cannot last. For, though the power of tyrants is great, it does violence to the free hearts of subjects and is of no avail against foreigners. Whoever, therefore, should in any way induce the lords of France to such tyrannical government, would expose the realm to great danger and pave the way to its end. For neither has the noble offspring of the French kings learned to be tyrannous, nor the people of Gaul to be servile ; therefore if the royal house decline from its ancient virtue, it will certainly lose the kingdom.

Thirdly, I submit, as a point already proved and often repeated, that to take or augment profit by alteration of the coinage is fraudulent, tyrannical and unjust, and moreover it cannot be persisted in without the kingdom being, in many other respects also, changed to a tyranny. Wherefore, it not only brings disadvantages of its own, but involves many other evils as either its conditions or its consequences. For this course can only be the advice of evil-minded men, ready to counsel any fraud or tyranny, if they see a prince inclined to it or willing to listen to it.

To sum up my argument, I say that a thing which tends to bring a realm to ruin is disgraceful and harmful to the king and his heirs, my first premiss ; that it extends and changes to a tyranny, my second ; and that it does so by alteration of the coinage, my third. Consequently a tax levied by means of such changes is against the king's honour and injures his posterity, which was to be proved.

All this, as I said before, is tentative and subject to correction by experts. For, as Aristotle says [1] : ' Civil

---

[1] Eth. Nic. i. 3. 2 (1094*b*14–16)

ciuilia negocia plerumque sunt dubia et incerta. Si quis igitur amore ueritatis inueniende hiis dictis uoluerit contradicere aut contrascribere, bene faciet ; et *si male locutus sum*, perhibeat *testimonium de malo*,[1] sed cum racione, ne ipse uideatur gratis et uoluntarie condempnare, quod non potest efficaciter impugnare.

Explicit Tractatus de mutacionibus monetarum a magistro Nicolao Oresme sacre pagine excellenti professore.[a]

[a] *So* W ; V *has* Explicit tractatus mag. N. O. de mutacione monete
[1] John xviii. 23

matters are usually doubtful and uncertain.' If anyone, therefore, in his love of truth, chooses to contradict or oppose what I have written, he will be doing well. And if I have spoken evil let him bear witness of the evil,[1] but with reason, lest he be seen needlessly and wilfully to condemn what he is not able effectually to refute.

Here ends the treatise of the worthy Nicholas Oresme S.T.P. on alteration of the Coinage

PART TWO

English Mint Documents

CAMBIUM

Temp. Henry III   (Red Book, fo. 231 v°.)

Genera argenti, uidelicet : de Monte Pessulano, quod est adeo bonum quod decidit libra examinata nisi in uno denario, uel in duobus ad plus. Argentum de Eregh[a] eodem modo. Argentum de Fuacg[io], unde libra decidit in iiij*d.* ad plus. Argentum de Seyngu[esa] et de Maclyne semper est purum et non decidens. Argentum de Alemannia, fere totum purum. Argentum de Brucela et de Flandria, de quo libra decidit iiij*d.* Argentum de Verona ; libra communiter decidit xij*d.* Argentum de Podio, de quo libra decidit xv*d.* Argentum de Valentino ; decidit libra viij*d.* Argentum de Pampeluna ; decidit libra ij*d.* Et hec omnia de argento in platis.

De denariis de Venitia ; non decidit libra nisi in j*d.* Similiter de Gennua. Similiter de Mylerensibus Yspanie. Colennenses legales ; unde libra decidit vj*d.* Colonenses falsi ; unde libra decidit iij*s.* Bruselenses decidunt in libra iij*s.* communiter. Marsilienses decidunt vj*d.* de libra. In hiis autem aduertat cambiator ut emat libram cuiuslibet argenti secundum quod sibi melius credidorit proficere quoniam respondebit de proficuo Regi, eo quod certa habet stipendia x*l.* Proficuum autem erit Regi, set dampnum non, eo quod aut est industrius aut non. Non industrio enim [non] indiget Rex. De uasis autem argenteis absque deauratione recipit Cambiator libram ad casum viij denariorum ; et consimiliter de deauratis. Et si fuerint uasa uenalia et integra, que

---

[1] Pence coined at Montpelier. *See* DuCange, s.v. *Moneta—Melgorensis.*

EXCHANGE

Temp. Henry III

Silver has the following varieties : from Montpelier, which is so good that a pound, when assayed, is only a penny or twopence at most short of purity. That from the Ariége is the same. Silver from Foix, a pound of which is at most fourpence short. Silver of Sangüesa and of Malines is always pure and does not fall short. Silver from the Empire is almost all pure. Silver of Brussels and Flanders, of which the pound is fourpence short. Silver of Verona, the pound is usually twelve pence short. Silver of Le Puy, of which the pound is fifteen pence short. Silver of Valenciennes (?), the pound is eightpence short. Silver of Pampeluna, the pound is twopence short. All these are silver in plate.

Of pence of Venice the pound is only a penny short. So also of Genoa. Likewise the *Mylerenses* [1] of Spain. Lawful pence of Cologne, a pound of which is sixpence short. Forged pence of Cologne ; the pound is three shillings short. Brussels pence are usually three shillings in the pound short. Those of Marseilles, sixpence.

In all this let the changer take care to buy a pound of any silver according to what he believes will bring him the best profit, since he shall answer for the profit to the king, because he himself has fixed wages of £10. But the profit will be the king's, but not the loss, because he is either diligent or not. For the king has no need of a man who is not diligent.

But of silver vessels without gilding the changer receives each pound at a discount of eightpence and gilt vessels likewise. And if the vessels are saleable and entire

10

possint uendi de lucro ultra pondus, debet respondere ; et similiter de excrescenti uasorum deautarorum, cum cuppa deaurata ualeat aliquando, ultra pondus, xx*s*., uel j*m*., uel x*s*.

[OFFICIA MINISTRORUM CAMBII]

c. 1248   (Red Book, fo. 246)

In baga inuenta in Thesauro, in qua continentur compoti diuersorum de cambio Monete Regis, inuenitur quedam cedula in hec uerba.

Officium Cambitoris iure tale est ; quod capiat de qualibet libra ueteris monete, xvj*d*., uidelicet, ad opus domini Regis et Comitis, per pondus, vj*d*. de recta et consueta firma, et x denarios ad opus monetariorum pro decensu ad ignem. Et eodem pondere quo ipse cambitor recipit ueterem monetam in cambiendo, eodem pondere ipsam liberabit monetario ad fundendam. Et si ipse Cambitor emerit argentum grossum purum, de qualibet libra capiat vj*d*. de recta et consueta firma ; et liberet idem argentum grossum monetariis eodem pondere quo emebatur ad fundendum. Et ipsi monetarii apponent cuilibet libre, vj*d*. de cupro, secundum rectam et antiquam consuetudinem ; de quibus vj*d*. ipsi monetarii dabunt operariis nouam monetam fabricantibus, iij*d*. de qualibet libra, et de aliis iij*d*., debent alocare domos fontorum, soldas operariorum, et conducent seruientes suos in suo officio, et inuenient cuneos et ement carbonem et omnia alia que suo pertinent officio. Et si ipse Cambitor emerit argentum grossum quod non sit purum per estimationem suam, et monetarii noluerint illud

and can be sold at a price higher than their weight, the changer must answer for the price and likewise for the extra value of gilt vessels, since a gilt cup is sometimes worth twenty shillings, a mark, or ten shillings beyond the weight.

[DUTIES OF THE OFFICERS OF THE MINT]

c. 1248

In a bag found in the Treasury in which are contained accounts of various officers of the Royal Mint, there is found a schedule in these words :

The office of the Changer lawfully is : to take in every pound of the old money sixteen pence, namely to the use of the king and the earl, by weight, 6d of the right and accustomed farm and tenpence to the use of the moneyers for loss in the fire. And by the same weight that the Changer receives and exchanges the old coin, he shall deliver it to the moneyer to melt. And if the Changer buys pure silver in bulk, he shall take 6d in each pound of the right and accustomed farm and deliver the same silver in bulk to be melted by the same weight by which it was bought. And the moneyers shall add to each pound 6 dwts of copper according to the right and ancient custom ; of which 6d the moneyers shall give to the workmen making the new money 3d in each pound, and from the other 3d they must hire the houses for the melters and pay the wages of the workmen and hire their servants in their office and find the dies and buy the charcoal and everything else belonging to their office. And if the Changer buy silver in bulk which is not pure by his estimate (of its value) and the

argentum per estimationem recipere, ipse Cambitor illud
argentum faciet purum per ignem ; ita quod si lucrum
inde ueniat, erit domini Regis et Comitis. Et conducent
ardorem de exitu cuneorum,[a] qui habet pro libra obolum.

In cambio erit unus assayator qui debet assayare
platas ante quam deferatur ad Cuneum, quod sint recti
ponderis et de bono argento, et faciet quamlibet assayam
de xx platis ponderantibus xx denarios legalis monete,
que assaia debet descidere unius oboli tantum et non
magis, neque minus. Et cum transierint per cuneum
plate ille, debet assayator facere j assayam xx*d*. in
cambio et coram clericis et cambitore et aliis circum-
sedentibus debet assaya illa judicari, quod sit legalis
ponderis et de bono argento, sicut dictum est de platis ;
et hoc facto, debet Cambitor cambire denarios illos.

Item officium custodum cuneorum tale est, quod
ipsi sedeant et uideant quod operarii bene percutiant
platas ad cuneum missas, et quod nulla plata percutiatur,
neque transeat per cuneum, nisi fuerit bona, legalis et
recta. Et ad istud officium faciendum, recipient de
qualibet centena libra xij*d*. de monetariis.

Item officium Hostiarii tale est, quod hostium Cambii
bene seruetur de intrantibus et exeuntibus ; et quod
uocet et congreget omnes ad officium monetariorum per-
tinentes, sicut fuerit ei iniunctum.

^a MS cun'um

moneyers refuse to accept it at that estimate, the Changer shall purify that silver in the fire, provided that if there come any profit from it, that shall accrue to the king and the earl. And they shall pay for the firing out of the issues of the dies and he (sc. the melter) has a halfpenny in the pound.

There shall be in the Mint an Assayer who must assay the blanks before they are brought to the die, that they are of right weight and of good silver and shall make each assay of twenty blanks weighing twenty pennyweights of lawful money, which assay should not be out more than a halfpenny more or less. And when the blanks have passed through the dies, the assayer must make an assay of twenty pence in the Mint, and that assay must be judged before the clerks and the Changer and other assessors, that it is of lawful weight and of good silver, as is said of the blanks. And after this the Changer must give these pence in exchange.

Also it is the duty of the Keepers of the Dies to sit and see that the workmen strike the blanks sent to the die well and that no blank be struck or pass through the die unless it be good, lawful and right. And for doing this duty they shall receive twelve pence from the moneyers in every hundred pounds.

Also the duty of the usher is to keep well the door of the Mint for men going in or out, and to call and assemble all belonging to the office of moneyers, as he may be commanded.

[EXAMINATIO NOVE MONETE]

A.D. 1248   (B.M. MS Hargrave, 313, fo. 96 v°)

Anno regni Regis Henrici filii Regis Iohannis xxxij°,
die Mercurii proxima ante festum Gregorii, facta fuit
examinatio tam noue quam ueteris monete Anglie
per breue domini Regis directum Maiori et ciuibus
Londonie sub hac forma :

Henricus, Dei gratia, Rex Angl', etc., Maiori et
ciuibus Londonie, salutem. Mandamus uobis quatinus
eligatis xij de discretioribus et legalioribus hominibus
Ciuitatis uestre Lond' et eis associetis xij bonos auri-
fabros eiusdem ciuitatis, ita quod in uniuerso sint xxiiij
discreti, qui simul eant coram Baronibus de Scaccario
nostro apud Westmuster et iurati examinent, una cum
eis Baronibus, tam ueterem quam nouam monetam
terre nostre et prouideant qualiter melius fieri ualeat ;
et quod fiat de bono argento ; et quod sit legalis et ad
commodum regni. Salua nobis firma nostra approbata
et antiqua.[1]

Concientibus igitur apud Westmonasterium predicta
die Mercurii dictis Maiore et ciuibus London', iuxta
formam predicti breuis, elegerunt ex se xij de discretioribus dicte ciuitatis, uidelicet, Michaelem Touy,
tunc Maiore[m] Londonie, Nicholaum Bat et Willel-
mum Vitalem, tunc uicecomites Londonie, Adam de
Basinges, Thomam de Dunelmo, Iohannem de Gisorz,
Stephanum Bukerel, Laurentium de Frowike, Iohannem
Adriani, Radulfum Hardel, Radulfum Fabrum, Radulfum Spiciarium, Hamonem de Castello, Iohannem le
Minur, Odonem Fabrum, ad predictam examinationem
faciendam. Qui xiij[2] in fidelitate qua tenentur domino
Regi, una cum xiij aurifabris iur', uidelicet, Thoma de

[ASSAY OF THE NEW MONEY]

A.D. 1248

In the thirty-second year of King Henry son of King John, on Wednesday before St Gregory's day (11 March 1248), an examination was made as well of the new as of the old money of England, by a writ of the king addressed to the mayor and citizens of London in the terms following :

Henry, by the grace of God king of England, etc., to the mayor and citizens of London, greeting. We command you to elect twelve of the more discreet and lawful men of our city of London and join with them twelve good goldsmiths of the same city, making twenty-four discreet men in all, who shall go before the Barons of our Exchequer at Westminster and examine, upon oath, together with the barons, both the old and the new money of our land, and make provision how it may be bettered ; and that it be made of good silver, and that it be lawful and for the good of the realm. Saving to us our approved and ancient farm.[1]

The said mayor and citizens of London, therefore, assembling at Westminster on the aforesaid Wednesday according to the tenor of the said writ, chose from among themselves twelve of the more discreet men of the said city, to wit, Michael Tony, then mayor of London, Nicholas Bat and William Vyel, then sheriffs of London, Adam of Basing, Thomas of Durham, John of Gisors, Stephen Bukerel, Lawrence of Frowick, John Adrian, Ralph Hardel, Ralph the Smith, Ralph the Spicer, Hamo de Castello, John le Minur, Odo the Smith, to make the aforesaid assay. And these thirteen,[2] in the

---

[1] Waltham. 23 February   [2] *Sic* in MS

Stanes, Ricardo Bonauenture, Roberto Pentecoste, Bartholomeo Ilger, Ricardo Abel, Iohanne Fiz, Ricardo le Bacheler, Reginaldo le Noir, Thoma de Wimburn', Adam de Stanes, Petro de Bristoll', Thoma Rosemud' et Petro de Standon'; in presentia domini Regis, Comitis Cornubie fratris domini Regis, Willelmi de Hauerhulle eiusdem domini Regis Thesaurarii, Edwardi de Westm', Willelmo Hardel, tunc custodis Camb' Londonie et Cantuarie, Radulfi de Ely, Baronis de Scaccario, et aliorum fidelium domini Regis tunc ibidem presentium, dictam examinationem, quam assaiam vocant, in hunc modum fecerunt, scilicet, sumpta coram predictis omnibus una libra, pluries, noue monete et noue incisionis, et in igne posita purgatura, et examinata et extracta et in statera posita; inuentum est quod non decidebat de libra nisi vj*d*.; unde, secundum consuetudinem regni Anglie, bona fuerat et legalis et a singulis approbata. De ueteri autem moneta, similiter, sumpta una libra, pluries, et modo premisso in igne missa et ponderata, decidebant de libra per examinationem predictam x denarii, unde uidebatur omnibus quod non erat bona neque legalis: et ideo prouisum est ab omnibus et concessum, quod qui de cetero uelint ad cambium domini Regis ueterem monetam cambire, dabunt pro qualibet libra, preter firmam domini Regis, x*d*., eo quod totidem denarii deciderunt de libra [in] illa moneta; aut in electione illius qui cambire noluerit huius modi monetam sit, quod moneta sua per ignem examinetur, uel quod det x*d*. pro qualibet libra ultra firmam predictam, sicut predictum est.

Et ne futuris temporibus posset fraus fieri de legali moneta regni, de consilio predictorum omnium pro utilitate reipublice, facta sunt duo assaia, pond[us] utri[us]que x*s*., quorum unum est de puro argento, et

fealty which they owe to our lord the king, together with
thirteen sworn goldsmiths, to wit, Thomas of Staines,
Richard Bonaventure, Robert Pentecost, Bartholomew
Ilger, Richard Abel, John Fitz, Richard le Bacheler,
Reginald le Noir, Thomas of Wimborne, Adam of
Staines, Peter of Bristol, Thomas Rosemud and Peter of
Standen, in the presence of our lord the king, the Earl
of Cornwall, his brother, William de Haverhull, his
treasurer, Edward of Westminster, William Hardel, then
warden of the Mints of London and Canterbury, Ralph
of Ely, baron of the Exchequer, and other of the king's
lieges then there present, made the said examination,
which they call an ' assay,' as follows : to wit—

One pound of the new money from the new dies
having been taken, more than once, before all the
persons named, placed in the refiners' fire, examined,
taken out and placed in the balance, it was found not
to weigh more than six pence less than the (standard)
pound ; wherefore by the custom of the realm of England
it had been good and lawful and approved by all. But
one pound of the old money having been taken likewise
more than once, and put to the fire and weighed in the
manner aforesaid, there was lacking from the pound, on
the aforesaid examination, ten pence ; wherefore it was
clear to all that it was not good nor lawful. It was
therefore provided and granted by all that those who
wish in future to come to the king's mint to exchange
their old money, shall pay for each pound, in addition
to the king's farm (i.e. seignorage and mintage) ten
pence, because that was the deficiency per pound in that
money ; or that anyone wishing to exchange such money
may choose to have his money tried in the fire, or to pay
ten pence beyond the farm as aforesaid.

And lest in time to come there should be deceit in

aliud de argento ad cuius exemplar debet fieri moneta,
que duo assaya[1] quodam quonio impressa, posita sunt
in thesauro domini Regis apud Westmonasterium sub
sigillo Maioris London.

Consimiliter facta sunt plura assaia in forma predicta, dicto conio signata per diuersa loca ubi erigitur
cambium liberata, scilicet, apud Lond' duo pondera
xl. denariorum, unum uidelicet purum ad argentum
cognoscendum, et aliud ad monetam ; apud Cantuar'
duo eiusdem forme ; apud Sanctum Edmundum,
Norwic', Oxon', Norh', Linc', Winton', Glouc', Exon' et
Eborac', Irencester, et eodem modo.

Postmodum uero mandatum est ex parte domini
Regis maioribus, prepositis et balliuis predictarum
uillarum in quibus fieri debet moneta extra ciuitatibus
London. et Cantuar, quod singuli in uillis suis eligant
de discretioribus et fidelioribus earundem uillarum iiij[or]
monetarios, totidem custodes cuneorum, duos assaya-
tores et unum clericum ; prouiso quod tales sint et tam
idonei quod de facto illorum tota uilla respondeat ; et
quod illos per litteras suas sigillo communitatis signatas,
Thesaurario et Baronibus et custodibus Cambii domini
Regis presentant. Qui maiores prepositi et balliui,
audito mandato domini Regis, et in huius modi elec-
tionem in forma predicta procedentes, homines ad
officia predicta electos, cum litteris suis patentibus, in
quibus nomina eorum electorum[a] continentur, et que
sint in Thesauro, predictis Baronibus presentauerint,
qui sacramenta eorum nominatim de omnimoda fidelitate in officiis suis faciendis admittentes, ipsos, sicut
inferius continetur, in officiis suis substituerunt.[2]

***

[a] *MS* clericorum
[1] See Plate II   [2] See Appendix II, p. 102

the lawful coin of the realm by the counsel of the persons aforesaid, for the good of the commonwealth there were made two trial-plates (*assaia*), each of the weight of ten shillings, one of which is of pure silver and the other of standard silver. And these two trial-plates [1] were stamped with a certain die, placed in the treasury of our lord the king at Westminster under the seal of the mayor of London.

There were likewise made several trial-plates after the same manner, stamped with the said die, and delivered to the various places in which mints were set up : to wit, at London two of forty pennyweights each, one of pure silver for testing the silver, and one for the coin ; at Canterbury two similar plates ; at Bury St Edmunds, Norwich, Oxford, Northampton, Lincoln, Winchester, Gloucester, Exeter, York and Ilchester, the same.

But afterwards the king's order was sent to the mayors, reeves and bailiffs of the aforesaid towns, where money is to be coined outside the cities of London and Canterbury, that each of them in their towns choose from the more discreet and loyal men of the towns four moneyers, as many keepers of the dies, two assayers and one clerk ; provided that they be such and so fit that the whole town will answer for their conduct ; and present them by their letters sealed with the seal of the community to the Treasurer and Barons and the Wardens of the King's Mint. The which mayors, reeves and bailiffs, having heard the king's command and proceedings to make choice as aforesaid, presented to the said Barons the men chosen to the said offices, with their letters patent containing the names of the persons chosen, which are in the Treasury ; and the Barons, taking their several oaths to perform their duties faithfully, appointed them to their posts as appears below.[2]

FORMA NOVE MONETE

A.D. 1279   (Red Book, fo. 245)

Premerement ke hom deit fere un estaundard ke deit demoerer al Escheker ou en quel lieu ke nostre Seignur le Roy voldra. E solum la forme del Estaundard serra fete la mone e de tel bonte cum le estaundart. Et deit estre merche, fete et ferue del enprente del vel coyn e du novel.

Enkore ke la grose mone de quatre esterlings deit estre de la bonte del estaundard sus dit.

Enkore ke les ferlings seient round, e doyvent touz estre fet a Londres, e nent aylurs, et serrunt appellez Lundreis ; issi ke en quatre ferlings, ky les vodra fundre, len y trose autant de fin argent cum en lEsterling, fors tant ke lenfaudra ceo ke il cousterayent plus a fere. E pur ceo ke ly ferling serroyt trop febles et trop petit de tel lay cum les sterling, si est purveu ke il eyt autant plus de lay. E est a saver ke il serrunt de peys de seysante cink souz e wit deners a la livere, e serrunt taile en tele manere ke en la unce puse aver cink fortz e cink febles ; e li plus forz ne pusent estre de meyns de seisante souz et wit deners a la livre, ne li plus febles de plus de sey-sante dis souz e wit d[eners] a la livre. E de ceo serra fet un estaundard, ausi cum des ferlings, e mis en Tresor cum le autre ; e deyt estre feru del coyn del ferling.

Enkore deit hom bailler al Mestre une garde, e cele garde deit garder ke les deners seient de peis e de taile, cest a saver ke en la livre ne deit aver ke sis fortz e sis

THE FORM OF THE NEW MONEY

A.D. 1279

First, a standard must be made which shall remain at the Exchequer or in such a place as our lord the king will. And the money shall be made according to the form of the standard and of the same fineness as the standard. And (the standard) must be marked, made and struck with the stamp of the old money and of the new.

Item. The groat of four sterlings must be of the same fineness as the standard.

Item. The farthings shall be round and must be made at London and nowhere else and shall be called ' Lundreis,' so that any one who chooses to melt down four farthings may find in them as much fine silver as in one sterling, except what is needed to cover the extra cost of making. And because the farthing would be too weak and small if it were of the same alloy as the sterlings, it is provided that it shall have so much more alloy. And be it known that they shall be of the weight of sixty-five shillings and eightpence to the pound and shall be cut in such a way that there may be five heavy and five light in the ounce ; and the heaviest shall not be fewer than sixty shillings and eightpence to the pound nor the lightest more than seventy shillings and eightpence to the pound. And there shall be made a standard for them as for the farthings and placed in the Treasury with the other ; and it must be struck with the stamp of the farthing.

Item. The Master must be given a Warden and the Warden must see that the pence be of [just] weight and

febles. Si ke le un ne peysera plus ke le autre de un greyn e demi del dreit dener. E cele garde deit peiser la monoye sus dite, e si ele est bien trove de soen dreit peys, li mestre est quites e delivere kant al dit peys de cele moneye ke serra livere de peys e de cunte. E si avenyt ke un dener fust trove a la livre fort ou feble plus ou meyns de un greyn e demi al dreit dener, pur ceo ne demore mie la moneye ke ne seit delivre. Et deit estre la livre de vint souz et treis deners. E si il avenit ke un dener fust plus ou meyns ala livere, pur ceo ne demore mie ke la moneye ne fust livre al Mestre pur payer as marchaunz. E le mestre est tenu a mender la defaute de plus e de meyns a la monoye ke il fera apres.

Enkore ke hom deit aver un boiste a deus clefs, dunt le un deit garder li Mestre de la monee, e le autre le gardeyn. E en la dite boiste deit em mettre de checun dis livres fetes, un esterling pur fere le essay. E cele boiste deit estre delivre quatre fiet par an par le assayur le Roy, e ce sayt a les Cheker.

Enkore ke nostre seignur le Roy deit aver un bon assayur et leal, e ke cel assayur face le assay de la moneye quatre feth le an, sicum il est ava[n]t dit. E si avenist ke les deners de la boiste seient trovez escharz de deus greyns e demy a la demy unce, ke pur ceo le Mestre ne seyt poynt greve, mes seit tenuz a restorer la defaute[a] a la deliverance de la boyste e de plus e de mayns al dist de le assayur e des gardes. Meymes la manere sayt fete des ferlings ke sunt apele Lundrays de grain, boyste e de tut cum de les deners.

Enkore ke le Roy face crier par tot soen reaume ke nul hom [ne] chaunge la monoye, ne nule plates, nenul

---

[a] Au tresor (*struck out*)

tale, i.e. that there must not be more than six heavy and six light in the pound. So that one may not weigh more than another beyond one and a half grains [above or below] the weight of the just penny. And the Warden must weigh the said money, and if it is found well of the right weight the Master is quit and free from blame as to the weight of this money which shall be delivered of (just) weight and tale. And if it should happen that a penny were found in the pound heavier or lighter than the just penny by a grain and a half, the money shall be accepted. And the pound must contain twenty shillings and three pence. And if there be one penny more or less in the pound, the money may still be accepted for the Master to pay to the merchants. And the Master is bound to amend the fault of excess or defect in the money he shall afterwards make.

Item. There must be a box with two keys, one of which the Master of the Mint must keep and the Warden the other. And in the said box must be put one sterling out of each ten pounds coined, to make the assay. And this box must be delivered four times a year by the assayer to the king, and this shall be at the Exchequer.

Item. Our lord the king must have a good and lawful assayer, and let the assayer make the assay four times a year as is aforesaid. And if it happen that the pence in the box be found two and a half grains short in half an ounce, the Master shall not be punished for that, but he shall be bound to make good the defect (at the Treasury) at the delivery of the box, and more or less according to the verdict of the assayer and the wardens. The same shall be done as to the farthings called Lundreis with regard to the grain, the box, and everything, like the pence.

Item. The king shall have it proclaimed throughout

autre manere de argent fors al chaunge le Roy, ou a teles
persones ke al ceo serrunt assignees ; e ke nul hom seit si
hardi de porter hors del reaume de Engletere la monoye
abatue ; e ky cuntre ceo fra, soen cors et ses biens
seyent a la volunte le Roy.

Enkore ke nul orfevre ne achate nul argent, fors de
vele vessele, si nun a chaunge ; ne en nule vile seit
overant nul orfevre fors en grant rues, a veue de gent,
sur greve forfeture a la volunte le Roy.

Nomina Ministrorum Cambii

Gregorius de Rokele
Orlandinus de Podio

Custodes Cambii. Idem sunt
Custodes Monete et respon-
deant Regi in forma, etc.

Magister Hubertus
Alion de Aste
Magister Willelmus
de Turnemire
Et Petrus frater eius
de Marcell[ia]

Isti sunt Magistri Monete et
respondebunt de moneta in
forma, etc. fideliter super
uita et membrorum.—Et
insuper inuenient fideiusso-
res citra festum Sancti Mi-
chaelis proxime futurum—
Jurati.

Bonifacius Galgani de Florentia, assayator Monete—
Juratus.

Iohannes de Maydenstane, Clericus Cambii, Contra-
rotulator sit ex parte Regis.

the realm that no man change money, plate or any other kind of silver except at the king's exchange, or with such persons as are there appointed ; and that no man be so bold as to take coined money out of the realm of England ; and whosoever shall contravene this, his body and goods shall be at the king's will.

Item. That no goldsmith buy any silver except old plate but at the exchange ; nor shall there be worker (in) silver or goldsmith in any town except in the main streets in public view, under heavy forfeiture at the king's will.

Names of the Officers of the Mint

Gregory de Rokesley Orlando di Poggio	Wardens of the Exchange. Also Wardens of the Mint and answerable to the king in the form, etc.
Master Hubert Alion of Asti Master William de Turnemire And Peter, his brother, of Marseilles	These are Masters of the Mint and shall answer for the money in the form, etc. faithfully, on pain of life and limb. And they shall also find sureties before Michaelmas next. —Sworn

Boniface Galgani of Florence, Assayer of the Mint.— Sworn.

John of Maidstone, Clerk of the Exchange, shall be controller on behalf of the king.

[DEFENSIO TONSURE]

c. 1280   (Red Book, fo. 245 v°)

Memorandum quod proclametur per totum Regnum quod nulla fiat tonsura de noua moneta sub periculo uite et membrorum et amissione omnium terrarum et tenementorum ac omnium rerum et bonorum quorum-cunque illorum quos inde per iudicium Curie domini Regis conuinci contigerit. Et Rex prohibebit ne aliqua tonsura fiat de eadem moneta sub pena predicta. Et similiter prohibebit Rex ne aliquis recipiat aliquam monetam de eadem tonsam sub pena predicta. Et ke le Roy defent ke nul orfevre . . .

DE MONETA

1279, December 8   (Red Book, fo. 247)

Conuentum est cum Magistro Willelmo de Turne-mire de Marcell[ia] die Veneris in festo Conceptionis Beate Marie anno regni Regis E[dwardi] octauo, in hunc modum ; uidelicet, quod idem Magister Willelmus erit magister monete Regis in Anglia, et operari faciet monetam in quatuor locis ad presens, uidelicet : Apud Lond', ubi habebit tot furnesias quot habere poterit. Apud Cantuariam, ubi faciet operari et sustinebit octo furnesias, cum illis tribus que sunt Archiepiscopi Cantuariensis. Apud Bristolliam habebit xij furnesias, et apud Eboracum habebit xij furnesias ; et in quolibet predictorum locorum trium, uidelicet, apud Cantuariam, Bristolliam et Eboracum, habebit sub se unum magistrum ad custodiendum predictam monetam et ea que ad monetam pertinent : et sustinebit, sumptibus suis,

[PROCLAMATION FORBIDDING CLIPPING]

c. 1280

Memorandum. That it be proclaimed throughout the realm that there be no clipping of the new money at peril of life and limb and of all the property and goods of whomsoever it shall befall to be convicted by judgment of the court of our lord the king. And the king will forbid any clipping of the same money under the aforesaid penalty. The king will also forbid anyone to receive any such clipped money under the said penalty. And the king forbids any goldsmith . . .

[INDENTURE OF WILLIAM DE TURNEMIRE]

1279, December 8

It was agreed with Master William de Turnemire of Marseilles on Friday, the feast of the Conception of St Mary, in the eighth year of king Edward, as follows :

Namely, that the same Master William shall be Master of the King's Mint in England and shall cause money to be worked for the present in four places, viz : at London, where he shall have as many furnaces as he can. At Canterbury, where he have working and maintain eight furnaces, together with those three which belong to the Archbishop of Canterbury. At Bristol he shall have twelve furnaces and at York he shall have twelve furnaces. And in each of the aforesaid three places, Canterbury, Bristol and York, he shall have under him a master to keep the said mint and its appurtenances ; and he shall at his own expense bear the

expensas et misas hominum suorum in eisdem locis, uidelicet, predicti magistri monetarii et custodis platarum et funditoris, garcionis in funtorio et aliorum ministrorum. Ita quod omnia onera et expensas portabit predictus Magister Willelmus in predictis quatuor locis, et monetam reddet domino Regi coctam et dealbatam et paratam in omnibus, sumptibus suis : et dominus Rex dabit ei pro qualibet libra sterlingorum, septem denarios, uidelicet, tres denarios et quadrantem pro stipendiis monetariorum percutientium et fabricantium monetam ; et allocabuntur eidem Magistro unus denarius et unus quadrans in decasu argenti ad ignem, et unus denarius et obolus in emendatione cuiuslibet libre monete. Ita quod pro emendatione monete et in decasu ad ignem, allocabuntur ei in qualibet libra undecim ferlingi ut predictum est : Item allocabitur eidem magistro unus denarius in qualibet libra pro stipendiis suis et expensis, et etiam aliorum magistrorum sub se, et aliorum ministrorum suorum, tam in cibis et potibus, quam robis eius et aliis, et pro carbone, et pro cuneis emendis et scindendis, et aliis expensis circa monetam. Et dominus Rex inueniet eidem Magistro Willelmo domos in quolibet predictorum quatuor locorum, aptas ad fabricandum in eis et sustinebit onus feodi domini Hugonis filii Othonis, custodis Othonis nepotis sui, quod clamat habere in custodia cuneorum uel satisfaciet eidem Hugoni pro illo feodo. Utensilia autem que dominus Rex habet Londonie in domibus suis monete liberabuntur prefato Magistro Willelmo, in statu quo nunc sunt, de prestito : et idem Magister Willelmus eadem restituet in fine anni, uel quando officium monete dimittet, in eodem statu in quo tunc fuerunt.

Conuentum est eciam cum eodem Magistro Willelmo

expenses and payments of his men in those places ;
namely the said master-moneyer, and the keeper of the
blanks, the melter, the foundry-man and the other
servants. So that the said Master William shall bear all
the charges and expenses in the said four places, and shall
deliver the money to the king made and blanched and
ready in every respect at his own expense. And the king
shall give him for every pound of sterlings seven pence,
namely three pence farthing for the wages of the moneyers
striking and making the coin, and there shall be allowed
to the same master one penny farthing for the loss of the
silver in the fire and one penny halfpenny for the remedy
of each pound of money. So that for the remedy of the
money and the loss by fire there shall be allowed him in
every pound eleven farthings, as aforesaid. There shall
also be allowed to the said Master one penny in each
pound for his own wages and expenses and those of the
other masters under him, and their servants, as well in
food and drink as in his robes and other things, and for
charcoal and for purchasing and cutting the dies and
other expenses concerning the mint. And our lord the
king shall find for the same Master William houses in
each of the said four places fit for working in and shall
bear the charge of Sir Hugh fitz Otho, guardian of Otho
his nephew, which he claims to have in the keeping of
the dies and shall satisfy the same Hugh for that fee.
But the tools which our lord the king has at London in
his houses of the mint shall be delivered to the said
Master William in their present condition on loan ; and
the same Master William shall restore them at the end
of the year, or when he resigns his office, in the same
condition as they then were.

It was also agreed with the said Master William that
he shall make the groat sterling, which is worth four lesser

quod grossum sterlingum qui ualet quatuor minores
sterlingos faciet per Angliam eodem foro et eadem
conditione quibus faciet predictum sterlingum minorem,
eo tamen adjecto quod, quia idem grossus denarius
fabricari potest leuius quam communis sterlingus, quicquid inde poterit comodi accrescere cedet ad proficuum
domini Regis.

Conuentum est etiam cum eodem Magistro Willelmo,
quod ipse similiter faciet ferlingos per Angliam qui
nunc sunt rotundi et Lundrenses uocantur. Ita quod
dominus Rex habebit de qualibet libra tantum pro-
ficui quantum habebit de communibus sterlingis, uidelicet, xij sterlingos. Et sciendum quod quelibet libra
continebit quatuor uiginti Londrenses, et tres solidos
ultra, numero, quoniam apponitur in ipsa moneta magis
de eslaio quam in sterlingis, propter magnas expensas
quas oportet ponere circa eandem paruam monetam
fabricandam ; et estimatur quod in qualibet libra
illius parue monete, oportet allocari predicto Magistro
Willelmo decem denarios et obolum pro factura et
omnibus custibus circa fabricam illius libre faciendis.
Et remanebunt domino Regi de proficuo de qualibet
libra, xij*d.* ad minus. Et sciendum quod predictus
Magister Willelmus incipiet fabricare in crastino cir-
cumcisionis Domini, anno predicto, iuxta formam irro-
tulatam in Scaccario, uidelicet de omnibus monetis
predictis.

Item conuentum est cum Fache mercatore quod erit
capitalis essaiator, emptor, et ponderator Monete, habens
unam clauem cuiuslibet pixidis denariorum de essaio.

sterlings, throughout England at the same rate and on the same terms as he shall make the aforesaid lesser sterling ; but with this addition, that because the same great penny can be made more easily than the common sterling, whatever profit may accrue shall be the king's.

It was also agreed with the said Master William that he shall likewise make farthings throughout England which are now round and are called ' Lundreis '. So that the king shall have of each pound as much profit as he will have of the common sterlings, to wit twelve sterlings. And be it known that each pound shall contain four score ' lundreis ' and three shillings over by tale, since more alloy is added in this money than in sterlings on account of the great expense which must be incurred in making this small money. And it is reckoned that in each pound of this small money there ought to be allowed to the aforesaid Master William tenpence halfpenny for the making and all the costs of manufacture. And there will remain to our lord the king a profit of twelve pence in each pound at least. And be it known that the said Master William shall begin to coin on the Morrow of the Circumcision of our Lord in the aforesaid year, according to the form enrolled in the Exchequer, all the aforesaid moneys.

It was likewise agreed with Boniface the merchant that he shall be chief Assayer, Buyer and Weigher of the Mint, having a key to every box of pence for assay.

DE MONETA

A.D. 1300, March 29   (Red Book, fo. 259)

Fait a remembrier que le xxix jour de Martz lan du regne le Roi Edward xxviij fui ordine a Westmostier par le Roi et son consail de mettre chaunge et overours de moneie en les lieus par mi le Reaume Dengleterre desuz nomez, cest a savoir ; a la Tour de Loundres xxx fornaises ; a Caunterbury viij fornaises, sicome avaunt ces houres unt este ; a Kyngestone seur Hulle, iiij fornaises ; a Neuechastel seur Tyne, ij fornaises ; a Bristuyt, iiij furnaises ; a Eccestre, ij furnaises. Et fait assavoir que Johan Porcher, Mestre de la Monoye Dengleterre, il meismes demoraunt a Loundres pur la moneie faire, deit mettre en chescun des autres lieus avaun nomez un homme en son lieu pur faire la moneye, et deit trover totes choses qui apent a Maistre, pur les queux il meismes vorra respoundre par autiel foer come il meismes prent pur la livre a Loundres. Et Roger de Frowyke, Chaungeour, demoraunt a Loundres, deit trover un Chaungur a Caunterbury et un autre a Bristuyt, pur les queux il voudra respoundre, et il deit prendre pur lui meismes et un clerk, del houre qe les Pollardes et les autres mauveises moneies contrefaites serront abatues, taunt qe la greignure presse serra passe, xl marcs par an. E pur le Chaungur de Caunterbury, del houre qil le mist, chescun an xxl. E pur le Chaungur de Bristuyt, del houre qil le mettra, chescun an xxl., tant come il demurront es lieus avauntditz. E Talde Janian et Coppe Cottenne et lour compaignons, marchauntz de la compaignie de Friscobald de Florence, averont les chaunges de Kyngestone seur Hulle, Neuchastel seur Tyne et

[THE RECOINAGE OF A.D. 1300]

A.D. 1300, March 29

Be it remembered that the 29th day of March of the 28th year of the reign of king Edward it was ordained by the king and his council at Westminster to set up Exchange and workers of money in the undermentioned places in the realm of England : namely, at the Tower of London, thirty furnaces ; at Canterbury, eight furnaces as there have been before ; at Kingston-upon-Hull, four furnaces ; at Newcastle-upon-Tyne, two furnaces ; at Bristol, four furnaces ; at Exeter, two furnaces. And be it known that John Porcher, Master of the Mint of England, himself dwelling in London to coin the money, must set in each of the other places named a man in his stead to coin the money, and must find everything necessary for a master, for which he himself will answer at the same rate to the pound as in London. And Roger de Frowyke, Changer, dwelling in London, must find a changer at Canterbury and another at Bristol, for whom he will answer, and must take for himself and a clerk, from the time when the Pollards and other bad counterfeit moneys are put down till the main press is over, forty marks per annum. And for the Changer of Canterbury, from the time of his appointment, twenty pounds a year ; and for the Changer of Bristol, from the time of his appointment, twenty pounds a year ; so long as they shall remain in the said places. And Taldo Janiani and Coppo Cottenni and their companions, merchants of the company of the Frescobaldi of Florence, shall have the exchanges of Kingston-upon-Hull, Newcastle-upon-Tyne and Exeter and shall find changers and pence in

Excestre, avantnomez, et troveront Chaungeurs, e deners
en les chaunges pur eaux sustenir, et totes autres choses
qe as Chaungeours apertenent ; issint qil des issues des
Chaunges avauntditz reddent acounte a Johan de
Sandale gardeyn des chaunges le Roi ; le quiel Johan
deit mettre Clerk's pur lui es ditz lieus pur contrerouller
e charger les avantditz marchauntz, e respoundrount a
dit Johan des issues, et le dit Johan en respoigne outre
au Roi.[1] E Lapyn Roger, assaiour, demoraunt a Loundres pur faire les essays de les countreboistes et totes
autres assays qi apertenent au Chaunge, deit prendre
par an, del houre qe la mauvoise moneie soit abatue, tant
qe la greignure presse soit passee, xl. marcs. E si par
aventure le dit Lapyn soit envoie hors de Loundres
aillours qe a Caunterbury pur faire assays, il en doit
avoir ses resnables despenses du Roi. E Johan de
Sandale gardeyn des chaunges le Roi avantditz deit
prendre pur lui et pur son clerk, demoraunt a Loundres,
autaunt de fee come les autres, qi unt este avaunt lui
on cel office, unt pris, et outre ceo, x marcs par an pur
un autre clerk qui li covendra tenir au chaunge de
Loundres tant come la presse durra. E pur les clerks
quil trovera a Caunterbury, Kyngestone seur Hulle,
Neuchastel seur Tyne, Bristuyt, et Excestre, les queux
serront aussint gardeyns des Coygns en meimes les
lieus, pour chescun de eaux xx marcs par an. E le
gardeyn des Coygns a Loundres deit avoir auxi come
autres gardeyns devaunt lui unt eu. E Usshiers des eus
a Loundre et a Caunterbury deivent prendre chescun
de eaux, iij*d*. le jour. E quel hour qe le dit Johan de
Sandale aille hors de Loundres en les bosoignes le Roi,
pur visiter les autres lieus, il deit prendre chescun jour
pur ses despenses, iij souz.

E estre ceo fu ordene meismes le jour qe Alisaundre

the said exchanges to maintain them and all other things which pertain to the changers ; provided that they render account to John de Sandale, Warden of the King's Exchanges ; which John must set clerks in his stead in the said places to control and charge the said merchants and they shall answer to the said John for the issues and John shall answer for them to the king.[1] And Lapyn Roger, assayer, dwelling at London to make the assays of the control boxes and all other assays pertaining to the mint, must take from the time that the bad money is put down till the main press is over, forty marks a year. And if it happen that the said Lapyn be sent out of London elsewhere than to Canterbury to make assays, he must have his reasonable expenses for it from the king. And John de Sandale, Warden of the King's Exchanges aforesaid, must take for himself and his clerk dwelling in London, the same fee that his predecessors in that office have taken, and besides that ten marks a year for another clerk whom he will have to keep at the London Mint as long as the press lasts. And for the clerks whom he shall find at Canterbury, Kingston-upon-Hull, Newcastle-upon-Tyne, Bristol and Exeter, who shall also be the keepers of the dies in those places, twenty marks a year each. And the keeper of the dies at London must also have as other keepers before him have had. And the ushers of the doors at London and at Canterbury must take each of them threepence a day. And whenever the said John de Sandale goes out of London on the king's business to visit the other places, he must take for his expenses three shillings every day.

And furthermore, on the same day, it was ordained that Alexander Norman of Lucca must be Master of the

---

[1] In the original draft the merchants were to answer directly to the king. The amendment was made by the Council of 11 April 1300.

Norman de Luyke deit estre mestre de la moneye le Roi
a Dyvelyn en Irlaunde, et deit mener ove lui, as custage
le Roi iiij furnaises, et deit prendre de chescune livre de
moneie qil fra, vj*d.* pur tutz custages ; issint qil deit
trover le gravour des coigns a ses custages, et totes autres
choses qi apertenent a Maistre, auxi avaunt come Johan
Porcher fait en Engleterre. E deit faire moneie dautieu
poys et dautiel allay come homme ad fait avaunt ces
houres. E a bien et loiaument respoundre au Roi des
totes choses qe lui serront baillez en garde et a overer.
Lavantdit Alisaundre ad trove la maynprise qi senswyt
al avauntdit Talde et ses compagnons qi deivent respoundre de tut, cest asavoir.[1]

E Talde Janian e Coppe Cottenne et leur compaignons avauntditz deivent aver la chaunge illoeques, e
troveront chaungeour et deniers et autres choses qi
apertenent au chaunge a Dyvelyn, e deivent rendre
acounte al Escheqer de Dyvelyn des issues du dit
Chaunge, et respoundre au Roi des issues ; issint qe le
Tresorer del Escheqer de Dyvelyn lur assignera un
clerk pur countrerouller a eaux et eaux charger des
issues avaunt dites. E pur ceo qe le veiage entre
Engleterre et Irlaunde est perilous et la boiste deit estre
porte en Engleterre pur assaier ; si est ordene qil facent
ij boistes, issint qe si lune feust perdue, qe homme
peusse aver recoverer en lautre. Endroit des gages,
mises et despenses des avauntditz marchauntz serront
taxez par lavisement le Tresorer et les Barouns del
Escheqer Dengleterre. E estre ceo est ordene qe
meismes ces marchauntz de Friscobald peussent chaunger
et achater argent, pollardz, crokadz et tutes manieres
dautres blaunches moneies countrefaites pur esterlings
par le Reaume Dengleterre, issint qe cel argent et les

King's Mint at Dublin in Ireland, and must take with
him, at the king's cost, three furnaces, and must take of
every pound of money that he shall make sixpence for all
costs, on condition that he must find the engraver of the
dies at his own cost and all other things pertaining to
the Master, as John Porcher does in England. And he
must make money of like weight and alloy as has been
made aforetime. And he has to answer well and lawfully
to the king for all things which shall be delivered to him
to keep and to work. The said Alexander has found the
following security to the said Taldo and his companions,
who must be answerable for everything, to wit : [1]

Taldo Janiani and Coppo Cottenni and their companions aforesaid shall have the exchange there and
shall find a changer and pence and the other things
which pertain to an exchange at Dublin out of the issues
of the said exchange, and answer for the said issues to
the king ; so that the Treasurer of the Exchequer at
Dublin shall assign them a clerk to control them and
charge them with the aforesaid issues. And because the
voyage between Ireland and England is perilous, and
the box must be carried to England to be assayed, it is
ordained that they make two boxes, so that if one were
lost it might be replaced by the other. As to the wages,
mises and expenses of the aforesaid merchants, they shall
be taxed by the judgment of the Treasurer and Barons
of the Exchequer of England. And it is further ordained
that these merchants of the Frescobaldi may change and
buy silver, pollards, crockards and all manner of white
money counterfeiting sterling throughout the realm of
England, provided that they bring such silver and the

---

[1] The particulars of the security appear to be omitted.

plates issauntes de celes monoies countrefaites portount as chaunges le Roi pur chaungier.[1]

E puis apres fust ordine par le Conseil qe chaunge feust a Cestre, e qe Johan de Sandale deit mettre illoeques un clerk pur lui, e Roger de Frowyke deit mettre illoeques un chaungeour pur lui, et Johan Porcher un maistre de la moneie pur lui, pur les queux il voudrent respoundre en la fourme desusdite.

TRACTATUS NOVE MONETE

c. 1280   (Red Book, fo. 259 v°)

Gaudens obsequi illorum laudabili desiderio qui amore iustitie noscere cupiunt causas et rationes faciende monete et examinationis sensuram, quamuis huiusmodi materia reputetur difficilis et subtilis, illam tamen, prout parvitas mei ingenii administrat, proposui declarandam et in scriptis sub compendio redigendam.

Dicitur quod Numa Pompeius, Imperator Romanus, monetam primus omnium fieri imperauit ; cuius singuli, a nomine ipsius Imperatoris, nummi uidelicet nuncupantur. Facti itaque fuerunt nummi cuprei, argentei et aurei. Set quia singuli nummi argentei ualebant decem nummos cupreos, ideo a numero denarii sunt vocati. Rursus quia singuli nummi aurei ualebant decem nummos argenteos, idcirco a numero denarii nominantur. Et inde inoleuit usus, ut omnis nummus denarius appelletur. A materia quoque argentei seu aurei sepius appellantur. Moneta uero fertur dicta fuisse a nomine artificis,[2] sicut sterlingi Anglie a nominibus opificum nomina contraxerunt.

---

[1] Q. R. Mem. adds : In witness of all the above Walter by the grace of God, Bishop of Chester, treasurer of our lord the King, of the one part, and

plate as results from such counterfeit money to the king's exchanges to be coined.[1]

It was afterwards ordained by the Council that there should be a mint at Chester, and that John de Sandale shall appoint a clerk there for himself, Roger de Frowyke a changer and John Porcher a Master of the Mint, for whom they shall be willing to answer in the form prescribed.

A TREATISE ON THE NEW MONEY

c. 1280

I am glad to comply with the praiseworthy wish of those who, through their love of justice, desire to know the reasons for and manner of making coined money, and the trial of the assay ; and although the subject is regarded as difficult and intricate, I propose, so far as my poor wits serve me, to explain it briefly in writing.

The Roman Emperor, Numa Pompilius, is said to have been the first to order the making of coins, and the several coins are called (in Latin) *nummi* from the name of the Emperor. But because one silver coin was worth ten copper ones, the silver coins were called *denarii* (pence) from the number ten. And thence arose the custom of calling any coin ' a penny ' and usually specifying its material as ' silver ' or ' gold '. Money (*moneta*) is said to have been so called from the name of the maker,[2] as the English ' sterlings ' have from the name of those who made them.

John de Sandale, Warden of the King's Exchanges, of the other, to this indenture have mutually set their seals. Written at Saint Albans, 11 April, 28 Edward I.

[2] Or rather from the temple of Juno Moneta where they were coined

In primis igitur oportet ut omnem monetam precedat
constitutio, allaii uidelicet ponderisque et numeri ipsius
monete distincte et aperte continens moderamen. Deinde
inchoanda est et perficienda ex edicto aut licentia principis speciali, et publicanda per proclamationem pre-
conis ipsius principis publice, ut mos exigit, faciendam,
et tunc usui apta erit, ita ut extunc non sit impune a
quoquam de populo recusanda. Quicunque autem clam
uel palam, absque licentia principis, cuiuscunque monete
contrafactionem attemptasse conuictus fuerit, corporaliter
plecti solet.

Hiis itaque in genere prelibatis, sciendum est quod
omnis moneta ex duobus efficitur, ex materia uidelicet
et forma ; ex materia, ut auro, argento et cupro, operando aptatur, et ex forma monetando perficitur, ut
cuditione cunei imprimentis formam monete cognosci-
bilem et discernibilem, que scilicet forma si defuerit,
nunquam erit moneta ; sicut cera non est sigillum donec
impressionem forme receperit. Hinc igitur primo de
cognitione ipsius materie ; secundo de dispositione
eiusdem ; tertio de examinatione facienda, specialius
de singulis est agendum. Sed quoniam pleraque ho-
rum in facto potius quam in ratione consistunt, que
uix intelligerent eloquio nisi fieri uiderentur, idcirco
mea dirigitur intencio ad ea que in hac parte possunt
discerni rationabiliter et intendi.

Cognitio materie, scilicet auri, argenti et cupri, ex
quibus fit moneta, habetur duobus modis, uidelicet, aut
discernendo per uisum, aut examinando per assaium.
Per uisum discernitur primo, utrum sit in massa uel in
moneta, et hoc quilibet nouit. Secundo, utrum sit
cuprum, uel aurum, aut argentum, et hoc etiam multi
sciunt. Tertio, an sit purum aurum uel purum argentum, aut mixtum cum alio metallo. Hoc autem plures

In the first place then, before there is any money, there must be a statute clearly and distinctly determining the proportion of alloy, the weight and number of the coins. It must then be put in hand and finished by the order or special licence of the prince and must be made generally known by public proclamation in the accustomed way by the prince's crier. It will then be ready for use and may not be refused by any of the public without penalty. But whoever, secretly or openly, without leave of the prince, attempts to counterfeit any coin and is convicted, is liable to suffer corporal punishment.

After this general preface, you must know that all money consists of two things, matter and form. Its matter is obtained by working in gold, silver and copper, and its form by coining, as by engraving a die which imprints a recognisable and distinguishable form on the coin, without which it can never be a coin any more than wax can be a seal until it has received the impression of its device. Hence we must treat separately in detail first, of the knowledge of material, secondly of its disposition, and thirdly of its testing. But since most of these points are matters rather of fact than of theory, which can hardly be described intelligibly unless they are seen, I must concentrate on the parts of the subject which can be distinguished and understood by the use of reason.

Knowledge of the material of which money is made, namely gold, silver and copper, is obtained in two ways, either distinguishing them by the eye or trying them by assay. We can distinguish by the eye whether the material is in bulk or in coin ; so much everyone knows. Secondly, whether it is gold, silver or copper ; this, too, many know. Thirdly, whether it is pure gold or pure

12

ignorant. Quarto, auri uel argenti mixti, quantum
quelibet marca uel libra metalli sibi adiuncti contineat.
Hoc soli experti et per excercitium edocti possunt
cognoscere. Verumptamen uix inuenitur quisquam
ita perfectus qui non in hoc sepissime falli possit.
Signa uero per que ipsa materia fit uisui cognoscibilis
uix absque exercitio possent exprimi aut intendi. Per
examinationem habetur certa auri et argenti cognitio ;
uerumptamen inter multimodas examinationes examen
per assaium certius reputatur, cuius certa signa uix
quisquam noscere poterit nisi per excercitium artificii
fuerit eruditus. Modernis ergo temporibus fieri consueuit assaium de pondere x sterlingorum, scilicet ex
dimidia uncia, cum subtilitate rectitudinis ponderata,
que in cineratis, ad hoc dispositis in igne, ponitur, et
cum sufficienti plumbo examinando ab omni alio tene-
mento cupri aut cuiuscunque alterius metalli purgatur,
cuius assaii pondus cuiuslibet grani per rectum compotum ualere probatur ad singulas libras unum denarium,
et sic per consequens dimidium granum ualet obolum
et quarta pars grani ualet quadrantem ; quod facile
ostenditur ; granum etenim est xxiiij^{ta} pars unius denarii.
Sicut ergo uiginti quatuor grana faciunt unum sterlingum, sic xxiiij^{or} dimidie uncie efficiunt unam libram.
Eundem igitur locum tenent singula grana in dimidia
uncia, quem singuli denarii tenent in libra. Cum autem
argentum possit faciliter in igne decrescere et nullatenus
au[g]mentari, sedulus examinator tenetur ad conserua-
tionem argenti summam ac studiosissimam diligentiam
adhibere. Et sic pro pondere cuiuslibet grani de decasu
in ipso assaio inuento, unus denarius ad quamlibet libram
conuenientius poterit computari. Et quia in Anglia, ac
nobilibus Anglie, cepi loqui, inceptus sermo percurrat
ad ea maxime que attendenda sunt circa monetam et

silver, or mixed with another metal ; but most people do not know this. Fourthly, how much the mark or the pound of mixed gold or silver contains of the metal with which it is alloyed ; this can only be known by experts who have learned by practice. But hardly anyone can be found so fully expert as not often to be mistaken in this. But the signs by which the material can be determined by inspection can scarcely be explained or understood without practical experience. A sure knowledge of gold and silver can be obtained by testing, but among a great variety of tests, examination by assay is considered the most certain and hardly anyone can know its certain signs unless he has learned it from practice in the art. Nowadays an assay is made of ten pennyweights, that is half an ounce, weighed with the greatest accuracy. This is placed in cupels arranged in the fire for the purpose and is purged by enough lead for the assay, from all the copper or other metal which it contains. The weight of each grain of the assay is proved by correct calculation to be equivalent to a penny in every pound, and consequently half a grain equals a halfpenny and a quarter a farthing ; which is easily proved, since the grain is the twenty-fourth part of a penny. Therefore, as twenty-four grains make one pennyweight, so twenty-four half-ounces make a pound. Each grain, therefore, bears the same proportion to a penny as each penny does to a pound. But since silver may easily be lost in the fire but cannot be gained, a diligent assayer is bound to take the greatest and most earnest care to preserve the silver. Thus for every grain that the assay loses in weight one penny can be accordingly reckoned in each pound.

And because I am addressing English noblemen, and in England, I must proceed to those points which are of

cambium Anglicanum. Scire ergo oportet ad euiden-
tiam dicendorum quod omnis massa aut moneta cuius
medietas et supra est argenti purissimi, argentea appellatur. A medietate uero infra, nequaquam argentea
est habenda. Igitur argenti cogniti aliud emitur tanquam purissimum, aliud tanquam mixtum. Et quia
multe sunt diuersitates argenti, quinque tantum ponam
exempla, quibus intellectis faciliter cognoscetur modus
emendi quodlibet genus argenti, secundum quod unumquodque plus aut minus de cupro uidebitur continere.
Primum exemplum est sterlingorum Anglie, quorum
standardi quelibet libra continet de cupro pondus
xviij sterlingorum et oboli ; et quodcunque argentum
equiual[u]erit eidem standardo emendum est per xiiij*d*.
ob., qui uidelicet de qualibet libra pro cambio retinentur.
Cuius rei causam fuisse arbitror quod cum olim Regi
Anglie de cambio cuiuslibet libre sex tantum denarii
prouenirent, in principio Noui Cambii consideratum
fuit et utiliter ordinatum quod Rex de singulis libris ix*d*.
recipere poterat, et Magister Monete unamquamque
libram pro quinque denariis et obolo fabricare. Cum
ergo ix*d*. et v*d*. *ob.* faciant xiiij*d*. *ob.*, plus nec minus
retinendum est pro cambio cuiuscunque argenti quod
paris bonitatis fuerit cum standardo. Eademque
consideratione debet cambiari et emi quodlibet genus
argenti, iuxta quod melius uel deterius reperitur ; ita
quod de exitu cambii cum sufficienti allaio Regi et
Magistro monete iuste ualeat responderi, et moneta
sufficiens inueniri. Verumptamen, de ueteri moneta
Anglie unus denarius et obolus pro cambio ulterius
retinentur, qui dicto Magistro ad emendationem Monete
deputati fuerunt, pro eo quod ad nouum standardum
Regis eadem uetus moneta dicebatur de totidem esse
peior ; unde etiam colligitur quod quicquid de peiori

the most importance in regard to English money and
the English mint. You must know then, to explain
what is to follow, that any bullion or coin half or more
of which is pure silver, is called ' silver.' But below
half it is by no means to be considered silver. Some
silver, recognised as such, is bought as ' pure,' some as
alloyed. And because there are many varieties of silver,
I will give just five examples, by understanding which
the method will be grasped of buying any kind of silver
according to the greater or smaller quantity of copper it
appears to contain. The first example is English
Sterlings, of which every standard pound contains
eighteen and a half pennyweights of copper ; and
whatever silver is equal to that standard is to be bought
at fourteen pence halfpenny, which are kept back from
every pound for the coining. I think the reason of this
is that, whereas the kings of England used to receive
only sixpence for the coining of each pound, at the
beginning of the new coinage it was considered and
profitably ordained that the king should receive ninepence from each pound and the Master of the Mint
should make each pound for fivepence halfpenny.
Therefore, since ninepence and fivepence halfpenny
make fourteenpence halfpenny, neither more nor less is
to be kept back for the coining of any silver of equal
goodness to the standard. All kinds of silver must be
coined and bought by the same method of reasoning,
according as they are found to be better or worse, so
that from the issues of the mint, with a sufficiently fine
alloy, the king and the Master of the Mint may be justly
answered and enough money found. But of old English
money another three halfpence are retained for coining,
because, compared with the king's new standard, the
old money was said to be so much worse ; from which it

argento ulterius retinetur ad emendationem eiusdem argenti est totaliter assignandum.

Secundum exemplum est Baudkynorum, quorum quelibet libra continet de cupro pondus xiiij sterlingorum, quodlibet autem argentum eiusdem ualoris emitur per x*d*., qui tantummodo de qualibet libra pro cambio retinentur ; quia, preter hoc, supra quamlibet libram pondus iiij sterlingorum et oboli de cupro potest recipere, et paris bonitatis existere cum standardo.

Tertium exemplum est Turonensium argenteorum et argenti de Gandavo, quorum quelibet libra debet continere de cupro pondus x sterlingorum et unumquodque simile argentum emitur per vj*d*., qui pro cambio singularum librarum inde solummodo retinentur, pro eo, uidelicet, quod unaquaque libra potest ulterius recipere pondus octo sterlingorum et oboli de cupro, et ualere equaliter ut standardus.

Quartum exemplum sit omne argentum continens tantummodo pondus iiij. sterlingorum de cupro in qualibet libra, tale enim argentum emendum est sine aliqua rententione pro cambio. Set pro pondere argenti, equale pondus debet tribui sterlingorum, quia supra quamlibet libram potest recipere pondus xiiij sterlingorum et oboli de cupro, et equalis ualoris existere cum standardo.

Quintum exemplum est argenti de Lemovicis, quod dictur esse purissimum ; tale ergo argentum potest emi et dari ad quamlibet libram, ultra pondus, quatuor sterlingi de avantagio ; quia supra quamlibet libram potest recipere pondus xviij sterlingorum et oboli de cupro, et equiualere standardo ; unde illi quatuor denarii, qui scilicet excedunt xiiij*d. ob.*, debent cedere in avantagium afferentis. Et cum non sit argentum purius inuenire ad huiusmodi officium ex[s]equendum, attendendum est quod quanto aliquod argentum bonitati

follows that whatever further is kept back from the worse silver is all to be assigned to the amendment of the same.

The second example is of Baudekyns, of which every pound contains fourteen pennyweights of copper. All the silver of this value is bought at tenpence, which is all that is kept back out of each pound for coinage, because it can take four and a half pennyweights of copper more in each pound and be of equal goodness with the standard.

The third example is of silver *Tournois* and silver of Ghent, each pound of which should contain ten penny-weights of copper and every pound of like silver is bought at sixpence, which is all that is kept back for the coining of each pound, because each pound can take eight and a half pennyweights of copper more and be as good as the standard.

Let the fourth example be all silver containing only four pennyweights of copper to the pound, for such silver must be bought without keeping back anything for the coining. But for the weight of silver must be given an equal weight of sterlings, because the silver can take fourteen and a half pennyweights of copper to the pound and be of equal goodness with the standard.

The fifth example is Limoges silver, which is said to be the purest, wherefore in buying it an *agio* of fourpence in the pound can be given in addition to the weight ; because it can take eighteen and a half pennyweights of copper to the pound and be of standard fineness ; where-fore the fourpence above the fourteen pence and a half should be the seller's advantage. And since no purer silver can be found for this purpose, you must observe that the nearer any silver attains to such fineness, the less must be kept back for the coining, and the farther

huiusmodi uicinius compertum fuerit, tanto minus erit
pro cambio retinendum ; quanto autem a bonitate magis
distiterit, tanto plus debet pro cambio retineri, iuxta
quod plus aut minus de cupro poterit sustinere.

Alibi uero fiunt emptiones cuiuscunque bilhonis seu
argenti secundum communem ualorem siue pretium
argenti ad monetam, per quam emptio compensatur.
Sciendum est igitur, quod quot solidis quelibet marca
puri argenti uenditur, totiens allaium bilhonis seu argenti emendi pro pretio marce cuiuslibet computatur.
Ponatur enim quod marca puri argenti ualeat Lvj*s*. iiij*d*.
Bilhonis igitur aut argenti ad vj*d*. de allaio, ualebit
quelibet marca quinquaginta sex uicibus vj*d*., qui faciunt
xxviij*s*. ; et pro iiij*d*. de pretio, computabo ij*d*. de allaio,
uidelicet pro tertia parte solidi de pretio, tertiam partem
de allaio. Et sic ualebit marca argenti, ad vj*d*. de allaio,
xxviij*s*. ij*d*. de pretio. Et eadem ratione pretium cuiuslibet bilhonis seu argenti poterit computari.

Sequitur de dispositione ipsius materie ad faciendam
monetam. Et primo de allaio, secundo de tallia et de
monetatione.

Compotus allaii computatur communiter per xij*d*. ad
dimidiam unciam,[1] et per xvj solidos ad marcam, et per
xlviij*s*., quibus appreciatur quelibet marca argenti ad
allaium comprobandum. Sciendum ergo est quod argentum purissimum dicitur esse ad xij*d*. de allaio, quia
singule dimidie uncie, ex quibus consueuit fieri assaium,
sunt argenti purissimi absque cuiuscunque alterius
metalli tenentia seu mixtura. Item moneta ad xj*d*. de
allaio tenet in singulis dimidiis unciis unum denarium
de cupro, unde sciendum est quod cuprum in allaio
appellatur nichil, quia, uidelicet, pro nichilo computatur.
De auro uero et de argento in moneta, proprie allaium
appellatur, unde quantum argenti in xij denariis, scilicet,

it departs from fineness the more is to be kept back for coining, according as it can bear more or less of copper.

But purchases are made elsewhere of bullion or silver according to the common value or price of silver at the mint in which the purchase is made. You must know, then, that at whatever number of shillings a mark of pure silver is sold, the silver content of the bullion or silver to be bought must be multiplied by the same number to get the price of a mark. Suppose that a mark of pure silver is worth 56s 4d. Then each mark of bullion or silver sixpence (in the shilling) fine will be worth fifty-six times sixpence, which make 28s ; and for the fourpence I shall reckon 2d, namely a third of a shilling in the price, for a third of the fineness of sixpence. And so a mark of silver, sixpence fine, will be worth 28s 2d. And in the same way may be reckoned the value of any bullion or silver.

We must next consider the disposition of the material in making money ; first, the alloy, next the shear and the coining. The fineness of the alloy is commonly reckoned at a rate of twelve pence to the half-ounce [1] and sixteen shillings to the mark, forty-eight shillings being taken as the value of the mark of silver in reckoning the alloy. You must know, therefore, that pure silver is said to be twelve pence fine, because each half-ounce (the customary weight of an assay) is of pure silver without any content or mixture of any other metal. Again, money eleven pence fine contains in each half-ounce one pennyweight of copper and you must observe that no mention is made of the copper because, of course, no account is taken of it. But the alloy gets its

---

[1] The weight used in purchasing silver is ' Tower ' weight, the pound being 5,400 gr., i.e. 12 oz. each of 20 dwt. and the dwt. of 22½ gr. But in reckoning fineness a mint-mark is used with a dwt. of 24 light grains and an ounce of 24 dwt. and 5,760 gr. to the pound.

in dimidia uncia reperitur, ad tantundem allaii existere
iudicatur. Et eadem ratione quodlibet argentum aut
moneta ad certum numerum allaii esse dicitur, secundum
quod continet de argento computando a xij denariis
usque ad nichil pro grana, et per denarios descendendo.
Cum autem quelibet marca xvj dimidias uncias contineat, computetur sexdecim uicibus allaium ad quod
dicetur esse moneta, et habebitur cetra summa quantitatis argenti, quantum, uidelicet, in qualibet marca
debeat contineri. Fit autem allaium monete per con-
uersionem alti ad bassum, et econuerso ; et dicitur esse
altum, quodcunque bilho siue argentum in allaio fuerit
supra monetam que inde extiterit allaianda. Bassum
uero dicitur quod sub eadem moneta inferius in allaio
reperitur. Et hoc patebit facilius per exemplum. Pono
quod debeam allaiare monetam ad ix*d*. de allaio, et
habeam bilhonem siue argentum ad xj*d*. de allaio et ad
iiij*d*. de allaio. Dicitur autem bilho moneta defensa
que uidelicet cursu caret. Ego igitur computabo quod
a ix usque ad xj est distantia de duobus. Item a ix usque
ad iiij est distantia de quinque. Facta autem con-
uersione de alto ad bassum, ponam duas marcas in allaio
de bilhone ad iiij*d*. de allaio, et quinque marcas de
argento ad xj*d*. de allaio. Et sic ille septem marce,
simul mixte, erunt ad ix*d*. de allaio plus nec minus. Et
hoc duobus modis ualeo comprobare. Primo modo
computabo quod bilho ad iiij*d*. de allaio, continet quelibet marca sexdecim uicibus iiij*d*., scilicet v*s*. iiij*d*. : et
sic due marce continent x*s*. viij*d*. de argento. Item,
computabo quod argentum ad xj*d*. de allaio, continet
quelibet marca sex decies xj*d*. ; qui sunt xiiij*s*. viij*d*., qui,
multiplicati quinquies, faciunt Lxxiij*s*. iiij*d*. de argento ;
quibus superadditis x*s*. viij*d*. pro duabus marcis predictis,
erunt in summa Lxxxiiij*s*., qui faciunt v^{que} marcas et duas

name from the quantity of gold or silver in the money,
so that according to the amount of silver in twelve pence
(i.e. half an ounce) it is adjudged to be so many pence
fine. And in the same way any silver or coin is said to
be of a certain fineness of alloy according to the silver
content, counting from twelve pence to nothing by the
grain, and going down by pennies. But since a mark
contains sixteen half-ounces, if you multiply the figure
of the fineness of the money by sixteen, you will arrive
at the quantity of the silver ; namely how much there
ought to be in each mark. And the alloy of coin is
made by changing high into low and vice versa. Any
bullion or silver is said to be ' high ' when its fineness is
above that of the money which is to be alloyed from it ;
it is called ' low ' when it is beneath that of the money.
An example will make this clearer. Suppose I must
alloy the money to be ninepence fine and have bullion
or silver elevenpence fine and fourpence fine. (Forbidden money, i.e. money not current, is called bullion.)
I shall therefore reckon that from 9 to 11 is a difference
of 2. Also, from 9 to 4 is a difference of 5. Turning
then from high to low, I shall put in the alloy 2 marks
of bullion fourpence fine and 5 marks of silver elevenpence fine. And so the seven marks mixed together will
be ninepence fine, neither more nor less. And this I
can prove in two ways. First, I shall reckon that the
bullion fourpence fine contains in each mark sixteen
times fourpence, namely 5s 4d, and so two marks contain
10s 8d of silver. I shall also reckon that each mark of
the silver elevenpence fine contains sixteen times elevenpence making 13s 4d ; this multiplied by five makes
73s 4d in silver. Adding to this 19s 8d for the aforesaid
two marks the sum will be 84s, which make five marks
and two ounces, reckoning the mark at 16 shillings.

uncias ; scilicet, pro qualibet marca, xvj$s$. computatis.
Item, computabo quod moneta ad ix$d$. de allaio, debet
continere quelibet marca sexdecim uicibus ix$d$. de
argento, qui sunt xij$s$. Septies igitur xij$s$. faciunt
Lxxxiiij$s$., qui sunt v^{que} marce et due uncie argenti, ut
supra. Et sic probatur sufficiens in argento.

Secundo modo computabo quod marca argenti appreciatur ad xlviij$s$. ad allaium comprobandum. Bilhonis
ergo ad iiij$d$. de allaio, ualet marca xlviij uicibus iiij$d$.,
qui sunt xvj$s$. Et sic due marce ualent xxxij$s$. Item,
argenti ad xj$d$. de allaio, ualet marca xlviij uicibus xj$d$.
qui sunt xliiij$s$. Ergo v^{que} marce ualebunt xj$l$. quibus
superadditis xxxij$s$. pro pretio predictarum duarum
marcarum, facient summam xij$l$. xij$s$. Item, computabo
quod moneta ad ix$d$. de allaio, ualet marca xlviij uicibus
ix$d$. qui sunt xxxvj$s$. Septies igitur xxxvj$s$. faciunt in
summa xij$l$. xij$s$. ut supra. Et sic per pretium argenti
ueritas allaii comprobatur. Eadem etiam ratione habet
fieri omne allaium et probari ; unde cum hee regule
allaiamenti et probationis allaii sunt infallibiles, discretus
allaiator ex sola materia falli poterit aut errare in facto,
si forte, ipso ignorante, argentum ex quo fiet allaium
sit deficiens quod idoneum reputabat. Hec autem
quacunque potui breuitate perstrinxi ut consequentia
tangantur expressius ea que spectant ad allaium con-
suetum in partibus Anglicanis.

Scire ergo oportet quod in allaio monete Anglie,
ad dimidiam unciam, decem sterlingi, et ad marcam
xiij$s$. iiij$d$. computantur, cuius allaii ratio ab illa, de xij$d$.
in dimidia uncia, et de sexdecim solidis in marca tantum
modo differre uidetur in numero. Verumptamen ambe
conueniunt in pondere et in forma, utrobique enim in
qualibet marca sexdecim dimidie uncie continentur.
Hinc est quod argentum ad x sterlingos de allaio dicitur

Again, I shall reckon that every mark of money ninepence fine must contain sixteen times ninepence of silver, which is 12s. Seven times 12s make 84s which is five marks and two ounces of silver, as above. Thus the silver is proved to be sufficient.

By the second method I shall reckon that a mark is valued at 48s for the purpose of checking the fineness. A mark of bullion fourpence fine is worth forty-eight times fourpence, that is 16s. And so two marks are worth 32s. Also, a mark of silver elevenpence fine is worth forty-eight times 11d which is 44s. Therefore five marks will be worth £11, and adding 32s for the price of the aforesaid two marks they make the sum of £12 12s. I shall also reckon that a mark of money ninepence fine is worth forty-eight times 9d which are 36s. Then seven times 36s make a sum of £12 12s as above. And so the correctness of the alloy is proved by the price of the silver. All alloy must be made and tested on the same principle; wherefore, because these rules of alloying and proof of alloy are infallible, the only error a skilled alloyer can make in his process lies in the material; if perchance, without his knowing it, the silver of which the alloy is made, and which he thought satisfactory, is not good enough. I have dealt briefly with all this in order to be more explicit in what follows, the alloy usual in England.

You must know, then, that in the alloy for English money, ten sterlings are reckoned to the half-ounce and 13s 4d to the mark; which only differs numerically from the ratio of twelve pence to the half-ounce and sixteen shillings to the mark. But both agree in weight and in pattern, since in both cases there are sixteen half-ounces in each mark. Hence pure silver is said to be ten sterlings fine, and the fineness of any money can

esse purissimum, et sic per numerum sterlingorum
allaium cuiuslibet monete recte poterit computari et
fieri, a nichilo, uidelicet, per grana et denarios, usque
ad decem sterlingos de allaio ascendendo, quo argento
non poterit melius inueniri. Subsequenter sciendum
est quod standardus monete Anglie est ad ix sterlingos
quinque grana et dimidium de allaio, et per hoc probatur quantum quelibet marca et libra contineant in
argento ; etenim ix sterlingi, v^{que} grana et dimidium
multiplicati sexdecies, faciunt xij*s*. iij*d*. *ob*. et quatuor
grana argenti ad marcam, quibus superaddita medietate tanti, uidelicet, vj*s*. j*d*. *ob*. *quadr*. et ij granis,
faciunt xviij*s*. v*d*. *ob*. argenti purissimi qui in qualibet libra standardi monete Anglie continentur.
Et preterea pondus xviij. sterlingorum et oboli de
cupro, per quos xx solidorum pondus et numerus
adimpletur.

Potest autem allaium monete Anglie fieri ex solo
bilhone ueteris monete Anglicane, que sola per se, et si
nec emendetur nec peioretur, sufficiens reddet allaium
in argento, et forte melius quam existat allaium de
standardo. De bilhonibus uero diuersarum monetarum
prout diuersimode emuntur, uel per xviij*d*. uel per ij*s*.
uel supra, quicquid retinetur de cambio de singulis
libris, ultra quod retineretur si essent sufficientis allaii,
totum illud est liberandum Magistro ad idem allaium
emendandum.

Sequitur[1] qualiter fit allaium de argento secundum
singulas emptiones. Ad argentum emptum per xiiij*d*.
ob. nullum est apponendum allaium, sufficit enim si
inueniatur sufficiens ad standardum.

Ad argentum emptum per xx*s*., scilicet, de quibus
nichil retinetur pro cambio, set pro pondere argenti
pondus tribuitur sterlingorum, siue argentum illud

be truly reckoned and effected by the number of
sterlings, namely by sterlings and grains, rising from
nothing to ten sterlings fine, than which no better silver
can be found. You must also know that the standard
money of England is nine sterlings, five grains and a
half fine, and by this is proved how much silver each
mark or pound contains. For nine sterlings, five and a
half grains multiplied by sixteen make 12s 3½d and four
grains of silver to the mark, and adding half as much
again, 6s 1¾d and two grains makes 18s 5½d of pure
silver in every pound of standard money of England.
Add to that 18½ dwt. of copper, which makes up the
weight and number of twenty shillings.

But the alloy for English money can be made entirely
from bullion of old money of England which by itself,
if it be neither made better nor worse, will give an alloy
containing enough silver, possibly even better than that
of the standard. But of the bullion of diverse moneys,
as they are bought at various prices, eighteen pence or
2s or above, whatever is kept back in the exchange of
each pound beyond what would be kept back if it
were sufficiently fine, must all be delivered to the
Master of the Mint to make good the fineness of the
alloy.

The following table [1] shows how the alloy is made
from the silver according to the several purchases. To
silver bought at fourteen pence halfpenny no alloy is to
be added, for it is enough that it be equivalent to the
standard.

As regards silver bought for 20s, namely that of
which nothing is kept back for the coining, but weight
for weight is paid in sterlings, whether the silver is good

---

[1] Given on p. 74

Ad argentum emptum		De cupro
Per xiiij*d*.		obolum
Per xiij*d. ob.*		j*d*.
Per xiij*d*.		j*d. ob.*
Per xij*d. ob.*		ij*d*.
Per xij*d*.		ij*d. ob.*
Per xj*d. ob.*		iij*d*.
Per xj*d*.		iij*d. ob.*
Per x*d. ob.*		iiij*d*.
Per x*d*.		iiij*d. ob.*
Per ix*d. ob.*		v*d*.
Per ix*d*.	Qui scilicet de singulis libris pro cambio retinentur, siue argentum illud bonum uerit siue malum, semper oneratur Magister Monete ad ponendum supra quamlibet libram eiusdem argenti, necnon ad respondendum in compoto suo per pondus.	v*d. ob.*
Per viij*d. ob.*		vj*d*.
Per viij*d*.		vj*d. ob.*
Per vij*d. ob.*		vij*d*.
Per vij*d*.		vij*d. ob.*
Per vj*d. ob.*		viij*d*.
Per vj*d*.		viij*d. ob.*
Per v*d. ob.*		ix*d*.
Per v*d*.		ix*d. ob.*
Per iv*d. ob.*		x*d*.
Per iv*d*.		x*d. ob.*
Per iij*d. ob.*		xj*d*.
Per iij*d*.		xj*d. ob.*
Per ij*d. ob.*		xij*d*.
Per ij*d*.		xij*d. ob.*
Per j*d. ob.*		xiij*d*.
Per j*d*.		xiij*d. ob.*
Per obolum		xiiij*d*.

[The table printed in the Latin text shows that to silver bought at 14d one halfpenny of copper is to be added. For each halfpenny that the silver price is reduced, a halfpenny of copper is added ; ending with one halfpenny for the silver and fourteen pence of copper. The words between the figures may be translated. 'Which (i.e. the pence held back in the exchange) are kept back in each pound for the exchange. Whether the silver be good or bad the Master is charged with them on every pound of silver and must also answer for them by weight.']

bonum fuerit siue malum, semper oneratur Magister
monete ad ponendum supra quamlibet libram eiusdem
argenti pondus xiiij sterlingorum et oboli de cupro et
tantundem in compoto suo inde cogitur respondere.
Ad omnem igitur emptionem argenti factam per reten-
tionem certe quantitatis de singulis libris pro cambio, a
xiiij*d*., uidelicet, et infra, usque ad emptionem factam
per xx*s*., ex qua ut dictum est nichil retinetur pro
cambio, set pro pondere argenti pondus tribuitur sterlingorum, siue argentum illud bonum siue malum existat,
semper oneratur Magister Monete ad ponendum supra
quamlibet libram eiusdem argenti tantum de cupro
quod, tam de quantitate que retinetur pro cambio,
quam de cupro, ad singulas libras xiiij*d*. *ob*. integre
compleantur. Et si forte aliquod purius argentum
afferatur ad cambium casualiter, et ematur, onerabitur
Magister pro qualibet libra altius de pondere certe
quantitatis de cupro iuxta exigentiam emptionis.

Per premissa igitur intelligendum est quod in allaio
monete Anglie nulla alia regula observatur nisi
forte Magister Monete in assaio suo aliquid uoluerit
emendare, scilicet, minus de cupro apponendo in argento
quam per compotum oneretur. Hoc autem faciens,
nullum in suo compoto inde sentiet relevamen, nisi forte
moneta inde facta propter hoc in argento standardum
excedere comprobetur. Per quod patet quod magna
pars sufficientie aut defectus allaii dependet a parte
argenti, et ex arbitrio comparantis. Impossibile enim est
monetam sufficientem effici nisi, ad perficiendum allaium,
habeatur uel melius argentum, uel eque bonum in allaio
ut moneta que inde fuerit allaianda. Et idcirco ipse
Magister debet argenti emptor existere, qui de compoto
et allaio monete cogitur respondere. Si uero, sicut in
Anglia, custos monete uel cambiator absque assensu

or bad, the Master is always charged with 14½ pennyweights of copper to be added to each pound, and must
answer for the same in his account. Therefore, for every
purchase of silver made by keeping back a certain
amount from each pound for the coining, namely from
14d or less down to purchase for 20s, of which, as we
have said, nothing is paid for coining but equal weight
in coin is given for the weight of silver, whether the silver
is good or bad, the Master is always charged with so
much copper to be added to each pound of silver as,
together with the amount kept back for the coining, will
come to 14½d to each pound. And if any purer silver
happen to be brought to the mint and is bought, the
Master will be charged with a higher quantity of copper
to each pound according to what the purchase requires.

It will be seen from the foregoing that no other rule
is observed in alloying the money of England, unless the
Master of the Mint, on his assay, chooses to make the
coin better, i.e. to add less copper to the silver than he is
charged with in his account. But if he does so he will
get no allowance on that score in his account, unless the
money so made be proved to exceed the standard. This
shows that the goodness or badness of the alloy depends
on the silver and on the judgment of the buyer. For it
is impossible for the money to be made up to standard
unless in making the alloy you have either better silver
or as fine as the money which the alloying is to produce.
And therefore the Master ought to be the buyer of the
silver because he has to answer for the count and the
fineness of the money. But if, as in England, the Warden
of the Mint, or the Changer, considers himself authorized

Magistri hoc sibi competere arbitretur, ac idem in emptionibus argenti, ad conservandam equitatem, sicut decet, solicitus non existat ; set si forte, accensus odio aut inuidia, de comoditate et honore Magistri contriste-tur et doleat, ac de ipsius iocundetur multiplici detri-mento, per quod, studio fraudulose malitie, non ad solam deceptionem Magistri, set etiam ad subuersionem monete Regis argentum fallaciter emisse conuinci ualeat, nulla lege debet impunitate gaudere quin tam Regi quam Magistro dampna restituat, necnon et pro delicto gravius redimatur.

Nunc dicendum est de tallia monete. Est autem tallia scissio siue diuisio argenti prout in partes equalius scindi potest, ita quod in pondere et numero constituto ad marcam conueniant ad libram ; uerbi gratia, moneta Anglie debet talliari ad xx*s.* iij*d.* ad libram, prout equalius potest scindi. Si uero fortiores uel debiliores inueniantur de uno denario ad libram, deliberabiles sunt. Fortiores dico, ut si sub pondere singularum librarum xx*s.* et ij tantum denarii per numerum habeantur. Debiliores dico, ut si sub cuiusque libre pondere, xx*s.* iiij*d.* per numerum teneantur. Item in qualibet libra potest transire unus denarius fortis et alius debilis sine numero, et duo alii denarii fortes aut debiles de uno grano et dimidio a recto denario xx solidorum et iij denariorum de numero sterlingorum. Hec autem tallia siue scissio argenti habet fieri ad preceptum Magistri per certos operarios deditos ad monetam, per quos etiam preparatur recoquendo et fabricando et prout expedit in flodonibus disponendo. Deinde, facta examinatione ponderis et numeri, sicut decet, iidem operarii dietas suas Magistro monete restituunt, ac de stipendiis suis, pro unaquaque libra ij*d. ob.* recipiunt ab eodem Magistro. Vero si necesse fuerit, eosdem flodones

to do this without the Master's assent, and is not concerned in his purchases of silver to be absolutely fair,
indeed if perchance, inflamed with hatred or envy, he
is saddened and grieved at the Master's comfort and
honour, and rejoices in the multitude of his misfortunes,
and so can be proved guilty by his malice and fraud, not
only of cheating the Master, but also of injuring the
king's coinage by his dishonest purchases of silver, no
law should hold him unpunished but should compel him
to make good the damage to the Master and pay a
severe penalty for his crime.

The next subject is the shear of the coin. Now the
shear is the cutting up or division of the silver as equally
as possible, so that it may correspond with the mark and
the pound in the appointed number and weight. For
example, the shear of English money is 20s 3d to the
pound, as evenly as it can be cut, but if the coins be
found to be not more than a penny stronger or weaker
than a pound, they will pass. By ' stronger ' I mean if
in the pound weight there are only found 20s 2d by tale.
By ' weaker ' I mean if in the pound weight there are
20s 4d by tale. Also in each pound one strong and one
weak penny may pass uncounted, and two other pence
stronger or weaker by one and a half grains than the
just penny of 20s 3d to the pound sterling. But this
shear or cutting of the silver must be done on the Master's
order by certain workmen on the staff of the mint, by
whom the silver is prepared by remelting and fashioning
and making into the required number of blanks. Then,
after a proper check of the weight and tale, the workmen
give back their day's work to the Master and receive for
their wages from the Master 2½d for every pound. But
the Master will, if necessary, have the blanks blanched

faciet candidari, quos et ad cudendum monetariis liberabit, qui etiam, monetatione completa, de singulis libris
singulos obolos pro stipendiis suis recipient a Magistro.

Insidenter autem sciendum est quod duo sunt officia
necessaria in unaquaque moneta, uidelicet, Magistri
Monete et Custodis eiusdem. Ad Magistrum Monete
pertinet bilhonis et argenti cognitio et eiusdem emptio
et allaiatio, ac omnimoda monete dispositio, necnon et
operariorum ac monetariorum suorum gubernatio et
cohercio ; in hiis enim que ad gerendum idem officium
requiruntur, a nemine possunt regi aut distringi conuenientius quam ab ipso. Idem quoque Magister tam
pro se quam pro omnibus operariis et monetariis, pro
omnimodis expensis et custagiis ac pro decasu argenti
de singulis libris, v*d. ob.* tantummodo accipere consueuit.

Ad Custodem Monete pertinet cognitio et peritia
assaiandi examinandi et omnium aliorum per que
sufficientia monete probari seu examinari ualeat et
cognosci, quod si custos hoc ignorauerit, habeat quem-
piam ad hoc ydoneum loco sui. Item, ad ipsum custodem summopere pertinet, per se uel per alium ubique,
etiam in manu sculptoris cuneorum siue ingrauatoris,
cuneos monete tanquam sigillum regium diligentissime
custodire et uidere quod in ipsis cuneis per monetarios
apte et recte denarii prout condecet monetentur ; ipsos
quoque denarios, monetatione consummata, conseruare
tenetur cum omni diligentia et cautela, ne a sua custodia
ullatenus transferantur donec per examinationem ydoneam fuerint liberati ; sic enim moneta tutissime cus-
toditur. Sit autem examinator circumspectus in facienda
qualibet examinatione monete eo studiosius, tenerius,
et attentius quod unde Magister Monete exoneratur in
examine, inde ipse Custos siue examinator totaliter

and deliver them to the moneyers to strike, who shall also after finishing the coining receive a halfpenny for each pound as their wages.

You must know, by the way, that there are two offices necessary in every mint ; those of the Master of the Mint and of the Warden of the Mint. It is the Master's business to appraise and purchase bullion and silver and to alloy it, and all the details of making the money and also the government and restraint of his workmen and moneyers, for in all that pertains to the exercise of their office they cannot be governed and kept in order by anyone more suitably than by him. The Master also has been used to receive only 5½d in every pound for himself and for all his workmen and moneyers, for all expenses and costs, and for the loss of silver in coining.

The business of the Warden of the Mint is knowledge and skill in assaying, testing and everything else by which the goodness of the money can be tested and known. And if the Warden be ignorant of this let him have some fit person in his place. It is also his supreme duty, in person or by deputy, most diligently to keep in every place and even in the hands of the cutter or engraver of the dies, as though they were the king's seal, the dies for the coin, and to see that the pence are rightly coined from the dies as they should be. He is also bound to keep the pence, after the coining is done, with all diligence and care, that they may not be taken out of his keeping in any way until they have been delivered by a fit assay ; for so is the coinage most safely kept. But let the assayer be careful in making any assay of coin, and all the more diligent, delicate and intent, because the charge of which the Master of the Mint is cleared by the assay, is entirely transferred to the Warden or the Assayer, so

oneratur, ita quod post deliberationis sensuram Magister
inde non tenetur amplius respondere. In potestate
enim et officio examinantis existit deliberare monetam
quam ydoneam inuenerit, et non ydoneam reprobare,
ac ipsam remittere ad funditorium, ad custus, uidelicet,
Magistri emendandam et, si necessitas exigerit, fundendam ac in omnibus reformandam.

Restat uidere qualiter monete examinatio sit agenda.
Et sciendum quod huiusmodi examinatio duobus modis
fieri consueuit. Primo, per pondus et numerum, ad
marcam seu ad libram, de denariis ipsius monete.
Secundo, per ignem et assaium de ipsius monete allaio
seu argento. Examinatio igitur de denariis monete per
pondus et numerum ad marcam seu libram semper et
ubique habet fieri antequam ipsi denarii exeant extra
manus custodis et examinatoris monete. Et siquidem
inueniantur sufficientes in recto pondere et numero, de-
liberabuntur tanquam ydonei. Si uero insufficientes
inuenti fuerint, hoc dupliciter potest esse, aut enim in
pondere et numero erunt fortiores aut debiliores quam
recti denarii. Et quia eadem ratio est utrobique de forti-
oribus in fortitudine, idem intelligatur per omnia quod de
debilioribus edicetur. Aut ergo denariorum debilium sua
debilitas erit infra terminum constitutum, infra quem
moneta est deliberabilis secundum constitutionem principis, et tunc non erit impedienda deliberatio cum tales
denarii apti usui discernantur ; aut debilitas erit extra
illum terminum. Tunc autem, aut debilitas illa erit mediocris, aut enormis. Si mediocris, ut si modicum distet a
moneta deliberabili, tunc quidem impedietur deliberatio,
tamen, facta leuissima emendatione, uel mixta cum alia
meliori moneta, deliberabitur absque impedimento. Si
enormis, ut si multum distet a moneta deliberabili, tunc
si aliter emendari non possit, erit fundenda tanquam

that after the verdict of delivery the Master is no longer answerable. For it is in the power and the duty of the Assayer to deliver the money which he finds fit, and to reject the unfit and send it back to the foundry to be made good at the Master's cost and if necessary melted down and completely remade.

We have still to see how the testing of the money is to be done. And you must know that it has been usual to test it in two different ways. First, by weight and tale of the pence against the mark and the pound ; secondly, by fire and assay of the alloy or silver of which it is made. The test of the pence by weight and tale against the mark or the pound must always and everywhere be made before the pence pass out of the hands of the Warden and Assayer of the Mint. And if they are found good enough in weight and tale, they shall be delivered as fit for use. But if they are found wanting, this may be in two ways ; for they will be either stronger or weaker than just pence. And because the principle is the same in both cases, what applies to the strong pence owing to their strength will also apply in what will be prescribed for the weaker. Consequently, the weakness of the weak pence will either be within the appointed limit, within which by the prince's ordinance the money is fit for delivery, and then its delivery must not be prevented because the pence are decreed to be fit for use ; or their weakness will be beyond the limit. In that case, the weakness may be either small or extreme. If it is small, as being only a little weaker than money fit for delivery, then its issue will be stopped, but if a slight improvement is made or it is mixed with better money, it will be delivered without difficulty. But if the weakness is excessive, as greatly differing from money fit for delivery, then if it cannot otherwise be mended, it must

reproba et ad custus Magistri ipsius monete cudenda
et totaliter emendenda.

Nota. Examinatio autem per ignem et assaium de
allaio seu argento monete potest fieri tripliciter ; secundum quod per principem fuerit ordinatum ; aut enim
examinabitur argentum antequam extra manus custodis
et examinatoris monete ipsi denarii in usus alios conuer-
tantur ; aut post, certo termino, facta una pixide de
una sola dieta, uel pluribus, quam uel quas sub illo
termino contigerit fabricari, aut utroque modo, si antequam denarii extra manus custodis monete transeant,
aut moneta inuenietur in argento seu allaio sufficiens aut
deficiens. Si sufficiens, deliberabitur moneta tanquam
ydonea, et Magister inde quietus erit. Si deficiens, aut
defectus ille erit infra terminum limitatum infra quem
moneta est deliberabilis secundum constitutionem principis, aut extra eundem terminum. Si sit defectus infra
illum terminum, tunc non est impedienda deliberatio
cum moneta sit apta usui ; sed precipiendum est
Magistro quod tantundem melioris monete faciat fabricari. Si uero defectus sit extra terminum limitatum, aut
defectus ille erit mediocris, aut enormis. Si mediocris,
ut si modicum distet a moneta deliberabili, tunc quidem
impedietur deliberatio ; tamen, mixta cum alia meliori
moneta, deliberanda erit sine impedimento. Si autem
defectus sit enormis, ut si multum distet a moneta
deliberabili, tunc erit moneta illa fundenda, cum aliter
emendari non possit, et ad custus Magistri ipsius monete
cudenda et totaliter emendanda. Et cum ex hoc idem
Magister nemini dampnum dedisse conuincatur, de
equitate non erit aliter puniendus. Semper enim est
locus emendationi monete, usque quo post deliberationis
examen ad utendum fuerit deputata. Tunc autem

be melted down as rejected and must be struck and completely amended at the cost of the Master of the Mint.

But the test by fire and assay of the alloy or silver of the money may be made in three ways, according to what the prince may have ordained. For the silver will either be examined before the pence pass out of the hands of the Warden and the Assayer of the Mint and are turned to other uses ; or afterwards at a definite time, a ' pyx ' being made up from one or more days' work [or ' journeys '] which have been done within the time ; or in both ways, if the money shall be found sufficient or the contrary in silver or alloy before the pence pass out of the hands of the Warden of the Mint. If sufficient, the money will be delivered as fit and the Master will be quit. If deficient, the defect will either be within the limit within which the money may be delivered according to the prince's ordinance, or outside that limit. If the defect is within the limit, the delivery of the money is not to be stopped, since the money is fit for use, but the Master must be ordered to make an equal quantity of better money. But if the defect is beyond the limit, the money being only a little short of being fit for delivery, then its delivery will be stopped, but if it is mixed with better money it shall be delivered without difficulty. But if the defect is excessive and it is much different from money fit for delivery, then it must be melted down, since it cannot otherwise be amended, and must be struck and entirely made good at the cost of the Master of the Mint. And since the Master is not convicted of damage to anyone by this, he is not fairly punishable in any other way. For there is always an opportunity of amending the money until it

examinator de ipsius sufficientia tenebitur respondere,
iuxta quod per ipsum in deliberatione fuerit iudicatum.

Si uero certo termino fiat examinatio de pixide,
prout una pixis fieri consueuit sub tribus clauibus seu
serruris de una sola dieta, uel pluribus, quam uel quas
fabricari contigerit a termino in terminum deliberationi
ipsius pixidis constitutum. Expeditis aliis que incum-
bunt, sumendum est assaium more solito de omnibus
denariis totius pixidis simul mixtis ; et sic assaii examinatio recte fiet, quam unicum equitatis iudicium
subsequetur. Inauditum est autem omnibus ubique
monetariis quod alicubi iudicium pixidis aliter unquam
fuerit terminatum. Semper enim faciendo pixidem
licitum est unam monetam in eadem pixide per aliam
emendari. Nam sufficit monetam totius pixidis uniuersaliter esse bonam et deliberabilem simul mixtam. Et
ad hoc suffragatur consuetudo communis tam in regno
Anglie, quam in aliis regnis hactenus approbata.

Aut igitur assaium rite factum inuenietur sufficiens,
aut deficiens. Si sufficiens inuenitur, tunc quietus erit
Magister omnino. Si deficiens, aut defectus ille erit
infra terminum limitatum, infra quem, scilicet, pixis
monete est deliberabilis secundum constitutionem principis, et tunc in deliberatione pixidis precipietur Magistro
quod tantundem melioris monete faciat, et aliter non
erit inde quietus quousque emendatio plenarie compleatur ; aut defectus ille erit extra terminum limitatum
extra quem pixis monete non est deliberabilis secundum
eandem constitutionem principis ; et tunc, cum non sit
locus emendationi, Magister Monete erit ad gratiam aut
uoluntatem principis de uita et membris. Princeps uero
considerabit utrum ille defectus sit mediocris uel enormis,
ac etiam si pixis effecta fuerit de paucis dietis aut de
pluribus, et utrum casualiter aut studio fraudis acciderit ;

has been assayed for delivery and put out for use. But then the Assayer will be held answerable for its goodness, according to his own judgement in issuing it.

But if a trial of the pyx be made at a certain term, as a pyx under three keys or locks has been used to be made of one or more days' work which happen to have been done between one term fixed for the delivery of the pyx and the next; after all the needful preliminaries an assay is to be taken of all the pence in the pyx mixed together in the usual way; and so the assay shall be rightly made and a single equitable judgment will result. For it is unheard of by moneyers everywhere that the trial of the pyx should ever be concluded otherwise. For in making up the pyx, it is always permissible for one batch of money to be made good by another in the same pyx. For it is enough for the money of the whole pyx to be good and fit to deliver as a whole when mixed together. And this is attested by common custom hitherto approved both in the realm of England and elsewhere.

The assay duly made will be found either satisfactory or defective. If it is satisfactory, the Master will be altogether quit. If it is defective, the defect will either be within the limit within which the pyx of money is fit to be delivered according to the prince's ordinance or not. If it is, on the delivery of the pyx, the Master will be ordered to make an equal quantity of better money and will not be quit until that amendment is completed. Or the defect will be beyond the limit beyond which the pyx is not by the prince's ordinance to be delivered; and then, since there is no place for amendment, the Master will be at the prince's mercy or will in life and members. But the prince will consider whether the defect was small or excessive, and also whether the pyx was

et sic consideratis circumstantiis, uel remittendum
descernet delictum cum laude misericordie, uel plecten-
dum cum laude justitie. Si autem utroque modo fiat
examinatio, uidelicet, et antequam denarii deliberentur
extra manus Custodis Monete, et iterum certo termino de
pixide, prout superius est notatum, tunc prima examinatio ad hoc tantummodo seruiet, ne Magister ualeat a
rectitudine deuiare. Secunda examinatio, scilicet de
pixide, crit per iudicium terminanda. Iustitia enim
non patitur quod duplex feratur iudicium in id ipsum.

NOTA

c. 1300 (?)   (Red Book, fo. 264)

Et notandum quod quotienscunque fiat examinatio
monete per assaium, oportet ad hoc, ut ipsius examinationis certius habeatur iudicium, quod ad minus inde
fiant tria assaia irreprehensibilia, uidelicet, ne propter
nimiam estuationem, uel aliter, ex aliquo ipsorum assaiorum argentum exilierit, et ne propter impetum uen-
torum uel defectum ignis assaium infrigidatum fuerit,
neue propter casum carbonum, uel alio modo, assaium
siue argentum fuerit diminutum. Et cum tria assaia
irreprehensibiliter facta fuerint, tunc primo sunt per
ipsum assaiatorem iudicanda quod, uidelicet, ipsorum
trium assaiorum preualeat, i[d est] purius in argento et
rectitudine sit, ad iudicium ex[s]equendum. Vel utrum
omnia in bonitate conueniant, et quodcunque assaium
sufficientius iudicabit, illud quidem primitus, dende alia
ponderentur. Et siquidem paris bonitatis fuerint iudi-
cata, et inueniantur equaliter ponderantia, recte exami-
natum et iudicatum est. Si uero inequaliter ponderent,

made up of few 'journeys' or of many, and whether the defect arose by accident or by deliberate fraud ; and after considering the circumstances will decide whether the offence should be mercifully pardoned or justly punished. But if the test be made both ways, namely both before the pence are delivered out of the hands of the Warden of the Mint and again at a fixed term by the pyx, as has been mentioned above, then the first test will only serve to keep the Master from straying from the right way. The second examination, by the pyx, will end with a judgment. For justice does not suffer two judgments on the same matter.

NOTE ON THE ASSAY

c. 1300 (?)

Note also that whenever the money is tested by assay, in order that the judgment of the test may be more certain, at least three impeccable assays should be made, lest through overheating or otherwise the silver should have spurted out from one of the assays and lest from draughts or a failure of the fire, the assay should have cooled, or by the fall of coals or in any other way the assay or silver should have been diminished. And when the three impeccable assays have been made, then first must they be judged by the Assayer himself, namely which of the three assays is to prevail (i.e. which is the purest in silver and most correct) in giving judgment, or whether they are all equally good. And whichever assay he shall judge the best shall be first weighed and then the others. And if they are judged equally good and are found to be of equal weight, the assay and judgment are correct. But if the weights are unequal,

semper pro illo assaio quod plus ponderat est judicium proferendum siue alia duo conueniant in pondere, siue distent. Et est ratio, quia argentum in igne faciliter potest minui et nunquam augeri, unde ubi plenius inuenitur argentum, ibi iudicium est aptandum.

Nota. Sciendum est quod assaium monete fit per dimidiam unciam, scilicet pondus decem denariorum que est xxiiij^{ta} pars unius libre, uidelicet xx$s$. ; in qua, scilicet, libra est pondus xvj$d$. allaii, sicut Regi responsum est de proficuo. Et quilibet denarius ponderat xxiiij grana argenti. Et sic quelibet dimidia uncia, que est xxiiij^{ta} pars libre, habebit de pondere cuiuslibet denarii allaii ad libram positi, unum granum argenti. Nam pondus xvj denariorum allaii apponitur libre, tunc dimidia uncia habebit xvj grana argenti, quod est xxiiij^{ta} pars allaii positi ad libram. Et dicitur quando assaium predictum fit de predicta dimidia uncia, quod apponuntur eidem xviij grana argenti, que sunt xxiiij^{ta} pars totius allaii libre, et ij grana ultra ; que quidem duo grana apponuntur pro eo, quod creditur, quod homo uelit computare consumptionem ponderis duorum denariorum argenti puri, que consumptio debet inesse allaio et non argento.

Nota. Notandum quod, proposito puro argento, dividatur in quatuordecim partes equales et addatur allaium toti, ad pondus quatuordecim partium. Verbi gratia, quatuordecies^{a} xvj denariorum faciunt xviij$s$. viij$d$. et sic pondus xvj$d$. est xiiij^{ma} pars ; que si toti addatur, faciunt unam libram, xx$s$. Et sic de iure Rex deberet responderi de xvj$d$. de proficuo de pondere xviij$s$. viij$d$. puri argenti, cuius contrarium sepe uidetur.

---

^{a} *MS* quatuordecim decies

judgment should always be given for the assay which weighs heaviest, whether the other two agree or differ. And the reason is, because silver can easily be lost and can never be gained in the fire, so that judgment must be given where the most silver is found.

You must know that an assay of money is made by the half-ounce, if that be the weight of ten pence, which is the twenty-fourth part of a pound of twenty shillings, which contains 16 dwt. of alloy, according as the king is answered for the profits. And each penny weighs 24 light grains. And so each half-ounce, which is the twenty-fourth part of a pound, will have for every dwt. of alloy added to the pound one grain. For 16 dwt. of alloy is added to the pound and so the half-ounce will have 16 light gr. which is the twenty-fourth part of the alloy added to the pound. And when the aforesaid assay is made of the said half-ounce, it is said that 18 light gr. are added to it, that is a twenty-fourth part of the alloy of the whole pound and 2 gr. over ; and these two grains are added to take into account the waste of two pence of pure silver in the pound, which ought to fall upon the alloy and not on the silver.

You should observe that if you take pure silver, it can be divided into fourteen equal parts, and the alloy for the whole added, of the same weight as the parts. For instance, fourteen times sixteen pence make 18s 8d, and so the weight of 16d is a fourteenth part ; and if that is added to all the rest they make one pound, 20s. And so the king should rightly be answered for 16d profit on the weight of 18s 8d pure silver, but the reverse is often the case.

[DE MONETA AUREA]

c. 1350   (Red Book, fo. 264 v°.)

Nota. Memorandum quod libra auri puri constat ex xxiiij caratis auri puri ; et quelibet carata equiualet in pondere cum dimidia uncia argenti continente x*d.* pondere ; que dimidia uncia est xxiiij^{ta} pars unius libre argenti ; et quelibet carata constat ex iiij^{or} granis auri ; unde quodlibet granum auri continet lx grana argenti subtilia ; unde xxiiij^{or} grana faciunt sterlingum in pondere ; que quidem lx grana faciunt ij*d. ob.* ; qui sunt octava pars unius uncie ; que uncia continet xx*d.* argenti pondere, et sic dimidium granum auri continet xxx grana subtilia, uidelicet, j*d. quadr.* Quod quidem dimidium granum auri, siue xxx grana subtilia, debent esse allaium ad libram puri auri, iuxta formam cuiusdem indenture inter Regem E[dwardum] tertium a conquestu et Magistros Monete auri et argenti super monetatione eorundem auri et argenti confecte, cuius datum est xxvij° die Januarii anno xxiij, et in qua inter cetera continetur quod libra auri monetati erit de xxiij caratis iij granis et dimidio puri auri. Et sic, ratione allaii, deficiet dimidium granum puri auri de xxx granis subtilibus, ut supra ; in libra, uidelicet, continente in toto xxiiij^{or} caratas puri auri, sicut superius continetur. Quibus xxx granis divisis in xij, est xij^a pars inde duo grana et dimidium subtilia, que per computationem predictam debent esse allaium unius uncie puri auri, que est xij^a pars libre. Ex xij enim unciis constat et libra auri puri et libra argenti pondere.

Nota. Et memorandum quod iuxta formam indenture predicte habebit Magister Monete remedium, ultra

[GOLD COINAGE OF EDWARD III]

c. 1350

Be it remembered that a pound of pure gold consists of 24 carats of pure gold ; and each carat weighs as much as half an ounce of silver containing 10 dwt., which is the twenty-fourth part of one pound of silver. And each carat contains four gold-grains, and every gold-grain contains sixty light grains, whereof 24 gr. make a pennyweight ; and these 60 gr. make 2½ dwt. the eighth part of an ounce, which ounce contains 20 dwt. and so half a grain of gold contains 30 light grains, namely, 1¼ dwt. And this half-grain of gold, namely, 30 light grains, should be the alloy for a pound of pure gold, according to the form of an indenture made between king Edward III and the Masters of the Mint of gold and silver as to the money made of the same dated 27 January, 23 Edward III, in which is contained among other things that the pound of coined gold shall be of 23 carats, 3½ gr. of pure gold. And so by reason of the alloy there will be wanting half a grain of pure gold, namely, 30 light gr., in the pound which contains 24 carats of pure gold, as stated above. Dividing these 30 light gr. by twelve, a twelfth is 2½ light gr. which by the previous reckoning should be the alloy of one ounce of pure gold, the twelfth part of a pound. For the pound of pure gold and the pound of silver both contain twelve ounces.

Be it also remembered that according to the form of the aforesaid indenture, the Master of the Mint shall have a remedy, beyond the aforesaid alloy, in every

allaium predictum, ad quamlibet libram auri xvj^am
partem carate, que se extendit ad xv grana subtilia, que
faciunt obolum et dimidium quadrantem argenti pondere, et que xv grana subtilia sunt quarta pars unius
grani auri, et quibus xv granis diuisis in xij, est xij^a pars
remedii conting[entis] unam unciam, unum granum et.
quarta pars unius grani. Et sic allaium et remedium
ad unam unciam auri se extendit ad tria grana et
dimidium et quartam partem unius grani ; et hoc modo
si uncia auri contineat plus de allaio quin sit purum
aurum preter predicta tria grana et dimidii, post examinationem, peccat in materia, et non fit moneta debite
iuxta indenturam predictam.

Nota. Et notandum quod allaium ponendum ad
aurum potest esse de cupro uel de argento ; quod si fiat
de argento quamquam postea rite purificetur aurum per
ignem de allaio, uidelicet, ut sit in igne per tres dies et
tres noctes, adhuc aurum sic emendatum et purificatum
semper continebit aliquem colorem de argento ; et sic de
cupro, pari forma habebit colorem aliqualiter cupreum
ut experti in huiusmodi scientia dicunt. Et debet
huiusmodi assaium auri fieri in igne per iij dies et iij
noctes in olla cum cimento de puluere tegularum bonarum et rubearum et sale de Peyto in quadruplici quantitate auri purificandi faciendo et ad hoc sumendo. Verbi
gratia, ad libram auri purificandi que continet in puro
auro xxiii caratas iij grana et dimidium, ut supra,
sumende sunt iiij^or libre cimenti unde vii^a pars uel viij^a
erit de sale de Peyto,[1] et totum residuum eiusdem cimenti erit de puluere bonarum tegularum et rubearum.
Ita, uidelicet, quod quando aurum plus continet de
allaio, maior quantitas salis est apponenda et si minus,
minor quantitas, etc. Et sic, consimili forma, ad purifi-

pound of gold, of the sixteenth part of a carat, amounting to 15 light gr. making a halfpenny and half a farthing's weight, which 15 light gr. are one quarter of a grain of gold ; and dividing these 15 gr. by 12, the twelfth part of the remedy for one ounce is $1\frac{1}{4}$ light gr. And so the alloy and the remedy for one ounce of gold amount to $3\frac{3}{4}$ gr. And so if an ounce of gold contains more alloy, on examination, than $3\frac{1}{2}$ gr. it is inadequate in material and cannot duly be coined on the terms of the indenture.

Note, also, that the alloy to be added to the gold may be either copper or silver, but if it be made of silver, even though the gold be afterwards duly purified from the alloy by fire, namely, by being in the fire three days and three nights, the gold so amended and purified will still retain some colour of silver ; and the same holds of copper also, the gold will have some sort of a coppery colour, as the experts tell us. And such an assay of gold should be made in the fire for three days and three nights, in a pot, with a cement of the dust of good red tiles and Bay salt to be made and taken for this purpose, to the quantity of four times that of the gold to be refined. For example, to a pound of gold to be refined, which contains of pure gold 23 carats $3\frac{1}{2}$ grains, as above, you must take four pounds of cement, a seventh or eighth part of which shall be of Bay salt,[1] and the rest of the dust of good red tiles : namely, so that when the gold contains more alloy, more salt must be put in, and if less, less, etc. And in the same way to refine silver, sterile lead, that is, pure lead without silver or other metal, must always be

---

[1] Salt from Poitou, made by evaporating sea-water.

candum argentum, etc., plumbum sterile, id est plumbum
purum sine argento uel alio metallo, semper sumendum
est in quadruplici quantitate. Verbi gratia, ad dimidiam
unciam argenti in pondere monetati, que se extendit ad
x*d.* pondere purificandi, sumendum est plumbum sterile
usque ad pondus xl*d.* et sic purificatur argentum per
plumbum tanquam per cimentum suum de allaio suo,
quod se extendit ad xviij*d.* ad libram pondere, sicut
aurum purificatur per cimentum suum superius anno-
tatum de allaio eiusdem auri.

Potest etiam assaium auri fieri per tactum ad petram;
set illud assaium non potest bene discerni nisi per ex-
pertos in excercitio huiusmodi artis, et vix per eos quin
sepius eos falli contigerit in discernendo.

CONTRA ABBATEM SANCTI EDMUNDI

1280, June 8   (Red Book, fo. 248 v°.)

Cum labbe de Seint Eumoun priat a nostre Seygnur
le Rey kil rendit le koing solum ceo ke ces predecessurs
le avaient eu avaunt; et nostre seygnur le Rey le coygn
li ad rendu a la fourme avauntdite; et mesmes celi Abbe
veint pus a notre seygnur le Rey et li priast kil com-
aundit kem li liverat le estandart com apurtenaunt al
koyng; acorde est par le consail ke le estandart ne le
seit point livere, mes kem die al Abbe, de bouche, com
ben de argent pur est en la lyvre de la novele monee le
Rey; et com ben de alai lem deit mettre ataunt de
argent; et comben la livre de argent monee deit peser;
et comben de deners il deit aver en la livre par acunte;
et puis li seit dit kil face sa monee si com fet le Rey.

used in four fold proportion. For example, to half an ounce of coined silver, that is, 10 dwt. to be refined, you must take 40 dwt. of sterile lead ; and so the silver is purified by the lead, as by its own cement, from the alloy, which amounts to 18 dwt. to the pound weight, just as the gold is purified by its cement as said above from the alloy in the gold.

An assay of gold may also be made by the touchstone ; but that assay can only be determined by experts in the art, and hardly by them without frequent failures.

AGAINST THE ABBOT OF ST EDMUNDS

1280, June 8

Whereas the abbot of Saint Edmunds besought our lord the king to restore to him the die, as his predecessors had it before ; and our lord the king has restored it as aforesaid ; and the same abbot afterwards came to the king and begged him to order that the standard should be given him as an appurtenance of the die, it was agreed by the council that the standard should not be delivered but that the abbot should be told, by word of mouth, how much pure silver is in the pound of the king's new money ; and how much alloy must be added to the silver ; and how much the pound of silver ought to weigh ; and how many pence there should be in the pound by tale ; and he should be told to make his money just as the king does.

DE CUNEO ET MONETARIO [a]

(B.M., Harl. MS. 645, fo. 152 ; Add. MS 14, 847, fo. 68 vº)

A.D. 1280

Cum post mortem regis Henrici filii regis Johannis facta esset mutacio monete in Anglia, anno viiº regni Edwardi filii ipsius regis Henrici, idem rex Edwardus concessit sancto Edmundo cuneum suum, uidelicet unum standardum ferri cum duobus trussellis. Pecierunt insuper conuentus sancti Edmundi a dicto domino rege standardum monete et assaium eiusdem, pondus eciam puri argenti cum numero denariorum libre fabricate. Set, quia ista hactenus inaudita fuerant, nec in aliquo domini regis rotulo huiusmodi peticionis pro tempore preterito aliqua inuenta fuit facta mencio, cepit res dilacionem usque ad annum ipsius domini E. regis viii. Re igitur interim per dominum regem et ipsius consilium plenarium diligenter discussa et examinata, tandem viiiº die mensis Junii, anno eiusdem E. regis viiiº, ad scaccarium presentibus tam ipsius scaccarii baronibus quam aliis consiliorum ipsius domini regis principibus, taliter pro cuneo sancti Edmundi est prolatum.

Cum le abbe de seint Esmon priast a nostre seignour le rey ke lui rendist le coyn solum ceo ke ses predecessurs avoyent en avant ; e nostre seignur le rey le coyn lui rendi a la furme avant dite ; e meymes cely abbe venist puis a nostre seignur le rey et ly priast kil comandast ke lem li liverast l'estandard cum aportenant al coyn ; acorde est par le conseil ke le staundard ne lui soit point livere, mes ke lem die al abbe de buche cum bien de argent puur est en la livere de la novele moneye le rey, e cum bien de alay lem deit mettre a tant de

---

[a] *Add. MS* De Novo Counes

[THE ST EDMUNDSBURY TRIAL PLATE]

A.D. 1280

When a change was made in the English coinage
after the death of king Henry son of king John, in the
seventh year of king Edward son of king Henry, king
Edward granted St Edmund his die, namely an iron
pile and two trussels. The convent of St Edmund further
petitioned the king for the standard and assay of the
money, and also the weight of pure silver and the
number of pence in the pound coined. But because
these demands were unheard of, and there was no
mention of any such petition in the past in any of the
king's rolls, the matter was postponed until the king's
eighth year. In the meanwhile it was discussed and
examined by the king and his full council, and finally,
on 8 June, in king Edward's eighth year, at the Exchequer, and of other the king's chief counsellors, the
following judgment was pronounced for St Edmund's
die.

Whereas the abbot of St Edmund's prayed our lord
the king to restore the die, as his predecessors had had it
before, and our lord the king restored him the die in the
form aforesaid ; and the abbot afterwards came to the
king and prayed him to command that the standard
should be given him as appurtenant to the die ; it was
agreed by the council that the standard should not be
delivered to him, but that the abbot should be told by
word of mouth how much pure silver there is in the
pound of the king's new money, and how much alloy
must be added to so much silver, and how much the
pound of coined silver must weigh, and how many

argent, et cum bien la livere del argent munee deit
peser, et cum bien de deners il deit aver en la livere
par acunte. E puis ly seit dit kil face sa moneye sicum
fet le reys.

Gregorio igitur de Rokesleye, tunc Londonie maiori
atque summo domini regis cuneorum magistro siue
ministro, ab ipso domini regis consilio fuit iniunctum,
quatinus in premissis nos certificaret. A quo talem
recepimus certificacionem, secundum quod idem non
scripto sed ore tantum nobis retulit.

La livere de la moneye contene xii unces.

En la livere deit estre de fin argent xi unces, ii esterlings, et j ferling, et lautre alay. E la livere deit peser
monee xx.*s.* et iij.*d.* Issint ke nule livere ne seit outre
xx.*s.* iiij.*d.*, ne meins ke xx.*s* ij.*d.* par cunte. E deit la
moneye estre talie ken la livere ne deivent estre ke vj.
forz et vj. febles, de un grein et demid le fort, et de un
grein e demi le feble, al dreit dener. Et cil avient ke set
seyent febles utre le grein et demi en la livere trove par
le assaiur ; ja pur ceo ne lesse kil ses ne delivere, si plus
ni seient.

E tele est la moneye le rey.

Uncia ponderat xx.*d.* Denarius ponderat xxiiij. grana.
Denarius fortis ponderat xxv. grana et dimidium granum.
Denarius debilis ponderat xxij. grana et dimidium
granum.

De quadrante, obolo, sive de denario precii iiij
denariorum nullam *a* adhuc fecimus mencionem.[1]

Item nota quod xi uncie, ij.*d.*, q*ᵃ*. debent esse de ita
puro argento sicut est illud de quo fiunt folia argentea.
Et dicitur uulgariter tale argentum, argentum de
Gutheron's Lane.*b*

a Add. MS ullam   *b Add. MS* Guerunlane

pence, by tale, there must be in the pound. He must then be told to make his money just as the king does.

Gregory de Rokesleye, then mayor of London and Master or Minister of the king's dies, was ordered by the council to inform us accordingly. He gave us the following information, not in writing, but by word of mouth.

The mint pound contains twelve ounces.

The pound must contain 11 oz. 2¼ dwt. of fine silver, and the rest alloy. And the pound should weigh 20s 3d. So that no pound be more than 20s 4d or less than 20s 2d by tale. And the money must be so cut that there are not more than six heavy and six light in the pound : the heavy [up to] a grain and a half heavier, and the light as much lighter than the true penny. And if there be found to be seven light, over the grain and a half, in the pound, by the assayer, he may nevertheless deliver them, if there are no more.

And such is the king's money : The ounce weighs twenty dwt. The penny weighs 24 gr. A heavy penny weighs 25½ gr. A light penny weighs 22½ gr.

We have not yet mentioned the farthing, the half-penny, or the groat worth 4d.[1]

Note also that 11 oz. 2¼ dwt. must be of pure silver, like that of which silver leaf is made. And such silver is commonly called silver of Gutheron's Lane.

---

[1] The Pinchbeck register (ed. Hervey, p. 2) adds : 'Anno domini igitur m⁰.cc.lxxx⁰., qui eciam fuit annus regni Edwardi filii regis H. viij, die uidelicet sanctorum Johannis et Pauli (*Jun.* 26), iuxta euidenciam, per preceptum domini regis in eius curia, ut supra dictum est, nobis factum, primo apud Sanctum Edmundum fecimus monetam.' (A.D. 1280 being the eighth year of King Edward, son of King Henry, on the feast of SS. John and Paul (Jun. 26) according to evidence, by the king's order in his court as aforesaid to us made, we first coined money at St Edmund's.)

[DE MUTATIONE MONETAGII]

1284, February 10   (Red Book, fo. 246)

Il fet a remembrer ke la ou lem dona a Mestre
Willeme Turnemyre, pur overage et pur moneage de
bilon de la tere de Angletere, set deners, lem ne donne
fors sis deners e maile ore aparmemes. E pur overage
e pur moneage de argent de outre mer, sinc deners
e maile, ausint le fet om uncore. E pur overage e moneage de mayles, viij*d. ob.* E pur overage e moneage de
ferlings, x*d. ob.* pur charbon e pur totes maneres de
custages. E pur ceo ke mayles e ferlings custent plus a
overer e a moneer ke ne funt les esterlings, pur ceo sunt
il de tant cum il custent plus de mendre peis ke les
esterlings. E fet a saver ke les gros deners e les esterlings, les mayles e les ferlings, serrunt de memes le alay
e de memes le assay ke le estandard. Done le dime
jur de Feverer, le an de regne le Rey Edward dozime.

TRACTATUS NOVE MONETE

(*Revised Version*)

(B M., Harl. MS 645, ff. 156 (olim 137) seqq.)

Quoniam cause et raciones monete faciende et sen-
sura examinacionis apud nonnullos dificilis subtilisque
reputetur ; illam tamen materiam, prout paruitas ingenii
mei administrat, in scriptis sub compendio declarabo.

Fertur enim quod quidam Numa Pompeyus, Romanorum imperator, primus omnium monetam fieri im-
peravit, a cuius nomine nummi nuncupa[n]tur. Factis

[CHANGE IN MINTAGE RATES]

1284, February 10

Be it remembered that whereas Master William Turnemyre was given seven pence for the working and mintage of English bullion, he is now only given six pence halfpenny. And for working and mintage of overseas silver, five pence halfpenny, as he still is. And for working and mintage of halfpence, 8½ pence. And for working and mintage of farthings 10½ pence. For charcoal and all manner of costs. And because the halfpence and farthings cost more to make and coin than the sterlings do, they are of as much less weight as they cost more. And be it known that the groats and the sterlings, the halfpence and the farthings, shall be of the same alloy and the same assay as the standard. Given the tenth day of February, the twelfth year of King Edward's reign.

TREATISE ON THE NEW MONEY

(*Revised Version*)

Since some people consider the causes and principles of making money and the judgment of its assay a difficult and abstruse subject ; I shall set it forth briefly in writing, so far as my limited faculties permit.

It is said that one Numa Pompilius, a Roman emperor, was the very first to order money to be made, and that a coin is called *nummus* from his name Numa. Now coins were made of copper, silver and gold ; and

itaque nummis cupreis, argenteis, et aureis, et quia
singuli nummi argentei ualebant decem nummos cupreos, et singuli nummi aurei ualebant decem nummos
argenteos ; ideo a numero denarii sunt uocati, et ab illo
hucusque utitur ut omnis nummus denarius appelletur.
A materia quoque argenti siue auri sepius appellantur.
Set moneta Anglie fertur dicta fuisse a nominibus opificum, ut florenus a nominibus Florentinorum, ita sterlingi
a nominibus Esterlingorum nomina sua contraxerunt.[1]

Verumtamen quia de obolo vel ferlingo,[a] quorum
disposicio et compotus denariorum multo est subtilior,
loqui non indiget, quia tantummodo in cambio London'
componuntur et non alibi, tantum de denariis qui uulgariter sterlingi uocantur perloquamur.

Incoandum in primis est de ministris cuiuscumque
cambii et de eorum officiis pertractare, ut de congnicione
materie unde moneta fit,[b] de disposicione, de allayo, et
de examinacione consequenter est agendum. Sciendum
est autem quod in omni cambio tria sunt officia necessaria, uidelicet Magistri Monete, Custodis, et Cambsoris
siue Assayatoris. Ad Magistrum... (etc. ut supra p. 77).
...v.d.ob. tantummodo accipere debet. Et si ipse Custos
cum minore cum ipso Magistro possit conuenire, bene
licet.

Ad custodem uero pertinet pericia computandi,
assayandi, et omnium officiorum aliorum congnicio per
que... (etc. ut supra p. 77) ...denarii monetentur, et ut
summam quam quolibet cuneo fuerit monetata,[c] custodi
cuneorum domini regis correspondere sciat. Et quia in
cambio Lond' ad cuneos regis custodiendos duo sunt
intendentes, unus uidelicet ex parte regis, qui ferrum et
asserum emere debet, et a fabro usque ad manus sculptoris lamina ferri formata portare, ipsosque cuneos

---

[a] *MS* sterlingo   [b] *MS* sit   [c] *MS* monetatam

because each silver coin was worth ten copper, and each gold coin ten silver, pence (*denarii*) were so called from the number ten ; and from that time until now it has been customary to call every coin a ' penny '. They are also often called gold or silver pieces from their material. But English money is said to get its name from the name of the makers ; as the florin takes its name from the Florentines, so does the sterling from the Easterlings.[1] But since we need not speak of the halfpenny or the farthing, of which the constitution and reckoning are more complicated, because they are only made at the London mint ; let us now only speak of pence, commonly called ' sterlings '.

We must first treat of the officers of any Mint, and their duties, and afterwards of acquaintance with the material of which money is made, of its disposal, of alloy and of its assay, in due course.

[Duties of the Master of the Mint]

. . . And if the Warden can compound with the Master for less, he is free to do so.

[Duties of the Warden]

. . . ; and that he may be able to answer to the keeper of the king's dies for the sum coined at each die.

And because there are in the London Mint two persons concerned with keeping the king's dies ; one on behalf of the king, whose duty it is to buy the iron and steel, and to have the finished plates conveyed from the smith to the hands of the engraver of the dies, and to deliver the dies engraved duly prepared for use as often as money has to be struck and coined, and to see that

---

[1] From this point the revised version will only be given when it differs from the original.

sculptos et rite paratos, quociens cudere et monetare
necesse fuerit, deliberare, et monetarios ut aperte flodones
cudeant superuidere[1] ; et alius ex parte Johannis de
Buttetourt', qui habet in uxorem filiam et heredem
Thome filii Ottonis, cuius est de foedo cudere cuneos
regis qui deseruiunt per totam Angliam ; qui capit pro
sculptura et fabricatura cuiuslibet duodene septem
solidos ; cuius uero officium est cuneos usitatos de-
formare ne amplius deseruiant, et penes se omnes ueteres
cuneos ad opus domini sui predicti, ut pro feodo suo
retinere. Set quia inter istos duos cuneorum custodes,
tam de nouis cuneis quam de ueteribus et usitatis, et
tam de liberacionibus quam de restitucionibus eorum,
indentura facta sit, et ipsis restet[a] respondere Baronibus de Scaccario domini Regis et Custodi suo quante
libre fuerint monetate cum quolibet cuneo usitato
Londonie, Cantuarie, Sancti Edmundi, Dunolmi, et
alibi, cum cambium cucurrerit per totam Angliam, per
predictam indenturam, et similiter per talliam inter
fabrum cuneorum et sculptorem et ipsos factam ; expediens et perutile est ut Custos cuiuscunque cambii,
quociens Londoniam pro cuneis habendis miserit, et ab
ipsis cuneorum custodibus nouos cuneos perceperit et
veteres restituerit, diem recepcionis nouorum et restitu-
cionis ueterum[b] irrotulet, et summam que[c] cum illis
fuerit[d] monetata, ut predicitur, in quantum poterit
memorari. Custos necnon, monetacione et dealbacione
peractis, denarios cum omni diligencia conseruare tenetur, ne a sua custodia usquam transferantur, donec per
examinacionem ydoneam fuerint assayati.

Et sit idcirco Cambsor circumspectus in qualibet
examinacione monete facienda eo tenerius, quia unde

[a] *MS* restat   [b] *MS* veterorum
[c] *MS* quam   [d] *MS* fuerant

the moneyers strike the blanks in view of the public [1] ;
and another on behalf of John de Botetourt, who is
married to the daughter and heir of Thomas FitzOtho,
who has the hereditary duty of cutting the king's dies
used throughout England, and receives for the engraving
and fashioning of every dozen dies, seven shillings. It
is also his duty to deface the worn-out dies so that they
may not be used again, and to keep in his hands all the
old dies to the use of his master, and for his fee. But
because an indenture is made between these two keepers,
both of the new dies and of the old and worn-out ones,
and both of their deliveries and their restitutions, and
because it is their affair to answer to the Barons of the
King's Exchequer and to their Warden how many pounds
have been coined with each worn-out die at London,
Canterbury, St Edmund's, Durham and elsewhere, when
coining has been going on all over England by the
aforesaid indenture and by a tally made between the
smith, the engraver and themselves ; it is expedient and
well worth while that the Warden of any mint, as often
as he sends to London for dies and receives new dies
from the keepers and restores the old ones, should enrol
the day of the receipt of the new dies and the restitution
of the old and the sum of money struck with them, to
the best of his recollection. The Warden also, after the
coining and blanching, is bound to keep the coins
carefully, so that they shall not be taken elsewhere until
they have been duly assayed.

Let the Changer therefore be careful and make every
trial of the coin more delicately, because of whatever
charge the Master of the Mint is acquitted in the trial,

---

[1] Perhaps ' properly ' ; reading *apte* for the *aperte* of the MS

Magister Monete in examinacione exoneratur, inde
tam Cambsor quam Custos totaliter onerantur*; ita
uidelicet quod post deliberacionem Magister inde non
tenetur amplius respondere, preter quam in pixidis sue
examinacione. In potestate uero Custodis uel officio
Cambsoris existit monetam... [etc. ut supra, p. 78]
... reformandam.

Restat uidere qualiter monete examinacio sit agenda.
Cum Magister Monete denarios monetatos, dealbatos,
et preparatos in examinacionis locum, ut in cambio,
portauerit ; singulos simul super scaccarium canabo
co-opertum reponat. Inde, denariis per manus Magistri
Monete et ipsius Cambsoris bene reuolutis et multipliciter mixtis, capiat Cambsor manum suam plenam in
medio cumuli *b* hinc et hinc undique per gyrum nouies
aut decies usque perceperit sex libras. Postea disponat
in quatuor partes bis aut ter, ita ut mixtura bene fiat.
Deinde ponderet de istis denariis sic mixtis et reuolutis
tres libras bene et subtiliter cum standardo xx. solidorum, quod efficitur per rectitudinem granorum. Et
sic, singulis libris singulariter prout rectius poterit pon-
deratis, tradat unam libram custodi computandam et
aliam Magistro Monete, terciam alicui assidenti aut sibi
ipsi, et computent diligenter. Et si [unus] ipsorum
inueniat xx.*s.* et ij.*d.* ultra, alius ij.*d.*, et tercius iij.*d.*,
ponendi sunt in indentura et compoto per ij.*d.* ob., et
semper sunt deliberabiles ; cum iustum est quod quilibet
mercator habeat ad quamlibet libram pro incremento
suo iij.*d.* Et si unus inueniat xx.*s.* et ultra iij.*d.*, alius
iij.*d.*, et tercius iiij.*d.*, ponendi sunt per iij.*d. ob.* Et si
unus inueniat xx.*s.* et ultra iij.*d.*, alius iiij.*d.*, et tercius
iiij.*d.* ; ponendi sunt per iiij.*d.* Et si casualiter acciderit,
ut semel in anno, quod unus inueniat xx.*s.* et ultra iiij.*d.*,

a exonerantur *MS*   *b* *MS* cumule

the Changer and the Warden are debited. Because, after delivery, the Master is not bound to make further answer except in the Trial of the Pyx. [The Warden can however send defective money back to the foundry at the Master's expense.]

We have still to see how the trial of the money is to be conducted. When the Master of the Mint has brought the pence, coined, blanched and made ready, to the place of trial, e.g. the Mint, he must put them all at once on the counter which is covered with canvas. Then, when the pence have been well turned over and thoroughly mixed by the hands of the Master of the Mint and the Changer, let the Changer take a handful in the middle of the heap, moving round nine or ten times in one direction or the other, until he has taken six pounds. He must then distribute these two or three times into four heaps, so that they are well mixed. Then he must weigh out, from these well mixed pence, three pounds, well and exactly, by a standard pound of 20s which is correct to a grain. And so, having weighed out each pound by itself as correctly as possible, he must hand one pound to the Warden to count, another to the Master of the Mint, the third to any of the company or to himself, and they shall count diligently. And if one of them find 20s and 2d over, another 2d and the third 3d the pence are to be entered in the indenture and the account at 2½d and they are still fit to deliver ; since it is just that every merchant have for his profit on every pound 3d. And if one find 20s and 3d over, another 3d and a third 4d, they are to be entered at 3½d. And if one find 20s and 3d over, another 4d and another 4d, they are to be entered at 4d. And if it happen by accident, say once in a year, that one finds 20s and 4d over, another 4d and another 5d, they are bad and unfit

alius iiij.*d*., et tercius v.*d*. ; reprobi sunt et indelibera-
biles. Tamen quia semel uel raro acciderit, ponendi
sunt per iiij.*d*., et rarius possunt deliberari. Ita quod
tallia siue scissio monete in pondere et numero constituto conueniat, scilicet ad libram xx.*s*. iij.*d*., prout
equalius uel rectius scindi potest ; tamen si forciores
uel debiliores inueniantur de uno denario ad libram,
semper sunt deliberabiles. Ita quod scissio excedens
duos denarios uel iiii. denarios ultra xx.*s*. per compotum
fiunt denarii semper deliberabiles modo supradicto et
non aliter. Hec autem cissio siue tallia habet fieri...
[etc. ut supra, p. 76] a Magistro pro stipendio, suo
recipiet. Caueat tamen omnino Cambsor ne monetam
excedentem *a* ultra iiij.*d*. ad libram deliberet, quia hoc
foret dampnum regis et rengni sui ; eo quod incrementum exedens ultra xx.*s*. per compotum cucurrit in auan-
tagium mercatorum deferencium argentum suum ad
cambium tantummodo.

De supra dictis tunc tribus libris sic computatis
capiat Cambsor xx.*s*. et quemlibet denarium cum
subtilibus balanciis singulariter ponderet primo cum
debili denario, et si inueniat tres denarios debiles in una
libra, inpedietur deliberacio. Tum facta leuissima emen-
dacione, i.e. mixta cum alia forciori moneta, iterum
ponderata et examinata, possunt deliberari. Similiter
quemlibet denarium cum eisdem balanciis singulariter
ponderet cum forti denario, et si inueniat duos denarios
fortes in una libra,*b* inpedietur deliberacio quousque
mixta sit cum alia debiliori moneta, iterum ponderata
et examinata, ut supra dicitur, possunt deliberari. Ita
quod, inter duos denarios debiles et unum fortem, ita
quod non attingant ad duos granos plenos, et duos
denarios fortes et unum denarium debilem, fit moneta

---

a *MS* exedens   *b* *MS* unam libram

for delivery. But as this hardly ever happens, they are to be entered at 4d and only very seldom delivered. Provided that the cutting or ' shear ' of the money agrees with the standard in weight and tale, i.e. 20s 3d to the pound, as near as possible ; still if they are found a penny in the pound heavier or lighter, they are still fit for delivery. Provided that a shear of fewer than two or more than four pence over 20s be only fit for delivery as specified above.

[Payment of shearers and moneyers.]

But let the Changer beware that he deliver no money exceeding the 20s by more than 4d for this would be to the damage of the king and the realm ; because the increment above 20s by tale goes to the profit of the merchant bringing his silver to the mint, and to no-one else.

Then let the Changer take 20s out of the three pounds so counted, and weigh each penny by itself with accurate balances, first against a light penny, and if he find three light pence in the pound the delivery is stayed. Then after making a small remedy, i.e. when it has been mixed with other heavier money, weighed and assayed, it may be delivered. He must weigh each penny separately with the same balances against a heavy penny, and if he find two of them in one pound, the delivery shall be stayed till it have been mixed with other lighter money, again weighed and assayed, as above, and may then be delivered. So that, between two light pence and one heavy (provided the difference is not more than two full grains), and two heavy pence and one light, the money becomes fit for delivery. However, in every

deliberabilis. Tamen in qualibet libra vj.*d.* debiles et
vj.*d.* fortes de uno grano et dimidio possunt preterire.
Et si aliqui denarii inepti usui discernantur propter
fortitudinem et debilitatem, ita quod multum distent
a moneta delibera[bi]li, tunc, si aliter emendari non
possunt, erit tota illa moneta fundata tanquam reproba,
et ad custus Magistri Moneta scindenda, cudenda,*ª* et
totaliter renouanda.

Deinde de denariis approbatis, usui aptis, ad quamlibet deliberacionem capiat Cambsor de singulis x.
libris unum denarium, ut de c. libris x. denarios, semper
secundum quantitatem deliberacionis ; quoniam de
minori quam de x. libris non potest pixis fieri nec denarius
capi. Et in quadam cincia de lineo panno unum
denarium de x.li. aut x.*d.* de c. li. de formosioribus
denariis inponat ; diem et annum deliberacionis in
quadam parua cedula his uerbis intitulet, ' Hic est
unus denarius captus de x.li.', aut ' Hii sunt x. denarii
capti de c. li. sterlingorum deliberatorum die tali,
mense tali, anno tali,' etc., super quam cinciam Magister
Monete apponat sigillum. Et contra pixidem capiat
Magister Monete aut Cambsor ad quamlibet deliberacionem unum assayum ad minus [si] fieri possit, unde
pixidem suam quociens necesse fuerit possit probare.
Et portantur tales cincie in quadam pixide sub tribus
seruris, de qua Custos habeat unam clavem, Magister
Monete aliam et Cambsor seu Examinator terciam ;
quia ibidem latet periculum et iudicium de uita et
membris. Pixis uero, in qua tales cincie recluduntur, ad
hoc deseruit, ut cum dominus rex monetam in rengno
suo fabricatam, monetatam, et usui liberatam per
communem assayatorem, unum ad hoc officium direc-

ª MS fundenda

pound six heavy pence and six light may pass. And if any pence are adjudged unfit for use as being too heavy or too light and so much different from money fit for delivery, then, if they cannot otherwise be bettered, all the money shall be melted down as rejected, and be cut, struck and entirely renewed at the cost of the Master of the Mint.

Then the Changer shall, at each delivery, take of the money which is approved and fit for use, one penny for each ten pounds, or tenpence for each hundred pounds according to the quantity delivered ; since from less than ten pounds the pyx cannot be made up nor pence taken. And he shall put a penny from each ten pounds, or ten pence from a hundred pounds, choosing the best coins, into a linen bag, and write the day and year of the delivery on a small label in these words : ' This is one penny taken out of ten pounds,' or ' These are ten pence taken out of a hundred pounds of sterlings delivered on such a day, in such a month, in such a year, etc.' ; and the Master of the Mint shall set his seal to the bag. And the Master of the Mint, or the Changer, should, if possible, have at least one assay made of each delivery against the Trial of the Pyx, whereby he can as often as necessary test his own pyx.

Now these bags are carried [to the assay] in a box or ' pyx ' with three locks, of which the Warden is to have one key, the Master of the Mint another and the Changer or Assayer the third, because it involves danger, and judgment of life and limb. But the pyx in which the bags are locked up serves this purpose : that when the king chooses to examine, by means of the common assayer, the only person appointed to the duty, the

tum, examinare uoluerit ; per examinacionem earundem cinciarum et cirograffi, uel indenture inter Custodem et Magistrum Monete, de liberacionibus monete per dietas factis possit probare et recongnoscere numerum librarum et monete sufficienciam ac insufficienciam ab ultima examinacione usque tunc, et iudicialiter discernere de huiusmodi examinacione. Et de iudicio plenius patebit in fine.

Congnicio materie de qua fit moneta habetur duobus modis... (ut supra, p. 66) ... nouit. Secundo, utrum argentum sit mixtum cum cupro uel plumbo : hoc eciam multi sciunt. Tercio argenti mixti quantum quelibet libra metalli sibi adiuncti contineat. Hoc per exercicium potest congnosci. Verumtamen uix inuenitur aliquis ita perfectus quin in hoc sepissime falli possit. Examen uero per quod quelibet materia sit uisui [a] congnoscibilis, uix absque maximo exercicio possit exprimi aut intendi.

Verissime inter omnimodas examinaciones examen per assayum x.d. ad libram certius et comprehensibilius reputatur ; cuius certus modus omnino [a] nullo [b] distincte possit nosci, nisi per exercicium subtilis artificis fuerit eruditus ; cuius subtilitas patebit inferius.

Cum Cambsor a mercatore argentum emerit et talliari fecerit ; hoc est cum hoc quod pro cambio et pro monetacione [debetur] de argento sic empto extraccerit : ut si aliquis mercator argentum in massa, aut argentum cismarinum, transmarinum, seu billonem, ponderis c. librarum ad cambium tulerit ; et (posito quod sit argentum de Gaunt, quod quidem sepius emitur per iij.d. ad libram) clericus irrotulabit hoc argentum in rotulo empcionis hoc modo, 'De tali

a *MS* usui   b *MS* n¹

money made, coined and issued for use in his realm, he may be able, by examining the bags, and the chirograph or indenture between the Warden and the Master of the Mint as to the deliveries of money made 'journey' (or day's work) by 'journey,' to test and determine the number of pounds coined and the goodness or badness of the money from the last trial to the present, and to give a judicial decision upon the trial. We shall speak more fully of the judgment later.

Acquaintance with the material [as above, p. 66] . . . Secondly, whether the silver is mixed with copper or lead. This many know. Thirdly, how much alloy a pound of such mixed silver contains. This can be known by practice. But scarcely anyone is found so perfectly skilled that he is not frequently deceived. But the test by which any such material can be judged by the eye can hardly be explained or understood without great experience.

But among all the tests the most certain and intelligible is considered to be that by an assay of 10d in the pound ; the correct method of which nobody can know unless he has had practical teaching from a skilful craftsman. The following description will show how delicate it is.

When the Changer has bought silver from a merchant and assessed it (that is, has deducted what is due for the exchange and coining), as for instance if a merchant has brought silver in bulk to the Mint, whether English, foreign or 'billon' (supposing it to be silver of Ghent which is usually bought at 3d the pound), the Clerk will enrol it in the Roll of Purchases as follows, 'Of

mercatore, die tali, mense tali, c. libras per iij.*d.*' Et sub-
trahere debet idem clericus et Custos de qualibet libra
iij.*d.*, qui faciunt xxv.*s.*, et tantum demere de predictis
c. libris. Et remanet tallia iiij^xx. xviij. li. xv.*s.* ; et hec
vocatur Tallia. Tunc Clericus componat mercatori hoc
argentum deferenti billam de predicta tallia in hunc
modum, ' Cambium talis loci. De tali mercatore iiij^xx.
xviij. li. xv.*s* ponderis, die tali, mense tali, et anno
r. r. E. etc.' Et hec billa ualebit mercatori tanquam
scriptum obligatorium. Et ponderibus quibus argentum
emitur, eisdem restituetur mercatori, exaccione tallie
excepta. Deinde facta indentura inter ipsum Custodem
et Magistrum Monete de argento ad monetandum
liberato, in eadem indentura intrato, liberet Custos
Magistro Monete argentum ; quod accipiens, Magister
accedat ad funditorem, et in sui periculum allayet
secundum estimacionem ualoris. Ad c. libras emptas
ad iij.*d.* ponat in crusiolo ad quamlibet libram viij.*d.*
ob., ita quod computatis predictis iij.*d.* allayi, qui latent
in illis c. libris, et viij.*d.* *ob.* ponderis cupri, simul
appositis, faciunt xj.*d.* *ob.*, quos dominus rex percipit
de qualibet libra monetata in cambiis suis. De quibus
soluit Magistro Monete de qualibet libra monetata,
uidelicet pro monetacione denariorum tantum, ut supra
dicitur, v.*d.* *ob.* Et sic remanent regi de singulis libris
vj.*d.*, de quibus soluit uadia Custodi, Clerico, Cambsori,
Custodi cuneorum, et hostiario.

Sequitur de titulo et de disposicione Rotuli Empcionis secundum quod utitur in Cambio Londonie.

such a merchant, on such a day, in such a month, 100 pounds at 3d.' And the Clerk and the Warden must subtract 3d from every pound, making 25s and take that from the said 100 pounds. And the assessment remains £98 15s od and this is called the Tally. Then the Clerk shall make out a bill of the said tally for the merchant bringing this silver as follows, ' Mint of such a place. From such a merchant £98 15s od by weight, on such a day, such a month, in the year of the reign of king Edward, etc.' And this bill shall be as good as a bond to the merchant. And repayment shall be made to the merchant by the same weights with which the silver is bought, except the deduction for the tally.

Then an indenture is to be made between the Warden and the Master of the Mint about the silver purchased for coining, and the amount entered in it, and the Warden shall deliver the silver to the Master, who shall receive it, go to the melting-house and at his own risk alloy the metal according his estimate of its value. For 100 lbs. bought at 3d he shall put in the crucible for each pound 8½ dwt. of alloy, so that, taking into account the aforesaid 3 dwt. in the 100 lbs. and the 8½ dwt. of copper, the whole amounts to 11½ dwt. which our lord the king receives from every pound coined in his mints. From which he pays : to the Master of the Mint for every pound coined, viz for coinage of pence only, as above mentioned, 5½d. And so there remain to the king 6d from which he pays wages to the Warden, the Clerk, the Changer, the Keeper of the Dies and the Usher.

We proceed to the title and the arrangement of the Roll of Purchases used in the London Mint.

Empciones Argenti tam Cismarini quam etc Transmarini et Billoni Facte in Cambios

a primo die Octobris a° r.r. etc. usque etc.

De Thedemanno atte Wych' primo die Octobris c. lx. li. per xx.*s.* Tallia c. lx. li.

De Johanne de Loo primo die Octobris c. lx. li. per j.*d.* Tallia c. lix. li. vj*s.* viij.*d.*

De Terrico le Vileyn xx. die Nouembris c. lx. li. per ij.*d.* Tallia c. lviij. li. xiij.*s.* iiij.*d.*

De Egidio de Herst' primo die Decembris c. lx. li. per iij.*d.* Tallia c. lviij. li.

De Baldewyno de Loueyne ultimo die Januarii c. lx. li. per iiij.*d.* Tallia c. lvij. li. v[j.]*s.* viij*d.*

De Petro de Bruges xxvj^{to}. die Februarii c. lx. li. per v.*d.* Tallia c. lvj. li xiij.*s.* iiij.*d.*

De Francisco Bardi v^{to}. die Marcii c. lx. li. per vj.*d.* Tallia c. lvj. li.

Ad argentum emptum... [ut supra, p. 73]... tribuitur sterlingorum, et semper oneratur... [ut supra]... pondus xj.*d.* et *ob.* de cupro... [ut supra]... respondere custodi suo. Ad omnimodam igitur... [ut supra]... pro cambio, ab xj.*d. ob.* uel infra... [ut supra]... tribuitur sterlingo-rum, semper oneratur... tam de cupro usque quantitas (*sic*) que retinetur pro cambio, scilicet ad singulas libras xi.*d. ob.* integre compleatur. Et si forte... [ut supra] ... empcionis. Per quod patet quod nulla alia regula... [ut supra]... releuamen. Et tum moneta inde facta in ualore standardum poteri texedere. Et hoc inueniet in pixidis sue examinacione.[1]

---

[1] The Pinchbeck Register adds, pp. 11 seqq. : 'Si certo termino fiat examinacio ... (ut supra, p. 81) judicium est aptandum' substituting 'tunc prima examinacio dematur' for 'tunc prima examinacio ad hoc

Purchases of Home and Foreign Silver and Billon made in the Mint

from 1 October in the year of the king's reign, etc.

From Tideman atte Wych, 1 October. 160 lbs. at 20s. Tally, £160 (wt.)

From John de Loo, 1 October. 160 lbs. at 1d. Tally, £159 6s 8d (wt.)

From Terry le Vileyn, 20 November. 160 lbs. at 2d. Tally, £158 13s 4d (wt.)

From Giles de Herst, 1 December. 160 lbs. at 3d. Tally, £158 (wt.)

From Baldwin de Loveyn, 31 January. 160 lbs. at 4d. Tally, £157 6s 8d (wt.)

From Peter de Bruges, 26 February. 160 lbs. at 5d. Tally, £156 13s 4d (wt.)

From Francis Bardi, 5 March. 160 lbs. at 6d. Tally, £156 (wt.)

Instructions as to the quantity of alloy to be added by the Master of the Mint [as above, p. 73], but substituting $11\frac{1}{2}$ dwt. for the $14\frac{1}{2}$ dwt. of the original. The Master will get no relief in his account if he makes money better than the standard. And then the money made may exceed the standard. And he will find this in the assay of his pyx.[1]

---

tantummodo serviet ut Magister valeat a rectitudine deviare' ('then the first trial shall be neglected' for 'then the first trial will only serve to keep the Master from going wrong').

Elsewhere (p. 2.) it adds : 'Plate de Gaunte puyt porter ix.d. ob. Plate de biloun xvj.d. Plate de Bruges vij.d. ob. Plate de Boeme xx.d. vel ij.s Bruschele iiij.d. ob.' ('Plate of Ghent can bear $9\frac{1}{2}$ dwt. of alloy. Plate of billon, 16 dwt. Plate of Bruges, $7\frac{1}{2}$ dwt. Plate of Bohemia, 20 dwt. or 2s (wt.). Brussels, $4\frac{1}{2}$ dwt.')

APPENDIX I

A

The French version of this treatise, made by Oresme himself, begins as follows :

A LITTLE TREATISE OF THE FIRST INVENTION OF MONEY,
ITS CAUSES AND ITS CHARACTER

Why money was made. How it should be used. Who may coin it, debase it or alter it, and what disadvantages may arise in consequence. Collected from various books, and now translated from Latin into French, in order to show the fault and misuse of it in these days by merchants and common people, which the King and Princes permit and endure ; from which will result many evils, discomforts and irreparable damage unless speedy provision and remedy be made as shall hereafter be specified.

Translator's Preface

Veritate manifestata, cedat oppinio veritati. Which is to say, in French, that when the truth is manifest, all opinions must yield and give place to truth. And this leads me to my purpose, since Some men hold *etc. ut supra. The preface continues :*

For certainly at this present time, there should be great need of it, seeing that everybody treats money as he chooses, assigning to it whatever arbitrary value pleases him, to the reproach and dishonour of the prince who permits it, and whose image it bears. For it is a direct offence against his highness and lordship, and results in the loss and entire confusion of the common wealth of his realm and country. For merchants nowadays have more trouble in agreeing on the price and value of money than of the merchandise in which they deal. Because gold and silver have now reached so high a price that, unless a remedy is shortly provided, there is reason to fear many grave and serious disadvantages in bearing this state of affairs ; as, for instance, from the materials of money, gold and silver, being carried to other countries, where their rate of exchange is higher, and thus impoverishing the realm, to the prejudice of

the prince and his subjects. By this export of the materials of money, merchants would lose on their merchandise and produce, and would cease to frequent the realm thus stripped bare of money. And again, what is worse, the money-changers and bankers, who know where each variety of gold coin, according to its stamp, is worth most, by their secret devices drain the land of gold and send or sell it elsewhere to merchants, receiving from them other gold pieces, impure and of base alloy, with which they fill the country. We may guess, then, that when the king of France shall be pleased to reform his coinage, those who are found encumbered with this bad money will have heavy losses. The *Postulats*,[1] for instance, recently struck in the Liégeois, which pass current in this realm for half a gold crown, are nevertheless of so base alloy that worse cannot be found ; and, what is even worse, have no definite proportion of alloy, or basic standard which can be observed. And this is true of other debased gold coins, whose alloy is uncertain. And concerning the course of silver money at the mint-price of the mark of silver, the impoverishment of the realm is also to be feared, because the mark is worth more in other countries than it is here. And the ratio of twelve marks of fine silver to one mark of fine gold is not observed, as is known to those who understand the science which it would be long and tedious to describe and hard to understand. So I pass over that and proceed to the rubrics of each chapter of the treatise.

[1] This reference to *postulati* does not occur in the earliest MSS of the French text (Bridrey, p. 65), and Bridrey (p. 59*n*) identifies them with the coins of this name struck by Rudolf of Diepholt in the early fifteenth century. This is certainly incorrect, for Rudolf was not bishop of Liége but one of the candidates for the bishopric of Utrecht after the death of Frederick of Blankenheim in 1423 ; he styles himself *postulatus* on coins struck between 1426 and his receiving papal approval in 1433. The *postulat* of Liége referred to in the French translation of Oresme is either the *vieux postulat* of John of Heinsberg (1419–55), struck in 1453, or the *nouvel postulat* of Louis of Bourbon (1456–82), struck in the early years of the latter's episcopate. They derive their name from the fact that they imitate precisely the type of the *postulaat-gulden* of Rudolf of Diepholt, and are of very base gold. See J. De Chestret de Haneffe, *Numismatique de la principauté de Liége*, Brussels 1890, pp. 190, 204 ; nos. 306, 342.

I am indebted to Mr P. Grierson for this note.

B

The French version continues as follows :

To render to Caesar that which is his, is nothing else than to render him obedience, as Saint Peter says in his second epistle (1 Peter ii. 13) ; but for some time past this obedience has been taken from him and been so changed in observance that any man will, in defiance of the King's commandment, sell or account for his gold or silver penny at any rate he pleases, without regard to the price appointed by the King and the Estates of his realm. Wherefore, it has come to this, that no man, whatever be his rank, can obtain a gold penny except at the seller's price, just as if it were a commodity ; which is directly opposed to the original object for which money was invented and ordained, as we have already mentioned. It is this lack of enforcement of the law which causes money to leave the country and transfer itself to another where it commands a higher price. And so, since no rule is kept, the kingdom is being so impoverished that great damage may in time ensue both to the king and the common wealth. Furthermore, what is worse, nobody pays attention to the king's coins which are clipped and robbed of their original weight, but those who hold them reckon at the same rate of exchange as good coins of full weight. This practice cannot last long owing to the confusion which it is bound to cause.

APPENDIX II

List of Officers

WINTONIA

Monetarii	Nicholaus Cupping
	Hugo Silvester
	Willelmus Prior
	Iordinus Drapparius
Custodes	Walterus Coleman
	Robertus de la Dene
	Walterus Ruffus
	Iohannes Aure[faber]
Assaiatores	Robertus Aure[faber]
	Petrus de Wormhole
Clericus	Robertus Poterel

LINCOLNIA

Monetarii	Willelmus de Paris
	Ricardus de Ponte
	Willelmus Brand
	Iohannes de Luda
Custodes	Alanus de Gaytone
	Iohannes Berne
	Iohannes filius Marenni
	Henricus Cocus
Assayatores	Thomas de Bello Fage (*sic*)
	Iohannes Aurifaber
Clericus	Hugo filius Iohannis

GLOUCESTRIA

Monetarii	Iohannes filius Simonis
	Ricardus le Francois

Monetarii	Rogerus [Le Enveyse]
	Lucas Cornub'
Custodes	Iohannes Marescallus
	Alexander le Bret
	Ricardus de Celario
	Iohannes de Esdrefelde
Asseyatores	Willelmus le Eiche
	Nicolaus de Theokebir
Clericus	Henricus de Glouc'

OXONIA

Monetarii	Henricus Simeon'
	Gaufridus de Stocwill'
	Adam Feteplace
	Willelmus Sarsorius
Custodes	Laurentius Whit
	Thomas sub Muro
	Walterus Aurivaber
	Iohannes Alegod
Assaiatores	Radulphus Aurifaber
	Iohannes le Fleming'
Clericus	Simon filius Rogeri

NORWIC'

Monetarii	Willelmus de Gaugy
	Thomas Kinne
	Philippus filius Roberti
	Lucas Parmentarius
Custodes	Philippus filius Roberti
	Adam de Stanford
	Willelmus filius Iohannis
	Gaufridus Espicer
Assayatores	Robertus de Arderne
	Robertus filius Nicholai
Clericus	Hugo filius Iohannis

SALOPESBR'

Monetarii	Ricardus Pride
	Nicholaus filius Ivonis
	Laurentius Cox *loco* Hugonis Champencis
	Petrus filius Clementis
Custodes	Robertus filius Iohannis
	Lucas filius Walteri
	Iohannes filius Rogeri le Parm'
	Hugo le Vilain
Assaiatores	Thomas Aurifaber
	Willelmus filius Hugonis
Clericus	Nicholaus filius Nicholai de Sancta Werbur'

WALLINGEFORDE

Monetarii	Clemens Clericus
	Ricardus Blaunc
	Alexander de Stanes
	Robertus Pecok
Custodes	Iohannes Robechild
	Simon Canon
	Iohannes Hentelowe
	Gaufridus de Wicke
Assaiatores	Iohannes Aurifaber
	Randulfus Aurifaber
Clericus	Nicholaus de Esteus'

YVECESTER

Monetarii	Gervasius Gris
	Hugo le Rus
	Stephanus le Rus
	Radulphus Fardein
Custodes	Robertus Fromund
	Henricus le Camerer
	Rocelin Barhud
	Walterus Witbred
Asseyatores	Rogerus le Norais
	Thurb[er] Aurifaber
Clericus	Walterus Love

NORWICUM [1]

Monetarii	Hugo de Brunham
	Iacobus Cocus
	Willelmus de Hapesburg'
	Iohannes Martini
Custodes	Gilbertus de Ley
	Iohannes Bartolomei
	Wilelmus de Chalvern
	Robertus Wenge
Assaiatores	Martinus Aure[faber]
	Henricus Aur[ifaber]
Clericus	Robertus le Tanur

EBORACUM

Monetarii	Iohannes de Seleby
	Alanus filius Sansonis
	Raynerius Taliator
	Geremias de Bedegate
Custodes	Robertus filius Thomas Verdenel
	Thomas Yoel
	Robertus filius Thome Alby
	Willelmus de Akaun
Assaiatores	Henricus Spari
	Ricardus Grusey
Clerici	Andreas de Sebeby [2]
	Petrus de Gannoc *ex parte Regis* [3]

KARLEL

Monetarii	Iohannes de Boltone
	Robertus de Chilay
	Willelmus de Thipatun
	Adam Caperun
Custodes	Thomas Speciarius
	Willelmus filius Ivonis

[1] *sic*, in MS, probably NORH'   [2] *sic*, probably for Seleby
[3] Probably as Controller

Custodes	Alexander le Clerk
	Henricus le Taliur
Assayatores	Willelmus Aurifaber
	Adam Garald
Clericus	Willelmus filius Ivonis

WILTONIA

Monetarii	Willelmus filius Radulfi
	Willelmus Mauger
	Iohannes Berte
	Hugo Goldrun
Custodes	Robertus filius Iohannis
	Adam Ace'
	Radulfus Hervici
	Rocelinus de Gube
[Assaiatores]	Iohannes Acer
	Matheus Bolegambe [1]
Clericus	Willelmus de Biscopestede

EXONIA

Monetarii	Robertus Picon
	Philippus Tinctor
	Iohannes de Egestone
	Walterus Okestone
Custodes	Walterus de Moletone
	Michael Pollard
	Robertus Cissor
	David de Medueye
Assayatores	Iohannes Hamelin
	Ricardus Bulloc
Clericus	Godefridus de Sowy

[1] Probably Folegambe

HERFORDE

Monetarii	Ricardus Mamworthe
	Walterus Siward
	Rogerus le Mercer
	Henricus Hathefet
Custodes	Gilbertus Seim
	Henricus Targ[isii]
	Iohannes Foliot
	Nicholaus de la Punde
Asseiatores	Ricardus Senior
	Ricardus Iunior
Clericus	Ingaimus de Sancto Mart'

BRISTOUE

Monetarii	Iacobus La Ware
	Henricus Langbord
	Walterus de Paris
	Elyas de Aby
Custodes	Iacobus le Clerk
	Robertus de Kilmain
	Henricus Adrian
	Willelmus Sevare
Assayatores	Petrus Aurifaber
	Walterus Aurifaber
Clericus	Willelmus de Bruges

NOVUM CASTRUM

Monetarii	Rogerus filius Willelmi
	Iohannes de Papede
	Henricus de Karlel
	Adam de Blakedone
Custodes	Thomas de Merlberge
	Thomas Toraud
	Iohannes Wichelarde
	Rogerus Russell
Assayatores	Ricardus de Westmel'
	Willelmus Aur[ifaber]
Clericus	Adam Clericus

Memorandum quod in Thessauro domini Regis sunt duo assaya, unum de moneta, et aliud de argento puro, sub sigillo Maioris Londonie, pondus utriusque x solidorum. Item dominus R[icardus], Comes Cornubie, habet unum assaium de puro argento ponderis decem solidorum.

Liberata assaiorum per diuersa loca, tam de moneta, quam de argento examinato ; scilicet, apud Londoniam unum de moneta et aliud de argento puro, signata cuneo apposito in Thesauro ; pondus utriusque xl*d*.

Apud Cantuariam, eodem modo
Apud Sanctum Eadmundum, eodem modo
Apud Norwicum, eodem modo
Apud Oxoniam, eodem modo
Apud Norhamptonam, eodem modo
Apud Lincoln', eodem modo
Apud Winton', eodem modo
Apud Glouc', eodem modo
Apud Exon', eodem modo
Apud Eborac', eodem modo
Apud Salopesbiriam, eodem modo
Apud Wallingford', eodem modo
Apud Karlel, eodem modo
Apud Wilton', eodem modo
Apud Hereford, eodem modo
Apud Bristoue, eodem modo
Apud Nouum Castrum, eodem modo
Apud Iuieucestriam, eodem modo

INDEX

Printed in Great Britain by
Thomas Nelson and Sons Ltd, Edinburgh